Samuel Beckett and the
End of Modernity

SAMUEL BECKETT AND THE
END OF MODERNITY

Richard Begam

STANFORD UNIVERSITY PRESS

STANFORD, CALIFORNIA

Stanford University Press
Stanford, California
© 1996 by the Board of Trustees of the
Leland Stanford Junior University
Printed in the United States of America

CIP data are at the end of the book

Stanford University Press publications are
distributed exclusively by Stanford University
Press within the United States, Canada,
Mexico, and Central America; they are distributed
exclusively by Cambridge University Press
throughout the rest of the world.

For Anne

Acknowledgments

Daniel Albright, Paul Cantor, and Michael Levenson provided guidance and direction when this book was in its formative stages; their advice, criticism, and support were invaluable. Richard Rorty has been remarkably magnanimous, both in helping me better to understand the Heideggerian aftermath and in reading over several versions of the manuscript. Eric Rothstein and Robert S. Baker reviewed my work thoroughly and made extensive comments, some theoretical, some interpretive, all useful. Todd Bender, Phillip Herring, David Loewenstein, James Nelson, Cyrena Pondrom, and Howard Wienbrot offered numerous improving suggestions and much needed encouragement. H. Porter Abbott and Angela Moorjani refined my thinking on the pentalogy and reminded me of the generosity and fellowship of Beckett scholars. James Soderholm, Lyell Asher, Michael Valdez Moses, Brian May, and Robin Grey extended my intellectual community beyond Madison and sustained me with their wit and humor. My family has shown understanding and indulgence through too many drafts and too few visits. Finally, Anne Birberick has read every word of this manuscript many times over. She has been a stern critic, a patient witness, an indefatigable supporter. This book is hers as much as it is mine.

I would also like to express my gratitude for the financial support I received while writing this book. The Woodrow Wilson Foundation granted me a Charlotte W. Newcombe Fellowship, which helped me get started; the Graduate School of Letters and Sciences at the University of Wisconsin provided me with summer research support, which helped me finish.

An earlier and much abbreviated version of Chapter 6 appeared as "Splitting the *Différance*: Beckett, Derrida and the Unnamable" in *Modern Fiction Studies* 38 (1992): 873–92. My thanks to *MFS* for permission to reprint portions of that article.

Contents

A Note on Texts

My citations for Beckett's five novels are to the American editions:

Murphy (1938; New York: Grove Press, 1957)
Watt (1953; New York: Grove Press, 1959)
Molloy (New York: Grove Press, 1955)
Malone Dies (New York: Grove Press, 1956)
The Unnamable (New York: Grove Press, 1958)

Samuel Beckett and the
End of Modernity

Not to be dead and yet no longer alive? A spiritlike intermediate being: quietly observing, gliding, floating? As the boat that with its white sails moves like an immense butterfly over the dark sea. Yes! To move *over* existence! That's it! That would be something!

—*Friedrich Nietzsche*

From a certain point onward there is no longer any turning back. That is the point that must be reached.

—*Franz Kafka*

Introduction

In 1979 Jean-François Lyotard published *The Postmodern Condition*, a book in which he argued that modernity—broadly defined as the Western Enlightenment tradition—had fallen into a "legitimation crisis" from which it could not deliver itself.[1] The time had come, Lyotard urged, to explore a postmodern alternative. A year later in "Modernity Versus Postmodernity," Jürgen Habermas took pointed issue with Lyotard, contending that modernity remained an "incomplete project" and that, rather than abandon it, "we should learn from the mistakes of those extravagant programs" that sought to replace it.[2] The debate on the "end of modernity" had been joined. There followed in quick succession Lyotard's "What Is Postmodernism?" (1982) and *The Postmodern Explained* (1988), Habermas's *The Philosophical Discourse of Modernity* (1985), and Gianni Vattimo's *The End of Modernity* (1985). The last two books were particularly valuable for the way they placed this debate in its larger context, relating it both to French poststructuralism and the philosophy of Nietzsche and Heidegger.

The present study expands upon that context by focusing on the five major novels Samuel Beckett wrote between 1935 and 1950: *Murphy*, *Watt*, *Molloy*, *Malone Dies*, and *The Unnamable*. It will be my claim that these novels provide the earliest and most influential literary expression we have of the "end of modernity." At the same time, I want to qualify the categorical distinction that is usually drawn between philosophy and literature, between theory and text, and I am therefore interested not only in reading Beckett through the discourse of poststructuralism but also in reading the discourse of poststructuralism through Beckett. Such an approach reveals that as early as the 1930s and 1940s Beckett had already anticipated, often in strikingly prescient ways, many of the defining themes and ideas of Barthes, Foucault, and Derrida. Indeed, we might begin to understand Beckett as a kind of buried subtext or marginalium in French poststructuralism, the writer who spoke most resonantly to those thinkers in France who came after Sartre and reacted against him.

My critical orientation in what follows has been substantially influenced by neopragmatism, especially the work of Richard Rorty. While this means that I have sought to avoid foundationalist or essentialist vocabularies, it does not mean that I have hesitated to use terms that generalize or conceptualize. To take one example, I occasionally make reference to the "Enlightenment tradition." In employing this phrase, I do not want to suggest that the Enlightenment has the status of a historical event, in the sense that the Treaty of Paris or the Lisbon earthquake are historical events; or that it consists of a set of assumptions and beliefs that were universally shared by Europeans in the seventeenth and eighteenth centuries; or that it possesses a single *archē, telos*, nature, structure, or spirit that confers upon it a monolithic and transcendent meaning. Rather, I understand the *Enlightenment* as a term of convenience that enables us, in rough-and-ready ways, to group together various people, events, and ideas according to a principle of family resemblance. Indeed, as I hope Chapter 1 makes clear, I am not offering a history or genealogy of this term so much as attempting to understand its significance for thinkers like Nietzsche, Heidegger, Foucault, and Derrida.

Two other terms require some comment here. The first of these is *poststructuralism*. While I am fully aware of the problems and limitations this word presents—the fact that, for instance, *postfoundationalism* or *antiessentialism* might better describe the work of Derrida—I have nevertheless retained the more familiar "poststructuralism" because my study focuses on the French intellectual scene in the 1960s and 1970s. Also helpful from my perspective are the quasi-literary associations this term carries with it, since I want to understand poststructuralism not as an alternative philosophy, a rigorously critical method for deconstructing metaphysics from beyond metaphysics, but as what Rorty calls a "kind of writing."[3] Hence, one of my motives in using a "literary" figure like Beckett to discuss the "philosophical" work of Foucault and Derrida is precisely to argue against treating poststructuralism as an *Aufhebung* of the metaphysical tradition.

A second term, which calls for more extensive elaboration, is *postmodernism*. A number of commentators have complained that this word has lost whatever explanatory force it once had. Rorty himself, who has described Heidegger and Derrida as "postmodern," now says that he has abandoned this term: "I have given up on the attempt to find something common to Michael Graves's buildings, Pynchon's and Rushdie's novels, Ashbery's poems, various sorts of popular music, and the writings of Heidegger and Derrida."[4] My own use of "postmodern" is primarily confined to philosophical discussions associated with the "end of modernity" debate. As a result, I have not attempted to assign a global meaning to the word or to examine studies that deal with it from the standpoint of sociology, history, politics, science, or architecture.[5] In other words, I am not proposing a unified field theory of the postmodern. I do, however, want to think through some of the theoretical implications of postmodernity, hoping in the process to avoid the conceptual pitfalls that have so often attended discussions of this term.

In particular, I am concerned with the tendency among critics to treat the postmodern as the antithesis or negation of the Enlightenment tradition, a form of "overcoming" in which the modern is ultimately replaced by the antimodern.[6] The problem with such an account of the postmodern—one that purports to establish the "foundations" of antifoundationalism or to disclose the "essence" of antiessentialism—is that it perpetuates precisely the kind of thinking it wants to free itself from. In the place of this antithetical approach to the postmodern, I propose a "*différantial*" approach. Here I have in mind Derrida's claim that there is never "any question of *choosing*" between modernism (what he calls "Western metaphysics") and some term of opposition (what he calls the "overcoming" of metaphysics).[7] Rather, Derrida recommends simultaneously practicing two forms of deconstruction—one that works critically within the tradition and one that projects itself imaginatively beyond the tradition. This "new writing" necessarily places its practitioner in the no-man's-land that lies between modernism and antimodernism, a self-divided ground that Derrida associates with *différance*.

Drawing on Derrida's analysis, I argue that the postmodern constitutes just such a *différantial* phenomenon. As Vattimo has observed, the very word *post(modern)* literally contains within itself what it seeks to displace. This sense that the postmodern is implicated in what it opposes, that it is marked by an internal split or *différance,* has led some critics to recognize the difficulty of articulating postmodernism, of treating it as a single and homogeneous discourse that can be readily "named." In this regard, it is worth remarking that Derrida himself has persistently connected *différance* with a figure associated with Samuel Beckett, a figure called "the unnamable."

In developing a *différantial* conception of postmodernism, I have chosen to focus on Beckett's five major novels because I believe they represent the most original and radical effort to date to move beyond the achievement of literary modernism.[8] For Beckett, the two figures who most fully epitomized that modernism were Marcel Proust and James Joyce. I argue that Beckett's five novels, which I treat as a group or "pentalogy," were conceived as a response to these writers and deliberately modeled on their multivolume, autobiographical works.[9] Thus, Beckett's heroes function as parodic versions of Marcel and Stephen: aging invalids who lie in bed, obsessively writing inventories of their past, or vagrant derelicts who wander from place to place, carrying a stick (instead of an ashplant) and seeking their alter egos. At the same time, Beckett supplements these "portraits" with familiar details from his autobiography: the story of his prenatal "memory," the anecdote of the first loop-the-loop, scenes from Foxrock, accounts of mental hospitals, and of course characters named Samuel and Lemuel.

But the pentalogy does not, in the final analysis, function as a record of either its creator or its creation, at least not in the sense that Proust's or Joyce's novels do. For Beckett there is no epic struggle to make the past and present cohere in a moment of self-revelation, no grand effort to "unite" the "hero and the narrator," to confront the man who ultimately will become "the author of his own story."[10] In other words, what Beckett gives us is not an autobiographical novel but its critical deconstruction. And yet this deconstruction continues to draw upon and to operate within the categories we traditionally associate with autobiography, even as it serves to dismantle those categories. Consequently, the pentalogy stands in a complicated relation to Proust and Joyce. Beckett uses these writers as representative figures, employing them in the five novels as points of reference in his own evolving dialogue with the modernism he seeks to overcome. But that overcoming does not occur—at least not in any ultimate sense—for the pentalogy "ends," in effect, by not ending ("I can't go on, I must go on"). Acknowledging that an absolute transcendence of modernism is impossible, Beckett turns to exploring the *différantial* space that lies between modernism and antimodernism.

Expanding on the material I have presented above, Chapter 1 investigates the theory of the postmodern as it develops out of Nietzsche and Heidegger and applies that theory to the genre of the novel, situating Beckett's own novelistic practice in relation to Proust and Joyce. I then go on to trace Beckett's evolving postmodernism, devoting individual chapters to each of the five novels. Chapter 2 sets the Foucault-Derrida exchange on Descartes and madness alongside *Murphy*, showing how Beckett attacks the idea that the cogito provides a "rational" basis for modernity and the "truth-telling" genre of the novel. Drawing on de Man's and Derrida's interpretations of Rousseau, Chapter 3 reads *Watt* as an extended critique both of the "self-presence" of the cogito and of its related literary form, the autobiography. Chapter 4 evokes Derrida's ideas of supplementarity and *différance* to explore the way *Molloy* immobilizes those oppositions (identity/difference, origin/copy) that have traditionally defined literary representation. Chapter 5 focuses on the "death of the author," examining how *Malone Dies* initiates, through its self-cannibalizing intertextuality, what Derrida later calls "the end of the book." Finally, Chapter 6 treats *The Unnamable* as part of the "end of man" debate, considering the ways in which literature might move beyond "man" as he has traditionally been conceived by the Enlightenment and humanist traditions. Replacing the "narrator" and "narrated" with a Derridean *écriture*, Beckett inaugurates literary postmodernism not by attempting to overcome modernism but by surrendering himself to a form of absolute textuality, the narrative equivalent of *différance* and "unnamability."

The criticism on Beckett is sufficiently voluminous that any systematic or comprehensive survey is impractical. We may, however, identify two approaches that were especially influential during the 1950s, 1960s, and 1970s. The first approach, which treats Beckett as a mimetic nihilist, argues that his literature mirrors the fragmentation and alienation of modern life by giving us works that are paradoxical, confusing, absurd. The second approach, which views him as an existential humanist, maintains that he acknowledges the "nothingness" of human existence but celebrates man's freedom to choose himself as an *être-pour-soi*.[11] Both approaches have proven valuable, not only because they shed light on difficult and obscure texts, but also because they established important affiliations between Beckett's work and such movements as existentialism and absurdism. Yet, as authoritative as these interpretations have been, they are by no means representative of all the scholarship produced during this period on Beckett's fiction. In two landmark studies, both dating from the early 1960s, Hugh Kenner and Ruby Cohn provided suggestive alternatives to the nihilist and humanist readings of Beckett.[12] Kenner was especially useful in revealing Beckett's fascination with mathematical paradigms and how they relate to issues of rationalism, Cartesianism, and the novel. Cohn performed the valuable service of illuminating the comic side of Beckett, helping to dispel the common view that his writing is nothing more than a despairing cri de coeur. More recently, Daniel Albright and J. E. Dearlove have argued that Beckett's literature should be understood as the effort to achieve a fully perfected act of nonrepresentation or antiexpression, and Albright in particular pointed out the antecedents for such an experiment in the symbolist tradition. Finally, Rubin Rabinovitz has tellingly investigated the problems of literary development and innovation in Beckett, while H. Porter Abbott and Angela B. Moorjani have done ground-breaking work—especially significant to the present study—on "autography" and "abysmal gaming" in Beckett's fiction.[13]

My own interpretive approach, however, is most closely aligned with three critics—Steven Connor, Leslie Hill, and Thomas Trezise—who have argued that we should begin to read Beckett through the discourse of poststructuralism.[14] Their work calls for a complete reexamination of the way we understand Beckett, especially on such fundamental issues as the subject-object dialectic, the metaphysics of presence, and the correspondence theory of truth. I am entirely in sympathy with their efforts to redirect Beckett criticism toward poststructuralism, and I regard the present book as an effort to continue the exploration of Beckett's relation to writers like Foucault and Derrida. At the same time, there are a number of points where my work differs from theirs, in both method and interpretation.

My first difference with Connor, Hill, and Trezise is theoretical and relates to their approach to poststructuralism, which tends to essentialize what is antiessential, to foundationalize what is antifoundational. For the most part, they take a line similar to that advanced by Jonathan Culler, Rodolphe Gasché, and Christopher Norris and treat poststructuralism as a powerful new tool for deconstructing the illusions of Western metaphysics, for "exposing" the false assumptions and false assertions of the Enlightenment.[15] Yet to the extent that poststructuralism seeks to disengage itself from the metaphysical tradition, it can no more affirm the "truth" of its own position than it can deny the "truth" of foundationalism or essentialism. As Rorty has observed:

> To say that there is no such thing as intrinsic nature is not to say that the intrinsic nature of reality has turned out, surprisingly enough, to be extrinsic. It is to say that the term "intrinsic nature" is one which it would pay not to use, an expression which has caused more trouble than it has been worth. To say that we should drop the idea of truth as out there waiting to be discovered is not to say that we have discovered that, out there, there is no truth.[16]

Connor, Hill, and Trezise largely apply the logic of an "essentialized antiessentialism" to their reading of Beckett. Thus, from their perspective, Beckett teaches us that the cogito is an "illusion," that words are "inherently falsifying," and that naming is an "imposition and falsehood."[17] Although I certainly agree that Beckett rejects traditional ideas of consciousness and language, he does not do this from a methodologically privileged point of view, a philosophical high ground that stands beyond human contingency and therefore enables him to speak in terms of "illusion," "falsehood," and "imposition." Or, to put the matter differently, Beckett is engaged not so much in the hermeneutics of suspicion as in the aesthetics of play; he is a Nietzschean who takes the "immense framework and planking of concepts" that we call Western metaphysics and then "smashes [it] to pieces, throws it into confusion, and puts it back together in an ironic fashion."[18]

Not surprisingly, my theoretical differences with Connor, Hill, and Trezise have led to a number of practical differences. Generally speaking, because these critics read the five novels in ways that are more antimodern than postmodern, they sometimes fail to recognize or appreciate the full range of Beckett's achievement. This is especially notable in three areas. First, the pentalogy develops what I call a "lapsarian epistemology," a retelling of the story of the fall as a loss of subject-object unity. While Beckett does not embrace the Romantic notion that we begin in wholeness and end in division, he does make use of this myth, initially to explore, and ultimately to deconstruct, the idea of primordial or unmediated consciousness. Lapsarian epistemology is of crucial significance to Beckett, but because his poststructuralist critics are wary of "origins" and "beginnings," either they have argued that there is "no fall from grace" in his work or they have simply ignored this issue.[19] Second, as I indicated earlier, the pentalogy depends on a variety of autobiographical devices that serve to parody self-inscription in Proust and Joyce. Beckett rejects the idea that the ego is a stable or narratable entity, but he is nevertheless willing to employ the language and logic of the self to, as he writes elsewhere, "dispel" the self. Hence autobiography, like lapsarian epistemology, becomes a key element in Beckett—yet it is an element that his poststructuralist critics frequently disregard, because their theoretical assumptions make them suspicious of forms of individual consciousness.[20] Third, considered in its larger contours, the pentalogy represents the attempt to work through an extended argument, one that is principally concerned with how we might critically engage the Western metaphysical tradition from within that tradition. While this argument is not carried to a definite or final resolution, it does follow a clearly articulated line of thought, a sequence of ideas that moves from one stage to another. Beckett's poststructuralist critics are, however, mistrustful of ends as well as beginnings, of teleology as well as archaeology, and they consequently emphasize the iterative structures in the five novels at the expense of their developmental structures.[21]

While I clearly have differences with Connor, Hill, and Trezise, I again want to stress that their criticism has been of tremendous importance to my own work, indeed to the entire field of Beckett studies. Nonetheless, one final qualification is necessary. For if the principal contribution of these critics has been to show how we might read Beckett through the discourse of poststructuralism, I would like to reverse this formulation—or rather expand upon it—and I therefore focus on how we might read the discourse of poststructuralism through Beckett as well. The larger claim of this study, then, is that much of what we associate with poststructuralism, both in its thematic preoccupations and its formal innovations, may be traced back to Beckett's five novels. This is most evident in Foucault's work on the "cogito and madness," the "death of the author," and the "end of man," and in Derrida's work on the "metaphysics of presence," supplementarity, *différance*, unnamability, and the "beginning of writing." The general approach I have outlined here strikes me as particularly desirable, since poststructuralism itself has sought to break down the rigid boundaries separating philosophy and literature. At the same time, this approach underscores the extent to which Beckett's own peculiar idiom has entered into, in a sense has become, the dominant cultural language of the last fifty years.

CHAPTER ONE

'Différance,' Unnamability, Postmodernity

Some twenty-five years ago, when the "problem of language" first burst upon the cultural scene and critics everywhere were scrambling to hurry their latest theory into print, one writer opened a major book on the subject by warning against the dangers of rhetorical excess. Lamenting the "devaluation of the word 'language,'" he insisted that "in the very hold [this word] has upon us, it betrays a loose vocabulary, the temptation of a cheap seduction, the passive yielding to fashion, the consciousness of the avant-garde, in other words—ignorance."[1] It will surprise some to learn that the writer in question was Jacques Derrida and that the book was *Of Grammatology*. Having arrived a generation later at a new cultural juncture, we may now say of "postmodern" what Derrida said of "language": it is a word whose overuse and misuse have so inflated its currency, and so debased its value, that it threatens to lose all significance, to become a word that comprehends everything and means nothing.

And yet, as Derrida wrote of "language," "this crisis is also a symptom."[2] Hence, the semantic instability of the word "postmodern"—its tendency to blur and fragment under the pressures of definition—represents not only a problem in nomenclature but also a solution of sorts. For one of the distinguishing characteristics of the postmodern is precisely the way it resists all efforts at delimitation, the way it presents itself as a taxonomical extravagance, what cannot be classified or specified. The problem before us, then, is to devise some means of conceptualizing the vast and disparate body of material that we call postmodern, while at the same time not only acknowledging the intransigence of this material but also incorporating that intransigence into—even identifying it with—the very idea of the postmodern. We must, in other words, "name" the post-modern, but we must name it as in some sense "unnamable."

In pursuing such an approach, I develop two separate but related lines of analysis. First, I focus on the theoretical discourse associated with the "end of modernity." The idea that the Enlightenment tradition has played itself out, that modernity has come to an end, is most often identified with Lyotard's celebrated exchange with Habermas. My interest here is not, however, in rehearsing the arguments of this exchange, in assessing the comparative merits of "performativity" and "paralogy" on the one hand, "intersubjectivity" and "communicative action" on the other. Rather, I want to understand the end of modernity in the broad philosophical and cultural terms proposed by Gianni Vattimo—namely, as a form of antiessentialist, postfoundationalist thinking, which begins with Nietzsche, extends through Heidegger, and finds its final, or at least contemporary, elaboration in such philosophers (to name only these) as Foucault, Derrida, Lyotard, Rorty, and Vattimo. While it goes without saying that these thinkers represent a wide range of intellectual attitudes and commitments, they nevertheless share the conviction that after Nietzsche, knowledge can no longer be "grounded" in those "first principles" that were so necessary to Descartes. For them modernity has come to an end precisely to the extent that the "philosophy of the subject" has come to an end.

Second, I examine Beckett's relation to the realist tradition in fiction and to his two most influential literary precursors, Marcel Proust and James Joyce. It will be my contention that Beckett regarded Proust and Joyce as modern insofar as he saw them employing methods and assumptions that were largely Cartesian. From Beckett's perspective, these writers revolutionized literature when they attacked the objectivity and scientism of the realist novel, but their own turn "within," toward "subjectivity" and "consciousness," meant that they were not so much leaving behind the philosophy of the subject as breathing new life into it. This is not to say, however, that Beckett believed he was, in some final sense, "overcoming" the modernism of Proust and Joyce. Beckett's conception of his undertaking, what we would now call his postmodernism, recognized that an absolute break with the past, a complete supersession of what had gone before, was itself the product of a teleological or modern form of thinking. Proust and Joyce therefore became not figures to be replaced or surmounted but telling points of reference in an ongoing dialogue between past and present.

My own effort to give a descriptive shape to the postmodern departs from the position most critics have taken on this subject. Rejecting a negative or antithetical approach, I argue that the postmodern tends to express itself in a language of equivocation and contradiction, a language that consistently describes itself in terms of what is "unthinkable" or "unspeakable." In this regard, two ideas are of particular importance to my analysis: *différance* and unnamability. It is the convergence of these two ideas in the pentalogy that marks Beckett as a crucial figure in the development of postmodernity.

�·

We might take as a useful point of entry into the problem of the postmodern some recent work in literary studies. Generally speaking, commentators in this field have been more successful in identifying the postmodern—deciding what does or does not fall under its general rubric—than they have been in charting its definitional or conceptual boundaries. Indeed, despite the controversy and debate that have attended this term, something like a consensus begins to emerge when the postmodern is thought of not as an idea or a theory but as a series of related literary attributes. Although it is doubtful that anyone could construct a definitive list of these attributes—its ten or so essential qualities—there is a surprising convergence of opinion on what such a list would include. Most critics seem to agree that it would offer some combination of the following themes, techniques, and devices: self-reflexivity, *mise en abyme*, metanarrative, surfiction, the death of the author, the end of the book, *écriture*, heteroglossia, intertextuality, the loss of the origin, the breakdown of the signifying chain, and the deferral of meaning.[3] It is especially significant, however, that what stands behind this list, what motivates and informs its various items, is an implicit anti-Cartesianism, a repudiation of any system of examination or classification that is grounded in subject-object relations.

Within the context of literary studies, Cartesianism has traditionally assumed two forms. One of these—what we might call mimetic Cartesianism—treats the work of art as a subjective creation that attempts to mirror or reflect an objective situation: the world, history, culture, or society. The other—what we might call expressive Cartesianism—treats the work of art as an objective artifact that refers back to, or seeks to recover, an antecedent, subjective condition: the author's intentions or state of mind, the conscious, preconscious, or unconscious.[4] In the case of both mimetic and expressive Cartesianism, the emphasis falls on establishing as accurately as possible a correspondence between a subjective and an objective state of affairs, on determining what kind of fit, if any, exists between mind and thing. Obviously, the catalogue of postmodern attributes we considered above tends to impede or frustrate these two kinds of Cartesianism. Various forms of self-reflexivity and intertextuality, for example, undermine the mimetic notion that literature mirrors what lies beyond it in the world, while ideas like the "death of the author" and the "loss of the origin" undermine the expressive notion that literature reveals what stands behind it in the mind of its creator. To put it another way, inasmuch as the postmodern rejects the effort to regulate and standardize subject-object relations, it involves turning away from a reality that is essentially understood as a matter of observation and representation.

We will better understand what is at stake in this turn away from empirical reality if we consider it as part of a more general critique directed against two aspects of the Cartesian inheritance: philosophical foundationalism and intuitional normativism. Philosophical foundationalism, or Descartes' famous Method, assumes that all genuine knowledge must be built upon the ground of some indisputable first truth—such as the cogito—and that everything that follows from this will, as long as it is soundly reasoned, necessarily be valid. Intuitional normativism, or Descartes' empiricism, assumes that reality is, in effect, transparent—that if we are perspicacious in our observations, we shall see the world as it is.[5] Postmodernists challenge both these assumptions, arguing that because we always perceive reality through linguistically and historically determined schemas, we can never know it directly and immediately, without reference to some cultural code. This, in turn, means that we are incapable of recovering some first principle, a knowledge that is true in itself, true independently of the languages and institutions that human beings invent. As a result, for the postmodernists empirical reality exists not as a universal truth but as one of the many "stories" that men and women tell.

This does not mean, however, that philosophical postmodernity is, as critics have often alleged, simply a form of radical skepticism.[6] Richard Rorty stresses this point in an important passage in *Contingency, Irony, and Solidarity*, one that is worth quoting at length:

> We need to make a distinction between the claim that the world is out there and the claim that truth is out there. To say that the world is out there, that it is not our creation, is to say, with common sense, that most things in space and time are the effects of causes which do not include human mental states. To say that truth is not out there is simply to say that where there are no sentences there is no truth, that sentences are elements of human languages, and that human languages are human creations.
>
> Truth cannot be out there—cannot exist independently of the human mind—because sentences cannot so exist, or be out there. The world is out there, but descriptions of the world are not. Only descriptions of the world can be true or false. The world on its own—unaided by the describing activities of human beings—cannot.
>
> The suggestion that truth, as well as the world, is out there is a legacy of an age in which the world was seen as the creation of a being who had a language of his own. If we cease to attempt to make sense of the idea of such a nonhuman language, we shall not be tempted to confuse the platitude that the world may cause us to be justified in believing a sentence true with the claim that the world splits itself up, on its own initiative, into sentence-shaped chunks called "facts." But if one clings to the notion of self-subsistent facts, it is easy to start capitalizing the word "truth" and treating it as something identical either with God or with the world as God's project. Then one will say, for example, that Truth is great, and will prevail.[7]

The crucial distinction to be drawn here is between the belief that "the world is out there . . . [and] may cause us to be justified in believing a sentence true" and the belief that "the world splits itself up, on its own initiative, into sentence-shaped chunks called 'facts.'" In other words, postmodernists recognize that we are fully capable of making statements that have "truth-value," but they also recognize that these statements only acquire meaning within culturally conditioned paradigms that determine such threshold questions as how we divide the world up, what we call a fact, where we perceive similarity, where we perceive difference. Michel Foucault cogently summarizes this point of view in the preface to *The Order of Things*: "The fundamental codes of a culture—those governing its language, its schemas of perception, its exchanges, its techniques, its values, the hierarchy of its practices—establish for every man, from the very first, the empirical orders with which he will be dealing and within which he will be at home."[8]

So far we have considered the postmodern as a form of anti-Cartesianism that rejects the idea that reality may be known in itself as what is given in the world or self-evident to the senses. In focusing on the discourse associated with the end of modernity, I want to expand on this view, showing how the postmodern involves an extended critique of the intellectual heritage of the Enlightenment, particularly those aspects of it that are identified with humanism, rationalism, and science. I therefore now turn to two thinkers who were among the first to undertake this critique: Friedrich Nietzsche and Martin Heidegger.

￪•

While much of Nietzsche's philosophy may be read as an protracted quarrel with the Enlightenment, I would like to concentrate my discussion on one essay, an early piece of writing entitled "On Truth and Lies in a Nonmoral Sense" (1873).[9] Nietzsche begins this essay by asking what has become one of the most familiar questions of poststructuralism: "Are designations congruent with things? Is language the adequate expression of all realities?"[10] He then goes on to reject the empirical paradigm, the idea that the "world splits itself up, on its own initiative, into sentence-shaped chunks called 'facts,'" as Rorty put it. But Nietzsche is not content to leave matters here. Rather, he suggests that empiricism itself functions as a form of humanism, pointing out that insofar as our observations of the world are necessarily mediated by language, they are necessarily circumscribed within a human perspective:

> The various languages placed side by side show that with words it is never a question of truth, never a question of adequate expression; otherwise, there would not be so many languages. The "thing in itself" (which is precisely what the pure truth, apart from any of its consequences, would be) is likewise something quite incomprehensible to the creator of language and something not in the least worth striving for. (82)

Truth is, to cite a well-known passage from the essay, nothing more than a "movable host of metaphors, metonymies, and anthropomorphisms: in short, a sum of *human* relations" (84; my emphasis). Obviously any proposition or assertion that is defined purely in human relations "contains not a single point which would be 'true in itself' or really and universally valid apart from man" (85). Nevertheless, we do not want to acknowledge the partiality of our own point of view, to admit that "the insect or the bird perceives an entirely different world from the one that man does, and that the question of which of these perceptions of the world is the more correct one is quite meaningless, for this would have to have been decided previously in accordance with the criterion of the *correct perception,* which means, in accordance with a criterion which is *not available*" (86).

Speaking in general terms, we may say that Nietzsche identifies two problems in the empirical tradition: it ignores the constitutive role that language plays in apprehending the world, and it assumes that a human perspective is universal, that all sentient beings perceive reality the same way man does. But, as Nietzsche observes, it is impossible to demonstrate that one perceptual framework is "true," while another is "false." In the absence of a God, there is no universal criterion, no higher authority, that transcends human and nonhuman perspectives, enabling us to determine which of these is ultimately "correct."

Nietzsche spends much of the remainder of the essay attacking the rationalism and scientism that he feels are also implicit in the empirical paradigm. Hence, the individual demonstrates that he is a "*'rational'* being" by placing "his behavior under the control of abstractions" and by "universaliz[ing] all these impressions into less colorful, cooler concepts, so that he can entrust the guidance of his life and conduct to them" (84). This, in turn, moves human beings toward more disciplined modes of thinking, with the result that the role language originally played in "the construction of concepts" is gradually taken over by science (88). But here again, Nietzsche is skeptical, arguing that science offers a no more "objective" account of reality than did the ancient myths, which once conceptually defined the universe:

> All that we actually know about these laws of nature is what we ourselves bring to them—time and space, and therefore relationships of succession and number. . . . We produce these representations in and from ourselves with the same necessity with which the spider spins.

> If we are forced to comprehend all things only under these forms, then it ceases to be amazing that in all things we actually comprehend nothing but these forms. (87)

Nietzsche's work effectively set the agenda for what was to become the "end of modernity" discourse. Not only did he attack the empiricism implicit in Descartes, but he extended his critique to humanism, rationalism, and scientism—in short, those habits of mind most often associated with the Enlightenment. As is well-known, Heidegger takes up and further develops the critique of truth that Nietzsche initiated.[11] For Heidegger, the advent of the Cartesian cogito constitutes the original sin of European philosophy, the intellectual event that precipitated our fall into subject-object thinking. Rather than elaborate on Heidegger's critique of truth, however—an enormous topic in itself—I would like to focus on what he has to say about science, particularly technology.[12]

As Heidegger sees it, modern or Enlightenment thinking is a by-product of the "age of the world-picture." After the dawning of this age, man is sundered from the world, no longer experiencing himself and what surrounds him as an indissoluble unity, what the Greeks called *hypokeimenon* or "that-which-lies-before."[13] Standing at a certain distance from man, the world becomes an objectifiable thing, a mere representation or picture, which is now susceptible to human manipulation and control. Plato and Aristotle were among the first philosophers to treat the world as representation (131), but it was Descartes who was most responsible for forging the distinctively modern compact between philosophy and science:

> This objectifying of whatever is, is accomplished in a setting-before, a representing, that aims at bringing each particular being before it in such a way that man who calculates can be sure, and that means be certain, of that being. We first arrive at science as research when and only when truth has been transformed into the certainty of representation. What it is to be is for the first time defined as the objectiveness of representing, and truth is first defined as the certainty of representing, in the metaphysics of Descartes. (127)

Of course, if the world is reduced to a mere representation or object, this means that man is reduced to a mere representer or subject. Again, Heidegger maintains that it was Descartes who secured the philosophical foundations for this kind of thinking: "With Descartes begins the completion and consummation of Western meta-physics. . . . With the interpretation of man as *subiectum*, Descartes creates the metaphysical presupposition for future anthropology of every kind and tendency" (140).

The division of human experience into subject and object is for Heidegger, as it was for Nietzsche, an expression of humanism, an anthropocentric mapping of the world, which defines reality entirely in terms of human profit and loss: "When man becomes the primary and only real *subiectum*, that means: Man becomes that being upon which all that is, is grounded . . . Man becomes the relational cen-ter of that which is as such" (128). As a result, technological man conceives of nature as a vast "standing-reserve" (*Bestand*), a series of potential forces and energies, which have, as it were, been stock-piled for his benefit and which can be unlocked, transformed, and redistributed at his pleasure. Such an approach—distinctively Carte-sian, as we have seen—has the effect of turning nature into a huge scientific laboratory: "Thus when man, investigating, observing, en-snares nature as an area of his own conceiving, he has already been claimed by a way of revealing that challenges him to approach na-ture as an object of research" (19).

At the heart of this kind of thinking is what Heidegger calls "En-framing" (*Ge-stell*), a word etymologically related to *herstellen* (to produce) and *darstellen* (to represent). This means that the process of placing things together (*stellen*) within a framework (*Gestell*), of rendering nature "identifiable through calculation" and "orderable as a system of information" (23), makes possible both representa-tion (*Darstellung*) and its corollary production (*Herstellung*) of goods and services. More generally, "Enframing" and the whole idea of technological thinking provide a paradigm for what have become the disciplines of the natural and social sciences, disciplines that treat reality as something capable of being charted along the Cartesian coordinates of scientific knowledge and then controlled and regu-lated.[14]

It is generally recognized that Derrida and Foucault, while criti-cal of certain aspects of Nietzsche and Heidegger, are themselves in-debted to the "end of modernity" discourse, which these earlier phi-losophers inaugurated.[15] We might say, simplifying greatly, that Der-rida's critique of truth owes its inspiration to Nietzsche's attack on a

Cartesianism that breaks up reality into subject-object dualisms and to Heidegger's elaboration on this critique. Thus, Derrida's famous "nonconcept," *différance*, is designed to resist antithetical thinking by showing how the clearly partitioned boundaries in binary oppositions can become blurred, shifting, unstable.[16] Foucault has been most original in attacking technology conceived as the "disciplines" of the social sciences—disciplines that, Foucault argues, function as forms of manipulation and domination.[17] Foucault's thinking obviously owes a great deal to Heidegger's attack on modern technology, especially his discussion of "Enframing." At the same time, it is indebted to Nietzsche insofar as the critique of science occupies a prominent place in the latter's work.

It should now be obvious that postmodernity, at least as it evolves out of the "end of modernity" debate, entails much more than a simple rejection of the empirical paradigm. It also involves a critique of the rationalist and humanist legacy, which developed in large part out of the Enlightenment. Yet here too there is a danger of oversimplifying. For, as we have seen, postmodernity participates in the intellectual heritage it criticizes, and this means that it is quite willing to employ the tools of reason and argumentation, if only to attack reason and argumentation. We observe just such a tendency in Nietzsche, Heidegger, Derrida, and Foucault: their philosophy is, at some level, divided against itself, at once working within a rationalist language (which relies on logic and analysis) and an aesthetic language (which ironically distances itself from logic and analysis). Postmodernity involves, in other words, a "mixed" discourse, a kind of writing that draws simultaneously on divergent, even opposing, traditions. And this raises the possibility that postmodernity includes the very modernity it is supposed to overcome—that postmodernity is, in some sense, identified with what it seeks to supplant and negate.

⌣·

Toward the end of "Structure, Sign, and Play," Derrida proclaims that there are "two interpretations of interpretation, of structure, of sign, of play."[18] Distinguishing between these two approaches, he argues that "one seeks to decipher, dreams of deciphering a truth or an origin which escapes play and the order of the sign," while "the other, which is no longer turned toward the origin, affirms play and tries to pass beyond man and humanism" (292). In effect, Derrida here draws a distinction between epistemology, which assumes that truth is something we discover in the world, and hermeneutics, which assumes that truth is something we create through language.[19] The "modern" and the "postmodern" have frequently—and usefully—been conceived of in terms of this opposition, whether we think of it as "legitimation through metanarrative" versus "incredulity toward metanarrative" (Lyotard), an "epistemological dominant" versus an "ontological dominant" (McHale), or "finding" versus "making" (Rorty).[20] Yet there is a problem in treating the postmodern as a simple or direct term of opposition to the modern. For if what postmodernity seeks to leave behind is categorical and teleological thinking, the kind of either/or proposition epitomized by the binary opposition, then it will not want to present itself as a mere reversal or negation of modernity. Derrida illustrates this problem—and indicates a possible response to it—when he declines to make a choice between the two interpretations of interpretation, between epistemology and hermeneutics:

> For my part, although these two interpretations must acknowledge and accentuate their differences and define their irreducibility, I do not believe that today there is any question of *choosing*—in the first place because here we are in a region (let us say, provisionally, a region of historicity) where the category of choice seems particularly trivial; and in the second, because we must first try to conceive of the common ground, and the *différance* of this irreducible difference. (293)

To put this another way, Derrida is generally skeptical of the notion that it is possible to transform radically our cultural horizon, to reposition ourselves through a single leap of transcendence outside the limits of the Western tradition. In his essay, "The Ends of Man," Derrida raises precisely this issue when he discusses various efforts to "overcome" the humanism or "anthropologism" that both Nietzsche and Heidegger criticized. Yet every attempt to move "beyond" the end of man, every attempt to get "outside" the humanist paradigm, depends on a series of ideas—similitude and difference, subject and object, inside and outside, *archē* and *telos*—which themselves participate in the anthropocentrism they are meant to transcend:

> The thinking of the end of man, therefore, is always already pre-
> scribed in metaphysics, in the thinking of the truth of man. What is
> difficult to think today is an end of man which would not be orga-
> nized by a dialectics of truth and negativity, an end of man which
> would not be a teleology in the first person plural.[21]

Derrida does not offer any definitive solution to the problem he poses—as he has stated it, there is no way he could—but he does suggest, given our relative fixity within the metaphysical tradition, that we are faced with two choices: on the one hand, a deconstruction of existing terms that, undertaken from the "inside," would assault founding concepts "without changing terrain" (135); and on the other, an effort to place "oneself outside," to affirm "an absolute break," a real change of terrain—while recognizing that this effort represents nothing more than a "*trompe-l'oeil* perspective" (135). Derrida concludes not by preferring one alternative to the other, but by recommending that we practice both at once: "It also goes without saying that the choice between these two forms of deconstruction cannot be simple and unique. A new writing must weave and interlace these two motifs of deconstruction. Which amounts to saying that one must speak several languages and produce several texts at once" (135). What Derrida encourages, then, is the pursuit of two forms of deconstruction: one that works critically within the tradition, and one that imaginatively projects itself beyond the tradition. This "new writing" places its practitioner in the liminal space that lies between modernism and antimodernism, a space Derrida consistently associates with *différance*.

Again, standing behind this conception of the postmodern is the work of Nietzsche and Heidegger. Vattimo makes this point when he specifically connects the turn away from a philosophy of "overcoming" to the ambiguity of the prefix in "postmodern":

> The first decisive step in making the connection between Nietzsche,
> Heidegger, and "post-modernism" consists in discovering why the lat-
> ter term employs the prefix "post-"—for "post-" signifies precisely
> that attitude which, in different but deeply related terms (at least ac-
> cording to my own interpretation), Nietzsche and Heidegger have
> tried to establish in regard to the heritage of European thought. Both
> philosophers call this heritage into question in a radical manner, but
> at the same time refuse to propose a means for a critical "overcom-
> ing" of it. For both philosophers, the reason for this refusal is that

any call for an "overcoming" would involve remaining captive to the logic of development inscribed in the tradition of European thought. . . . Both philosophers find themselves obliged, on the one hand, to take up a critical distance from Western thought insofar as it is foundational; on the other hand, however, they find themselves unable to criticize Western thought in the name of another, and truer, foundation. It is this that rightly allows us to consider them to be the philosophers of post-modernity.[22]

Vattimo explains this peculiarly divided approach to the metaphysical tradition in terms of what Heidegger calls *Verwindung*, a word that is related to *Überwindung* (overcoming) but that functions as a dislocation or distortion of that word, because it "has none of the characteristics of a dialectical *Aufhebung* . . . because it contains no sense of a 'leaving-behind' of a past that no longer has anything to say to us" (164). Like any number of Derridean expressions, *Verwindung* is semantically overdetermined, unable to contain its various and diverse meanings:

The lexical meaning of the term in German provides two other shades of meaning: it is a convalescence (in the sense of "*ein[e] Krankheit verwinden*": to heal, to be cured of an illness) and a distorting (although this is a rather marginal meaning linked to "*winden*," meaning "to twist," and to the sense of a deviant alteration which the prefix "*ver*" also possesses). The notion of "convalescence" is linked to another meaning as well, that of "resignation." . . . Metaphysics, to put it another way, is not something which can "be put aside like an opinion. Nor can it be left behind us like a doctrine in which we no longer believe"; rather, it is something which stays in us as do the traces of an illness or a kind of pain to which we are resigned. (172–73)

Verwindung is a Heideggerism that has, at it were, been infected by *différance*, a word that simultaneously evokes notions of "overcoming" and "resignation," of "cure" and "convalescence," of "deepening" and "distortion." As Vattimo puts it, "*Verwindung* . . . defines Heidegger's basic position and understanding of the task of thought at the moment in which humanity finds itself today, namely at the end of philosophy in the form of metaphysics" (173).[23]

Now if the postmodern is, as I have been arguing, a *différantial* phenomenon, characterized by internal contradiction, self-discrepancy, and incongruity, then this creates practical problems for the critic who wishes to articulate the postmodern, who wishes to treat it as a coherent discourse that can be readily, or at least meaning-fully, defined. For if postmodernity actively resists classification, if it stands outside our received intellectual and conceptual boundaries, then it is, at some level, "unnamable."

Among the scholars writing about the postmodern, few have con-fronted the predicament of its "unnamability" as consistently or as ingeniously as Ihab Hassan. Practicing what he calls "de-creative" writing,[24] Hassan engages not in "criticism" but in "paracriticism," a form of discourse that does not aspire to the "objectivity" or "transparency" of what Barthes calls *écriture blanche*. Rather, Has-san's "paracriticism" insists on its own "textuality," whether this means employing experimental typography and layout to remind us of the physical (hence writerly) quality of what we read, or deploy-ing texts that are fragmentary, discontinuous and abyssal, thereby breaking down conventional notions of the literary work as unitary and proprietary. "What evidence," he asks, "may we expect from our (postmodern) culture? Perhaps only evidence circumstantial: so-cial bric-a-brac, intellectual *bricolage*, bright shards of a dis-estab-lished imagination, all jangling their peculiar themes and variations" (65).

Indeterminacy is the term Hassan repeatedly uses to indicate the difficulty that attends any effort to narrate or name the postmodern, any effort to put the fragments together into some more significant or revelatory order: "Indeterminacy often follows from fragmenta-tion. The postmodernist only disconnects; fragments are all he pre-tends to trust. His ultimate opprobrium is 'totalization'—any syn-thesis whatever, social, epistemic, even poetic" (168). Thus, although Hassan is one of the earliest critics to have "made sense" out of the postmodern, a critic who has consistently shown a willingness to "define" this difficult and obscure term—even to employ diagrams, schemas, or binary oppositions—he always qualifies these clarifying gestures with something like an admission of bad faith, as though he had betrayed his subject precisely by bringing it to light—or, per-haps more accurately—as though his various efforts at definition had, according to a Heisenbergian logic, altered the object it had meant merely to observe. In a characteristic essay, "Pluralism in Postmodern Perspective," Hassan offers eleven "definiens" of postmodernism, but then ironically distances himself from his own act of definition: "These eleven 'definiens' add up to a surd, perhaps absurd. I should be much surprised if they amounted to a definition of postmodernism, which remains, at best, an equivocal concept, a disjunctive category, doubly modified by the impetus of the phenomenon itself and by the shifting perceptions of its critics" (173).

While Hassan does not explicitly "name" the postmodern as "unnamable," he intimates as much when he evokes Beckett's earliest anticipation of the "unnamable," Murphy's "third zone," described as a "matrix of surds."[25] A number of French poststructuralists have, however, addressed this issue more directly, specifically using the word "unnamable" (*innommable*) in their discussions of the postmodern. The case of Lyotard is particularly notable. Like Hassan, Lyotard is capable of making statements about the postmodern that are lucid, straightforward, and highly quotable ("I define *postmodern* as incredulity toward metanarratives").[26] But also like Hassan, Lyotard feels the need to remind us that such statements are themselves subject to the "truths" they enunciate, and this means that if we are incredulous toward metanarratives, we should also be incredulous towards Lyotard's metanarrative on metanarratives.

Thus, almost despite himself, Lyotard concludes "What Is Postmodernism?" with a warning about the dangers of definition: "Finally, it must be clear that it is our business not to supply reality but to invent allusions to the conceivable which cannot be presented. . . . The answer is: Let us wage a war on totality; let us be witnesses to the unrepresentable; let us activate the differences and save the honor of the name".[27] Here, Lyotard suggests that the postmodern is characterized by two features: it is a conceptual extravagance, something that stands beyond the categories of thought and imagination, that can only be represented as "unrepresentable"; and it is produced out of a process of self-abnegation and self-consumption, a willingness to allow its own identity to dissolve amid an upsurge or backwash of "differences." Lyotard goes on to elaborate on the idea of the "unrepresentable" in *Heidegger and "the jews,"* calling it that "presence" that every representation misses or forgets. In an effort to descriptively locate this elusive "presence," to specify its radical nonidentity, he has recourse to a single but now familiar word:

The true object of literature (to speak only of that) has always been to reveal, to represent in words, what every representation misses, what every representation forgets. This "presence," whatever name we give it, which persists not so much at the limits as in the heart of representations. This *unnamable* in the secret of names.[28] (my emphasis)

Julia Kristeva is another critic who has memorably described the postmodern in terms of what cannot or should not be named. In an essay entitled "Postmodernism?" Kristeva evokes both ideas of unrepresentability and difference (what she calls "multiplicity") when she argues that the "language-defying style" of postmodern writing leads to a "multiple, heteroclitic and unrepresentable idiolect." Explaining how this "unrepresentable idiolect" manifests itself, Kristeva tells us that "as far as writing is concerned, it has since set out to blaze a trail amidst the *unnamable.*" Then, lest there by any doubt as to the pedigree of this particular "unnamable," Kristeva informs us that "Beckett is the best example" of this new kind of writing.[29]

It is in the work of Derrida that the idea of *différance* is most significantly, and most resonantly, joined with the idea of the "unnamable." As Derrida writes in his title essay on the subject, *différance* is "literally neither a word nor a concept."[30] It therefore is unwritable, unspeakable, and unnamable: "*Différance* has no name in our language. But we 'already know' that if it is unnameable [*innommable*], it is not provisionally so, not because our language has not yet found or received this *name*, or because we would have to seek it in another language. . . . It is rather because there is no *name* for it at all."[31] Because I examine the relation between *différance* and the "unnamable" at length in Chapter 6, I shall not review it here. The larger point to be made is that insofar as postmodernity wishes to abandon teleological and categorical thinking, insofar as it embraces the peculiar logic of *différance,* it is inevitably drawn into a discourse of unnamability. Certainly this does not mean that the postmodern exists as a kind of intellectual vapor, forever lost in the realm of the ineffable or the unknowable. It does mean, however, that our efforts to understand this volatile and resistant term should acknowledge the difficulties that necessarily attend any effort to "name" it.

We have been examining the modern and the postmodern from

a perspective that is almost exclusively theoretical, but I would now like to shift the ground of our discussion and consider these terms in relation to the genre of the novel. Beckett once remarked that he was "interested in the shape of ideas."[32] In the 1930s and 1940s this interest translated itself into a fascination with the forms and conventions of fiction, especially those associated with two literary types: the traditional nineteenth-century novel, as represented by Balzac, and the avant-garde twentieth-century novel, as represented by Proust and Joyce. All the same, it is important to understand that Beckett's approach to questions of literary form—often couched in the language of subject-object dialectics—was clearly influenced by the sort of theoretical issues we have been discussing. For Beckett the novel was preeminently an epistemological genre, and this viewpoint had important consequences for his response to the realist and modernist traditions.

∽•

In *The Rise of the Novel*, Ian Watt famously argued that "modern realism, of course, begins from the position that truth can be discovered by the individual through his senses: it has its origins in Descartes."[33] Hugh Kenner carried this proposition a step further in *Samuel Beckett: A Critical Study*, contending that Descartes not only provided an epistemological model for the novel but also produced an example of that genre when he wrote the *Discourse on Method*:

> It is Descartes who leads the Western mind to the place where realistic fiction, its accuracy checked by "many particular experiments," becomes a focal mode of art. His journey to the famous room with the stove foreshadows the novelist's journey to the room where one writes day after day, alone. Beckett would seem to be the first to have read the *Discours de la Méthode* as what it is, a work of fiction. (81)

Recent criticism has generally resisted the notion that the novel possesses any single origin, that it progresses toward any final destination.[34] Yet if the empirical heritage does not constitute the only point of departure for the novel, its unique and defining source, it certainly stands as one of the genre's shaping influences. For our purposes, this influence takes on special significance, not only because Descartes was crucial to Beckett's intellectual development but also because the basic situation in the *Discourse*—a man alone in a room, thinking—is the basic situation in much of the pentalogy. At the same time, Kenner's assertion that the *Discourse* is a work of fiction is neither as extravagant nor as implausible as it might seem. Indeed, Descartes seems to bear out Kenner's claim when he describes his intentions at the beginning of the *Discourse* as more "literary" than "philosophical"[35] and then goes on to cast his personal *histoire* in the form of a memoir or confession, organizing the events of his life into a sequential narrative, including his school days at the Collège de Flèche (1: 112–13), the revelation in the heated closet (1: 116–22), and the genesis and composition of the *Discourse* itself (1: 126–27). Yet, despite these autobiographical and novelistic elements, Descartes makes it clear that he attaches little or no value to "histories" and "fables," preferring scientific knowledge, which is based upon "certainty" and "self-evidence" (1: 114).[36] It is for this reason, Descartes tells his readers, that "as soon as I was old enough to emerge from the control of my teachers, I entirely abandoned the study of letters," resolving instead to "seek no knowledge other than that which could be found in myself or else in the great book of the world" (1: 115).

Descartes's peculiar invitation to read the *Discourse* as both a piece of fiction and an exercise in scientific inquiry helps us locate the outer boundaries of the realist novel.[37] On the one hand, there is the mainstream Cartesian tradition described by Watt, a tradition that is rigorously empirical in both its method and practice. On the other hand, there is the Beckettian rewriting of Descartes as told by Kenner, a rewriting that nullifies Descartes's carefully constructed method, replacing the will to truth with the will to play. Somewhere between these Cartesian beginnings and this Beckettian end lies the vast middle ground of the realist novel.

Within a French context, that ground is primarily represented by nineteenth-century fiction—especially the work of Balzac and Zola—and it is here that we must turn if we wish to see how Beckett responded to the challenge the realist novel posed.[38] Certainly there is no simple or direct correlation between Descartes and nineteenth-century fiction—nor do I wish to make such a sweeping claim. But there are, in the case of both Balzac and Zola, a number of significant affiliations with the Cartesian inheritance, two of which are particularly worth emphasizing. First, both writers seek to give their analysis of society a quasi-scientific status by modeling it on the research methods of eighteenth- and nineteenth-century biology. Balzac expresses this idea most memorably in the "Avant-propos" to *La Comédie humaine* where, evoking the great naturalist Buffon, he argues that his own novels provide a taxonomical system for understanding Social Man: "There has therefore existed, there will therefore exist in all times, Social Types just as there are Zoological Types. If Buffon has created a magnificent piece of work by attempting to represent in a book the whole of zoology, does there not remain a work of this kind to be done for Society?"[39]

In Zola this scientism, carried even further, begins to resemble a form of mechanistic determinism, especially when he takes up Balzac's zoological metaphor in his own essay "De la description": "To describe is not our goal; we want simply to complete and *determine*. For example, the zoologist who, in speaking of a certain kind of insect, would find himself forced to study for a long time the plant on which this insect lives."[40] Second, the scientism that Balzac and Zola profess largely functions according to the logic of Cartesian dualism, a logic that enables us to translate epistemological terms, such as subject and object, into novelistic terms, such as character and environment. Seen from this perspective, the task of realism begins to look not unlike the task of Cartesianism: to record, catalogue, and analyze, much as the scientist might, the various interactions that connect and define either side of the dialectical exchange.

It is important to understand, however, that for Balzac and Zola subject and object, or character and environment, are interdependent: each determines the other. We might refer to this sense of mutuality and reciprocity as the "Maison Vauquer effect," recalling the famous opening of *Le Père Goriot* where the narrator treats Mme Vauquer as the logical extension of her boarding house, and the boarding house as the logical extension of Mme Vauquer: "Her face as fresh as the first frost of autumn, her wrinkled eyes, her expression alternating between the fixed smile of a ballerina and the bitter scowl of a discounter of bills—in short, her entire person explains [*explique*] the boarding house, just as the boarding house implies [*implique*] her person."[41] Again, in "De la description" Zola carries Balzac's determinism even further, casting it in a rigidly materialist mold, one that ultimately operates more as a form of biology than sociology: "Character has become a product of air and soil, like a plant" (232).

Obviously, such an abbreviated account of the French realist novel produces reduction and distortion. Yet, despite the inaccuracies this involves—indeed, perhaps, because of them—the view I have developed here was widely accepted in France by writers both of Beckett's generation and of the preceding one.[42] I therefore now want to consider how Beckett and his two most influential precursors, Proust and Joyce, responded to the challenge of literary realism, and how Beckett in particular sought to rewrite what he regarded as the Cartesian novel. Even though Proust and Joyce represented a striking departure from the realist tradition, they continued to work in a mode that was—from Beckett's perspective—predominantly mimetic. We may begin to understand why this was the case by considering Proust and Joyce within the larger context of literary modernism.

~·

Literary modernism has often been viewed as an attempt to acknowledge the dominant role consciousness plays in apprehending reality, and both Proust and Joyce are frequently cited as examples of modernists who "subjectivized" the realist tradition.[43] Speaking in broad terms, we may say that this turn toward the subjective produced two large effects. First, if we understand the self as a bundle of "impressions, unstable, flickering, inconsistent," caught in its own "perpetual weaving and unweaving," then it will be difficult to think of character as possessing a fixed identity, one that is static, unitary or essential. Second, if we understand reality as the endless "movement . . . of impressions, images, sensations," a "tremulous wisp constantly re-forming itself on the stream," then it will be equally difficult to conceive of plot as an orderly and sequential progression, a development from a clearly defined beginning to a clearly defined ending.[44] The literary revolution that Proust and Joyce helped bring about consisted, at least in part, of translating this sense of reality as subjective event into a number of innovations in novelistic form, innovations that freed character and plot from what was largely a materialist ground. No longer held hostage by a Cartesian conception of time-space relations, character became less a fixed type and more an experiment in individuation, while plot moved away from the horizontal logic of chronology and toward a more fluid and variable mode of presentation.

At the same time, the new interest in subjectivity opened up the vast territory associated with the preconscious, subconscious, and unconscious, which in turn meant that myth and archetype began to emerge as increasingly important methods for organizing experience. If Balzac saw himself as the "secretary to society," Proust and Joyce saw themselves as the "secretary to the tribe," taking down dictation from a transhistorical and transcultural ego, through which they ultimately hoped to define the nature of "man."[45] Considered from this perspective, the *Recherche* seeks to sound human consciousness to its depths, recovering what Proust thought of as a "deep self," while *Finnegans Wake* undertakes the retelling of all human history through the story of five archetypal characters.

Beckett's account of what Proust and Joyce meant to modernism and how they responded to the realist tradition is most readily available in three of his early writings: a critical essay, "Dante . . . Bruno . Vico . . Joyce"; a monograph, *Proust*; and an aborted first novel, *Dream of Fair to Middling Women.*[46] "Dante," published in 1929, was commissioned by Joyce as part of a collection of essays to focus on "Work in Progress." Because the subject of the essay had been assigned—Joyce's relation to the three Italian writers of the title—and because much of its content was influenced by conversations with the master, it cannot be read as a simple or straightforward expression of how Beckett saw Joyce.[47] Nevertheless, the essay gives us considerable insight into two areas germane to our present discussion: Joyce's understanding of history and his treatment of language.

With regard to history, Beckett identifies in Joyce a Viconian or cyclical view of human development, which posits six stages of "social progression" corresponding to six essential "human motives" and six fundamental personality types.[48] Although the typological and deterministic aspects of this scheme call to mind the scientism of Balzacian realism, it is fundamentally different in the sense that Balzac's views are grounded in sociology, while Joyce's are grounded in myth and, by extension, anthropology. In other words, Joyce rejects the nineteenth century's faith in materialism, just as surely as he rejects Ireland's faith in the Church:

> Thus we have the spectacle of a human progression that depends for its movement on individuals, and which at the same time is indepen-

dent of individuals in virtue of what appears to be a preordained cy-
clism. It follows that History is neither to be considered as a formless
structure, due exclusively to the achievements of individual agents,
nor as possessing reality apart from and independent of them, ac-
complished behind their backs in spite of them, the work of some superior force, variously known as Fate, Chance, Fortune, God. (21)

As Beckett reads him, Vico condemns both the views offered here,
"the materialistic and the transcendental," preferring instead the notion that "individuality is the concretion of universality, and every
individual action is at the same time superindividual. The individual and the universal cannot be considered as distinct from each
other" (21–22).[49]

Beckett's other major point in the "Dante" essay touches upon
Joyce's use of language, which, like his use of history, is archetypal.
In Beckett's view, Joyce revolutionized literary language not by rendering it more sophisticated—as is usually thought—but by freeing
it from verbal abstraction and refinement.[50] Hence, Joyce has "desophisticated language" (28), returned it to its primal origins in sign,
symbol and gesture:

> The root of any word whatsoever can be traced back to some prelin-
> gual symbol. This early inability to abstract the general from the par-
> ticular produced the Type-names. It is the child's mind over again.
> The child extends the names of the first familiar objects to other
> strange objects in which he is conscious of some analogy. The first
> men, unable to conceive the abstract idea of "poet" or "hero," named
> every hero after the first hero, every poet after the first poet. (25)

Again, in Vico and Joyce the individual and the universal are treated
as one: Homer, the author of the *Iliad* and the *Odyssey*, and Homer
the archetype of all poets are identical. When language is used in this
way, blurring the distinction between the individual and the universal, we have left the realm of scientific description and entered the
realm of myth. Here the kind of sociological taxonomy that Balzac
proposed becomes impossible precisely because the individual specimen is rendered indistinguishable from its class or genus, making
the latter useless as a vehicle for explaining the former.

What follows from this Viconian notion of language is an entirely
new conception of the relation between literary form and literary
content: "Vico asserts the spontaneity of language and denies the

dualism of poetry and language. . . . In such direct expression, form and content are inseparable" (25). In this regard, it is worth recalling that the nineteenth-century novel depends on the dualism that Vico seeks to overcome. The realist or Balzacian novel aims not at equivalence but at adequation, not at identity but at similitude; and this means that the word must not *become* the thing, any more than character *becomes* environment or environment *becomes* character. In other words, while each term in any dialectical pairing is mutually defining, each term remains discrete and separate. Where Balzac seeks a language that functions at the "zero degree" and is therefore "transparent," Joyce seeks a language that is incarnational, a language that attempts, at some primal level, to reconnect word and thing:

> Here form *is* content, content *is* form. You complain that this stuff is not written in English. It is not written at all. It is not to be read—or rather it is not only to be read. It is to be looked at and listened to. His writing is not *about* something; *it is that something itself*. . . . When the sense is sleep, the words go to sleep. . . . When the sense is dancing, the words dance. (27)

If Beckett sees Joyce's revolt against the nineteenth-century novel as involving a movement outward, toward myth and archetype, he sees Proust's revolt as involving a movement inward, toward consciousness and the self. Thus, Beckett's 1931 monograph, *Proust*, examines the "excavatory" procedures of the *Recherche*, focusing on issues of narrative presentation, such as description, temporal structuring, and point of view, and on issues of character, such as psychology and identity. Marcel confronts the first of these issues when he realizes, toward the end of his book, that he does not live among, and therefore cannot write about, the external realities of life:

> The narrator has ascribed his "lack of talent" to a lack of observation, or rather to what he supposed was a non-artistic habit of observation. He was incapable of recording surface. So that when he reads such brilliant crowded reporting as the Goncourts' Journal, the only alternative to the conclusion that he is entirely wanting in the precious journalistic talent is the supposition that between the banality of life and the magic of literature there is a great gulf fixed. Either he is devoid of talent or art of reality. And he describes the radiographical quality of his observation. The copiable he does not see.[51]

Of course if Marcel is not a writer of the "surface," this implies that he is a writer of the "depths," a writer for whom "the only world that has reality and significance [is] the world of our own latent consciousness" (3). In rejecting the "realists" (59) and their "miserable statement of line and surface" (57), Proust turns instead to what Beckett describes as a form of "impressionism" (62), "the non-logical statement of phenomena in the order and exactitude of their perception" (66), and this means that in the *Recherche* "instinctive perception" or "intuition" achieves "primacy" (63). Thus, from Beckett's perspective, Proust is not ludic, self-inventing, self-constructing—in a word, postmodern—but an author for whom "the work of art is . . . discovered, uncovered, excavated, pre-existing within the artist, a law of nature" (64). To put it another way: the *Recherche* does indeed seek the ultimate ground of "reality" (the "law of nature"), but it is a reality located in the deepest substrate of human consciousness. Hence, "for the artist, the only possible hierarchy in the world of objective phenomena is represented by a table of their respective coefficients of penetration, that is to say, in terms of the subject" (64).[52]

The narrative techniques that Proust developed, techniques designed to "excavate" and "uncover," begin by making certain assumptions about consciousness and the self. Proust rejects what Beckett saw as the mechanical creations of nineteenth-century fiction, characters who are determined in advance, stamped out from the mold of "race, moment et milieu" and reducible to catchphrase definitions ("Père Grandet, l'avare"). Proust's conception of character is, of course, less fixed, more fluid. Because we inhabit time—time that endlessly deforms and transforms—the individual is not a single or unitary being but a series of selves, a complex of personalities: "We are not merely more weary because of yesterday, we are other, no longer what we were before the calamity of yesterday" (3); "the individual is a succession of individuals" (8). This does not mean, however, that for Proust the self is radically indeterminate or ultimately unknowable, a mere play of surface effects without any underlying structure or logic. If we can break through the outer shell of daily custom and routine, if we can penetrate to the "ideal core" of the individual, then we shall find the "gouffre interdit à nos sondes," the deep "essence of ourselves" (18). Thus Albertine, that protean creature of the sea, exists as a "*pictorial* multiplicity" that "will duly evolve into a *plastic* and moral multiplicity" (32). But behind her mobile beauty mark, her ever-shifting contours of appearance and affection, the narrator discovers a character of substantial inner resource, a character who is ultimately transformed from a "creature of surface into a creature of depth" (35).

Although we can find Beckett's responses to Joyce and Proust in his critical writings, we must turn to an abandoned work of fiction, *Dream of Fair to Middling Women* (1932), for his comments on nineteenth-century fiction. Here Balzac emerges, as he later will for Sarraute and Robbe-Grillet, as the principal target of an unrelenting attack on novelistic realism:[53]

> To read Balzac is to receive the impression of a chloroformed world. He is absolute master of his material, he can do what he likes with it, he can foresee and calculate its least vicissitude, he can write the end of his book before he has finished the first paragraph, because he has turned all his creatures into clockwork cabbages and can rely on their staying put wherever needed or staying going at whatever speed in whatever direction he chooses.[54]

What Beckett gives us in these pages is largely a caricature: this is Balzac, the keeper of the literary laboratory, the novelist as naturalist who studies the raw material of society the way a taxonomist studies the raw material of nature. According to this view, what Balzac hopes to achieve is nothing less than a comprehensive system of characterology, one in which each type is as determined by its environment, as predictable in its behavior, as any specimen fresh from the field. In arguing against the Balzacian novel as lifeless ("chloroformed"), as mindless and mechanized ("clockwork cabbage")—qualities that follow from a predictability whereby everything is determined in advance ("he can write the end of the book before he has finished the first paragraph")—Beckett is, in effect, already arguing for an indeterminacy of character and a contingency of narration. He does this, at least in part, by renouncing the realist equation between inside and outside, between character and environment. In speaking of one of his characters, Smeraldina-Rima, Beckett insists that she "is not demonstrable" and, with a passing glance at Taine, he refuses to inform the reader of her "milieu, race, family, structure, temperament, past and present and consequent and antecedent back to the first combination and the papas and mammas and paramours and cicisbei and the morals of Nanny and the nursery wallpapers and the third and fourth generation snuffles."[55] The summary view, which finally emerges in *Dream*, is a sweeping dismissal of the whole paraphernalia of realism, whether that involves locating character within a particular historical setting or shaping events into a narrative and verisimilar coherence. As Rubin Rabinovitz has observed:

> The narrator of *Dream* refuses to indulge in . . . artifices of plot manipulation: he claims he is "neither Deus enough nor ex machina enough . . . " (p. 104). A cohesive plot makes him uncomfortable: "The only unity in this story," he says, "is, please God, an involuntary unity" (p. 118). After listing a few possibilities for a character's final scene he says, "that ought to dénouer that"—as if he really had provided a denouement (p. 132). When the narrator finally does revert to old-fashioned methods, he cannot help grumbling. It is with very bad will indeed, he says, that he approaches "the gehenna of narratio recta."[56]

We might summarize Beckett's critical response to Proust, Joyce, and the Balzacian tradition as follows: while he sees his two masters reacting against nineteenth-century realism, challenging its assumptions and developing alternatives to its techniques, he still regards them as writers who are working within a Cartesian paradigm, one that is based on dualistic and mimetic assumptions. Rather than dismantle the logic of foundationalism or the aesthetics of representation, Proust and Joyce have simply brought into the foreground the role consciousness plays in "apprehending reality." In their hands the object is not destroyed as an epistemological unit but subjectivized and psychologized. It is, therefore, quite possible in their work to imagine that we are getting back to the "ground of reality," recovering from the flow of time a complex but unified character, a varied but consistent plot. Far from removing the reader from the binary oppositions that have informed the realist novel, Proust and Joyce go, as it were, underground, urging us to descend into the subterranean world of consciousness, psychology, and archetype in order that we may better understand the configuration at the surface.

All of this is to say that Beckett regards Proust and Joyce as what I have been calling "modern" writers, while he himself is struggling to become a "postmodern" writer.[57] Of course, such a view runs counter to a good deal of recent criticism on Proust and Joyce. The *Recherche* has, for instance, been read as postmodern to the extent that it deals with an "absent I" that generates itself through an act of writing—an act of writing that is, significantly, deferred until the end of the book.[58] The case of Joyce is complicated by the fact that we are dealing with two related but highly distinctive novels: *Ulysses* and *Finnegans Wake*. *Ulysses* has itself often been treated as a self-divided work, modern in the first half ("Telemachus" through "Scylla and Charybdis"), postmodern in the second ("Wandering Rocks" through "Penelope").[59] Critics have been more willing to identify *Finnegans Wake* as a thoroughly postmodern text, but it also appears to straddle the modern/postmodern divide. Thus, insofar as its language is self-referential and self-generating, constructed on a principle of linguistic combination and permutation, the text can be seen as postmodern; but insofar as its plot and characters are primal and archetypal, designed to utter "deep truths" about the nature of "humanity," it can be seen as modern.

Of course, our concern is not to determine whether Proust and Joyce are better read as modern or postmodern, but to understand what they meant to Beckett. As I have attempted to show, he viewed these two writers as brilliant innovators who dramatically rearranged the elements of the novel within an old paradigm, revitalizing the genre by returning it to the subjective origins of the cogito. Beckett, however, hoped to achieve something quite different: not the resurrection of the old paradigm but its dissolution, not a subjectivized account of reality but an end to foundationalism and the mimesis of traditional fiction.

The initial problem for Beckett was how to move beyond the old paradigm from a position that nevertheless began within that paradigm. Could one deconstruct Descartes by using the language of subject and object, the categories of reason and madness? This was to become the point of departure for *Murphy*, a novel that quite consciously deals with many of the philosophical and literary concepts we have been discussing but in ways that attempt to work both within and beyond those concepts. Thus, although *Murphy* evokes the Cartesian legacy more directly than any of Beckett's other novels, it discovers at the heart of the cogito not the rationalism of the Enlightenment but the derangement of the lunatic asylum. At the same time, as we will see, it represents Beckett's most elaborate experiment in nineteenth-century novelistic construction—but here realist technique does not so much establish the coherence and stability of the world as plunge it into an epistemological vertigo. As Beckett wrote some years later in a review of Thomas McGreevy, "There is at least this to be said for mind, that it can dispel mind."[60] *Murphy* may be read as Beckett's first attempt to give a fictional shape to this proposition.

CHAPTER TWO

Madness and the Cogito in 'Murphy'

Samuel Beckett's novels are haunted by images of the madhouse. Watt and Macmann become patients in a mental hospital; Molloy and Malone endure what appears to be an institutional confinement; even Worm, surrounded by a "committee" that files reports, suffers under a clinical gaze of sorts. If standing behind Beckett's fiction is all the accumulated weight and tradition of the Enlightenment—extending from Descartes's empiricism to Balzac's scientism—then rising before it, beckoning to it, is the Enlightenment's mad inversion, the dark netherworld of insanity, where all the carefully articulated structures of the *ratio* collapse into chaos and unmeaning. It is in the space that lies between these poles, the space that separates Reason from Unreason, the cogito from madness, that Beckett stages his first novel, *Murphy*.

In the last thirty years or so, that space has been most memorably explored by Michel Foucault in his celebrated study *Madness and Civilization*. Foucault's basic argument is well known: during the Middle Ages and the Renaissance, madness was stigmatized by society but not excluded from it. There consequently developed in this period relatively free converse between the "sane" and the "mad," with the latter playing a role that was socially visible and culturally significant.[1] However, with the coming of the Enlightenment—what I have broadly defined as modernity—all of this changed. The mad underwent what Foucault describes as the Great Confinement: their citizenship within the community of man was revoked, and they were hustled away, often under seal of a *lettre de cachet*, into an internment designed to deny their very existence. Madness now became the negation of Reason, its antithetical Other, a condition associated with the "nonbeing" that stood at the heart of the madman's experience and that was most immediately apparent in his habit of seeing and hearing what-was-not-there.[2]

Especially important for our purposes is the fact that Foucault draws an explicit parallel between the way the Enlightenment sought to eliminate madness from society and the way Descartes sought to eliminate it from philosophy. Focusing on the famous opening to the *Meditations*, Foucault argues that in "the economy of doubt" Descartes discovers a "fundamental disequilibrium between madness on the one hand and dream and error on the other."[3] While the latter are "surmounted within the structure of truth," measurable against criteria external to themselves, madness knows only itself and is therefore "excluded by the subject who doubts." As Foucault explains: "It is not the permanence of a truth which secures thought against madness, as though it permitted one to detach oneself from an error or to emerge from a dream; it is the impossibility of being mad, essential not to the object of thought but to the subject who thinks."[4] Given Foucault's reading of Descartes, madness cannot count as one of the conditions under which thought (*pensée*) occurs, because madness is, strictly speaking, unthinkable, the outer boundary of the cogito, its negative extreme:

> The progress of Cartesian doubt seems to demonstrate that in the 17th century . . . madness is placed outside the domain of appurtenance where the subject holds its rights to the truth—this domain which for classical thought is reason itself. From that point forward, madness is exiled. If *man* can always be mad, *thought*, like the exercise of the sovereignty of the subject which gives itself the task of perceiving the true, cannot be mad. A line of partition is traced that will soon render impossible the familiar experience in the Renaissance of an unreasonable Reason, of a reasonable Unreason.[5]

In his essay "Cogito and the History of Madness," Derrida takes the position that Foucault has badly misconstrued Descartes. The whole point behind evoking madness as an extreme case of doubt, Derrida contends, is to show that even if the thinking subject is insane, the truth of *cogito ergo sum* nevertheless remains valid:

> The certainty . . . [of the cogito] need not be sheltered from an emprisoned madness, for it is attained and ascertained within madness itself. It is valid *even if I am mad*—a supreme self-confidence that

seems to require neither the exclusion nor the circumventing of madness. Descartes never interns madness, neither at the stage of natural
doubt nor at the stage of metaphysical doubt.[6]

As Derrida sums up this argument, "whether I am mad or not, *Cogito, sum*. Madness is therefore, in every sense of the word, only one
case of thought (*within* thought)."[7]

It is of course irrelevant to our present purposes which of these
two interpretations we decide more accurately represents Descartes's
Meditations.[8] I am using Foucault and Derrida to lay out a problem
that Beckett explores at some length in *Murphy*, a problem that depends on understanding what kind of relation, if any, exists between
the cogito and madness. As we have seen, for Foucault the cogito
excludes madness from the outset, establishing a kind of *cordon san-
itaire* designed to protect Reason from the contaminating influence
of its demented Other—while for Derrida, the cogito not only includes madness, but also is, in an important sense, constructed out of
it, thus revealing the extent to which the Enlightenment rests upon
the quicksands of Unreason. Beckett, I argue, anticipates the Derridean position that the cogito and madness are not strictly partitioned, that they do not function merely as the affirmation or negation of Reason. Yet from Beckett's perspective the danger is not so
much that the cogito will be tainted by madness, but that madness
will be tainted by the cogito. Yes, Beckett concedes, the subject can
say *cogito, sum* even if it is mad, but—alas—it cannot say I am mad,
even if *cogito, sum*. And it is this second proposition that Murphy
spends an entire novel vainly struggling to utter.

It will be my contention, then, that *Murphy* provides a kind of alternate history of the cogito, one which invites us to imagine that
Descartes has retired to the heated closet not to think his way beyond doubt but to think his way back into the most radical form of
doubt there is—madness. Not *cogito, sum* but *cogito, demens sum*.[9]
Hence, Murphy accepts employment at the Magdalen Mental Mercyseat only after he discovers that his room will be a tiny mansard—
a rough approximation of the philosopher's closet—and only after
it is agreed that his quasi-Cartesian enclosure will be heated. This is,
as Derrida suggests of the *Meditations*, to build one's *poêle* on the
foundations of a madhouse. And, in a sense, that is precisely what
Descartes himself appears to have done. For there is certainly a kind
of madness at work in a dualism that radically dissevers mind from

body, that schizophrenically splits experience into utterly disjunct realms. Obviously, for Descartes such dualism is motivated by a desire to coordinate subject and object, to observe and record their various points of intersection and correspondence. Out of this will come, Descartes assures us, a system of rationalism, empiricism, and science. Beckett, however, wants something entirely different: a Descartes who locks the door on his closet and turns up the heat—a cogito that withdraws from the big world into the little world and systematically doubts its way to madness.

Such a decisive inversion of Descartes suggests that Beckett's preoccupations in *Murphy* are almost exclusively philosophical. Yet these preoccupations, philosophical as they are, raise two important problems concerning literary form. The first problem, which relates to character, involves Murphy's desire to move from the cogito to madness, to escape subject-object dialectics by solipsistically withdrawing into himself. At stake here is an epistemological experiment, one in which Murphy attempts to enter self-consciously into a state of anti–self-consciousness, to will himself into the will-less indeterminacy of the "third zone." Yet if Murphy is able to achieve his goal, if he succeeds in dissolving himself as an individual, then he will cease to exist as a character. The second problem, which relates to plot, concerns Beckett's struggle to overcome the dualism inherent in the realist tradition. What results from this struggle is a novel that divides itself into two parts, which I call the "inner" and "outer" novels. Because this division represents an effort not to articulate subject and object but to radically separate them—indeed to undermine the very dialectic that defines them—it is anti-Cartesian in spirit. And yet the fact that it leads precisely to the dualism it seems to transcend makes for an irony very much to Beckett's purposes. For in the final analysis, *Murphy* demonstrates just how difficult it is for the cogito to escape into madness, and insofar as the novel ultimately delivers its hero into the "superfine chaos" of the "third zone," it is only through a piece of narrative intervention as deliberately and artificially contrived as anything out of Balzac.

From the outset, Murphy finds himself caught in the grip of a Cartesian dualism that he struggles to overcome, or at least to redefine. So it is that the opening of the novel divides itself between two separate and distinct spheres, what the narrator calls the "big world" and the "little world": "The sun shone, having no alternative, on the nothing new. Murphy sat out of it, as though he were free, in a mew in West Brompton" (1). Here an opposition is established that will accrete significance as the novel progresses: the external, physical world—represented by the sun's clocklike movements through the heavens—functions like an oversized machine, enmeshed in the gears and levers of chronometric time; the internal, mental world—represented by Murphy's rocking chair accelerating, impossibly, toward stasis—unfolds as a series of entropic transformations suspended in a Bergsonian *durée*. The first is deterministic and closed to change ("having no alternative, on the nothing new"); the second seeks its own freedom and is open to change ("Murphy sat out of it, as though he were free").

Murphy himself begins from a position of dualism. This position is explicitly articulated in chapter 6 of the novel, when we are told "Murphy felt himself split in two, a body and a mind" (109). And it is implicitly suggested at other points—when, for instance, Murphy comments to Celia, "What have I now? . . . I distinguish. You, my body and my mind" (39–40)—or when we are informed that his suit is "bodytight": "It admitted no air from the outer world, it allowed none of Murphy's own vapours to escape" (72). It is important to understand, however, that while Murphy starts from a Cartesian position, he carries its assumptions to a logical extreme that is anything but Cartesian. Hence, the dualism that attracts Murphy is a particularly radical kind advocated by Descartes's Occasionalist disciple, Arnold Geulincx, whose "ubi nihil vales, ibi nihil velis" the narrator approvingly quotes (178). In contrast to Descartes's assertion that mind and body intersect at the conarium or pineal gland, Geulincx argues that these two spheres are absolutely separate, that no immediate or direct commerce unites them. In effect, Neary is calling Murphy a Geulincxian when he remarks "your conarium has shrunk to nothing" (6), a point that is made even more emphatically in chapter 6: "They [the body and the mind] had intercourse apparently, otherwise he could not have known that they had anything in common. But he felt his mind to be bodytight and did not understand through what channel the intercourse was effected nor how the two experiences came to overlap. He was satisfied that neither followed from the other" (109).[10]

In separating inside from outside, mental from physical, Murphy seeks what is, in effect, the philosophical analogue to schizophrenia, a cogito founded on madness. His efforts toward this end are anatomized in chapter 6, where we are introduced to the three zones of his mind. While there have been numerous critical commentaries on this chapter, I would like to emphasize the extent to which Murphy's three zones are hierarchically arranged according to a principle of increasing freedom.[11] Thus, in the first zone, "the forms with parallel" (111), Murphy is limited to the material of physical reality, but he possesses the freedom he would lack in the outer world to arrange it according to his lights: "here the kick that the physical Murphy received, the mental Murphy gave" (111). The second zone offers greater freedom than the first because in it Murphy is constrained neither by the intractability of the outer world nor by the forms that define it: "In the second were the forms without parallel. Here the pleasure was contemplation. . . . Here was the Belacqua bliss and others scarcely less precise" (111). Again the narrator emphasizes that it is precisely freedom that is at issue in retreating to these two zones, in severing the little world from the big: "In both these zones of his private world Murphy felt sovereign and free, in the one to requite himself, in the other to move as he pleased from one unparalleled beatitude to another" (112).

But all of this is as nothing in comparison to the third zone where Murphy discovers an entirely new order of freedom:

> The third, the dark, was a flux of forms, a perpetual coming together and falling asunder of forms. . . . Here there was nothing but commotion and the pure forms of commotion. Here he was not free, but a mote in the dark of absolute freedom. He did not move, he was a point in the ceaseless unconditioned generation and passing away of line.
>
> Matrix of surds.
>
> It was pleasant to kick the Ticklepennies and Miss Carridges simultaneously together into ghastly acts of love. It was pleasant to lie dreaming on the shelf beside Belacqua, watching the dawn break crooked. But how much more pleasant was the sensation of being a missile without provenance or target, caught up in a tumult of non-Newtonian motion. So pleasant that pleasant was not the word.
>
> Thus as his body set him free more and more in his mind, he took to spending less and less time in the light, spitting at the breakers of the world; and less in the half light, where the choice of bliss intro-

duced an element of effort; and more and more in the dark, in the
will-lessness, a mote in its absolute freedom. (112–13)

Here notions such as the self or the unitary ego fall away or collapse
into themselves, like a kind of phenomenological antimatter, creating a world where determinate individuals yield to transpersonal
states, where static forms and fixed outlines dissolve into metamorphoses of becoming. In the third zone, Murphy is "free" not in the
limited sense, which we might attach to an individual, but in a
broader sense, which extends beyond the restrictions of personality,
which comprehends the self as "a mote in the dark of absolute freedom."[12]

Opposed to this radical indeterminacy is the character who is
fixed in a world where outside and inside are causally related, where
environment becomes personality and the fate of the individual is
decided in advance. Determinism of this sort is consistently associated in Beckett with the figure of the puppet in the box, a mindless
and mechanized creation that serves as a counterpart to Balzac's
"clockwork cabbages." In *Murphy* the narrative marionettes include
those characters who are most clearly the parodic remains of a realist tradition, characters like Mr. Kelly, Miss Counihan, and Wylie,
who are compared, respectively, to a doll (12), a traffic signal (55),
and an empty-headed automaton (226–27). It is Murphy alone who
appears to rise above this determinism, to transcend the wobbling
rigidities of the mannequin: "All the puppets in this book whinge
sooner or later, except Murphy, who is not a puppet" (122).[13]

Reducing Murphy to a puppet is presumably something Beckett
wants to avoid, and one way to read the novel is as an extended attempt on Beckett's part to preserve his hero from the mechanization
that defines the other characters. Whether we should understand this
as the central project of *Murphy* or merely a framework for exploring problems that grow out of the nineteenth-century novel remains
to be seen. But we may, in any event, begin to consider these alternatives more closely by examining how Beckett's novel divides itself
between the little world and the big, between the inner world and
the outer.

⌣ᐧ

In good Geulincxian fashion, the inner and outer worlds of *Murphy* have intercourse—otherwise we would not know "that they

have anything in common"—but "through what channel that intercourse [is] effected" (109) remains mysterious. The inner world, which tells the story of Murphy and his psychotic withdrawal, promises an absolute freedom, whereas the outer world, focusing on Neary and company in pursuit of Murphy, guarantees a rigid determinism. As the chief representative of the outer world, Neary acts as Murphy's opposite. Thus, while the former is a strict "Newtonian" (201) who believes that "all life is figure and ground" (4), the latter yearns to enter into a "tumult of non-Newtonian motion" (113); while the former works to define boundaries and assure stability, to discover, as the title of his tractate—"The Doctrine of the Limit" (50)—suggests, the latter strives to transcend all limits, to become a "missile without provenance" (112).

The motive force behind Neary's analytic assault on the world, behind his predilection for breaking things up into figure and ground, is not the detached cerebration we might expect, but an erotic desire, which has inspired him, as the novel opens, to a Gestaltian rhapsody on the subject of Miss Dwyer: "Murphy, all life is figure and ground . . . the face . . . or system of faces, against the big blooming buzzing confusion. I think of Miss Dwyer" (4). Beckett is here giving us, to vary one of Murphy's formulations, a "critique of impure love" (103). According to this view, desire functions like a wheel in a squirrel cage: the lover thinks that he is actively pursuing the love object, when in fact he is merely retracing his steps through the same circuit. Of course, he may in the vulgar sense possess the love object, but not in any significant sense; as Beckett writes in *Proust*, "No object prolonged in this temporal dimension tolerates possession, meaning by possession total possession" (41). Hence, Neary's discovery that winning Miss Dwyer leads to the disappointment rather than the realization of his desires: "No sooner had Miss Dwyer, despairing of recommending herself to Flight-Lieutenant Elliman, made Neary as happy as a man could desire, than she became one with the ground against which she had figured so prettily" (48).

The larger point is that Neary has not genuinely possessed Miss Dwyer, because desire cannot break free of its self-enclosed orbit; it cannot move beyond itself, move beyond its own logic of anticipated yet deferred gratification, and still remain desire. Trapped within a libidinal economy that is anchored in a deterministic world, Neary may occasionally succeed in transgressing its limits, but the results will always prove illusory and unsatisfactory—a host of tantalizing daydreams, which recede at the least touch. This is the lesson of Wylie's story of the horse leech's daughter ("For every symptom that is eased, another is made worse. The horse leech's daughter is a closed system. Her quantum of wantum cannot vary" [57]), a story that invokes the passage in Proverbs 30.15 about "things that are never satisfied," about the insatiability of desire. But if desire is a closed system and the love object a mere pretext for its invariable operations, something to keep the wheel in the squirrel cage spinning, then it is of little consequence who, or even what, the love object is. Accordingly, love becomes a kind of merry-go-round in which what matters is not who is chasing whom but that the chasing not stop, that the machine be kept going: "[Neary loved] Miss Dwyer, who loved a Flight-Lieutenant Elliman, who loved a Miss Farren of Ringsakiddy, who loved a Father Fitt of Ballinclashet, who in all sincerity was bound to acknowledge a certain vocation for a Mrs. West of Passage, who loved Neary" (5). As Neary wittily puts it, "Love requited . . . is a short circuit" (5).

The whole problem of desire is illustrated by the parable—it is hardly less than that—of the five biscuits. Each day Murphy's lunch consisted of a cup of tea and a packet of biscuits, and each day it raised a difficulty: in what order should he eat the biscuits?

> They were the same as always, a Ginger, an Osborne, a Digestive, a Petit Beurre and one anonymous. He always ate the first-named last, because he liked it the best, and the anonymous first, because he thought it very likely the least palatable. The order in which he ate the remaining three was indifferent to him and varied irregularly from day to day. On his knees now before the five it struck him for the first time that these prepossessions reduced to a paltry six the number of ways in which he could make his meal. . . . But were he to take the final step and overcome his infatuation with the ginger, then the assortment would spring to life before him, dancing the radiant measure of its total permutability, edible in a hundred and twenty ways! (96–97)

Of course, experiencing the biscuits in all 120 combinations means purging them of any material reference, means reconceiving them as a set of formal counters that are exclusively defined by their relational possibilities. Like the first zone of Murphy's mind, the permutation draws on the "elements of a physical experience," which it then makes "available for new arrangement" (111). This trans-mutation of the "dog's life" into a "radiant abstract" is possible, however, only if Murphy can overcome what attaches him to phys-ical reality, which is to say, the discriminations of his appetite and the will to satisfy them: "Murphy fell forward on his face on the grass, beside those biscuits of which . . . he could not partake in their fullness until he had learnt not to prefer any one to any other" (97).

By leaving behind those parts of himself that are anchored in the external world, Murphy can enter into an abstracted free play with the stuff of reality ("the world of the body broken up into the pieces of a toy," 112), beyond desire ("without love or hate," 112), beyond will ("in the will-lessness," 113). For in the absence of will and de-sire, the self is no longer obliged to move along any particular tra-jectory, to pursue a certain set of objects, to enter into a series of worldly negotiations that have the effect of constraining and defin-ing it. Under such conditions, the self, dispersed simultaneously in all directions, quite simply ceases to be, leading to what is, in Mur-phy's terms, the end of individuality: "Here he was not free, but a mote in the dark of absolute freedom" (112).

But the indeterminacy this involves raises the problem of how one self-consciously seeks anti–self-consciousness, of how one willfully achieves will-lessness. Murphy struggles with these difficulties, as he struggled with his five biscuits and, in attempting to resolve them, turns to astrology and Geulincx.

⌣˙

It may strike the reader as odd that a character as obsessively pre-occupied with freedom as Murphy should submit himself to an or-der as rigidly deterministic as astrology, and yet he describes it as "the only system outside his own in which he felt the least confi-dence" (22–23). If, however, we read "outside his own" as meaning not merely "other than" but more precisely "external to," then we may begin to understand the appeal of astrology, which, precisely because it is arbitrary and mechanistic, represents the appropriate means for dealing with an arbitrary and mechanistic world. Put an-other way, if Murphy is forced into commerce with what he else-where calls the "colossal fiasco" (178), astrology has the advantage of at least acknowledging its own determinism, of making no pre-tenses to freedom.

Standing behind this sensibility is a Geulincxian point of view that utterly renounces the outside. In a memorable metaphor, which compares the body to a ship and the mind to its passenger, Geulincx describes the limited freedom accorded man in his transactions with the material world: "While the ship headed towards the West speedily drags the passenger away, nothing prevents him from walking towards the East on that very ship."[14] We are sovereign only in the little world of the mind, not in the big world of physical reality; we can move within the bounds of the ship, but the ship moves whither it will. Of course, this is to say that Murphy has not so much submitted to astrology as forged it into a kind of Geulincxian armor with which he protects himself against an importunate world; hence, Murphy's exchange with Celia on the subject of his horoscope:

> "Pandit Suk has never done anything better."
> "Can you work now after that?" said Celia.
> "Certainly I can," said Murphy. "The very first fourth to fall on a Sunday in 1936 I begin. I put on my gems and off I go, to custode, detect, explore, pioneer, promote or pimp, as occasion may arise."
> "And in the meantime?" said Celia.
> "In the meantime," said Murphy, "I must just watch out for fits, publishers, quadrupeds, the stone, Bright's——"
> She gave a cry of despair intense while it lasted, then finished and done with, like an infant's.
> "How you can be such a fool and a brute," she said, and did not bother to finish.
> "But you wouldn't have me go against the diagram," said Murphy, "surely to God." (34)

Coming from Murphy, the "surely to God" is priceless. He has, as Celia knows full well, perverted his horoscope from a plan of action into a "corpus of deterrents" (34), from a guide for commerce with the big world into a justification for sanctuary in the little world. True, Celia finally prevails upon Murphy to find work, but even then astrology provides a Geulincxian absolution, one that enables him to treat his dealings with the outer world as though they were an accident of birth rather than a consequence of choice. Thus, although Murphy accepts the post at the Magdalen Mental Mercyseat on the basis of a "sudden syzygy in Suk's delineations of lunatic in paragraph two and custodian in paragraph seven" (93), he recognizes that the forecast is a fraud and the story it tells his own invention: "This six-pence worth of sky, from the ludicrous broadsheet that Murphy had called his life-warrant, his bull of incommunication and corpus of deterrents, changed into the poem that he alone of the living could write" (93). Astrology does not, then, provide a regimen that, by denying will and desire, enables Murphy to transcend a coherent and limited self. It is, rather, a makeshift device for holding the world at arm's length, for keeping it at a distance while Murphy pretends not to see it. As he comes to recognize toward the end of the novel, "he was the prior system" (183) and his stars were his "vitagraph" (183), the "superfluous cartoon of his own" (189).

By the same token, Geulincxian renunciation leads not to the expansive freedom of Murphy's third zone but to a melancholy caricature of it, and when Beckett quotes the Geulincxian boat metaphor in *Molloy*, he cynically transforms the passenger into a galley slave who crawls rather than walks toward his freedom: "I who loved the image of old Geulincx, dead young, who left me free, on the black boat of Ulysses, to crawl towards the East, along the deck" (68).[15] The inadequacy of Geulincx is more explicitly worked out in *Murphy*, where Beckett's hero can admire the "beautiful Belgo-Latin of Geulincx," particularly his famous "ubi nihil vales, ibi nihil velis" (178), while rejecting it as a solution to his predicament:

> But it was not enough to want nothing where he was worth nothing, nor even to take the further step of renouncing all that lay outside the intellectual love in which alone he could love himself. . . . It had not been enough and showed no signs of being enough. These dispositions and others ancillary, pressing every available means (e.g. the rocking-chair) into their service, could sway the issue in the desired direction, but not clinch it. (179)

At Magdalen Mental Mercyseat, though, Murphy wants to move beyond the desired direction to the clinch itself, and he wonders if he might not achieve this by embracing the psychosis he finds all around him: "Suppose he were to clinch it now, in the service of the Clinch clan" (179).

∿·

If astrology and Geulincxian philosophy require that Murphy submit to a system outside the self, Magdalen Mental Mercyseat represents the opposite alternative—a turn toward interiority, which, like the madness it emulates, restricts itself to the narrow circle of consciousness:

> Stimulated by all those lives immured in mind, as he insisted on sup-posing, he laboured more diligently than ever before at his own little dungeon in Spain. Three factors especially encouraged him in this and in the belief that he had found his kindred at last. The first was the absolute impassiveness of the higher schizoids, in the face of the most pitiless therapeutic bombardment. The second was the padded cells. The third was his success with the patients. (180)

Descartes locked away in his heated closet, ceaselessly revolving mind about itself, serves as the paradigm for this kind of detach-ment, only here the cogito not only does not exclude madness but is itself identified with it. Hence, the very name and situation of the asylum, suggestive of both sedentary cerebration ("mental mercy-seat") and radical dualism ("ideally situated . . . on the boundary of two counties," 156), punningly pay tribute to Descartes. At the same time, the heart of the asylum consists of the padded cells, those sanc-tuaries from the big world that, in their warmth and self-enclosure, constitute a kind of lunatic's *poêle*:

> The pads surpassed by far all he had ever been able to imagine in the way of indoor bowers of bliss. . . . The temperature was such that only total nudity could do it justice. No system of ventilation ap-peared to dispel the illusion of respirable vacuum. The compartment was windowless, like a monad, except for the shuttered judas in the door, at which a sane eye appeared. (181)

However, as appealing as Murphy finds the physical organization of Magdalen Mental Mercyseat, the asylum's chief attraction proves to be its patients, and its chief patient proves to be Mr. Endon:

> It seemed to Murphy that he was bound to Mr. Endon, not by the tab only, but by a love of the purest possible kind, exempt from the big world's precocious ejaculations of thought, word and deed. They re-mained to one another, even when most profoundly one in spirit, as it seemed to Murphy, Mr. Murphy and Mr. Endon. (184)

"Most profoundly one in spirit," Murphy sees in Endon a reflection of his own solipsistic intentions, a medium through which he can glimpse his third zone. He is consequently drawn to Endon as to a mirror image of himself ("as Narcissus to his fountain," 186), and their encounter comes to represent a confrontation between Murphy and—as *endon* translates from the Greek—Murphy's own "within."[16] Here, at last, the novel appears to have arrived at its epistemological destination, as we are presented with an image of Cartesianism schizophrenically withdrawing into itself.

The encounter between Murphy and Endon, between the cogito and madness, comes in three stages, the first of which involves the wonderfully comic chess game of chapter 11. Endon, playing Black, wheels his pieces through a series of configurations, which alternately shape themselves into symmetry and disperse themselves into randomness, while never acknowledging the existence of another player or the larger goal of a game to be won or lost. Meanwhile, Murphy begins by imitating Endon and then attempts, with increasing desperation, to engage him. Murphy resigns when Endon, in blissful disregard of the check, threatens King to King 1, a move which, by restoring each of his major pieces to its original position, would complete the circuit of his permutation.

There follows the second stage in which Murphy, about to lift out of subject-object dialectics, hallucinates Endon as an aestheticized image of his own transcendence, a kind of bird-man in pre-Raphaelite plumage:[17]

> Following Mr. Endon's forty-third move Murphy gazed for a long time at the board before laying his Shah on his side, and again for a long time after that act of submission. But little by little his eyes were captured by the brilliant swallow-tail of Mr. Endon's arms and legs, purple, scarlet, black and glitter, till they saw nothing else, and that in a short time only as vivid blur, Neary's big blooming buzzing confusion or ground, mercifully free of figure. (245)

Murphy goes on to encounter, if only briefly, his Within or third zone, a place where the bounding line and the limiting form become conceptual impossibilities, where the distinction between figure and ground, subject and object, mind and body become as superfluous as Murphy's chess game was to Endon's:

> Then this also faded and Murphy began to see nothing, that colourlessness which is such a rare postnatal treat, being the absence (to abuse a nice distinction) not of *percipere* but of *percipi*. His other senses also found themselves at peace, an unexpected pleasure. Not the numb peace of their own suspension, but the positive peace that

comes when the somethings give way, or perhaps simply add up, to the Nothing, than which in the guffaw of the Abderite naught is more real. (246)

Emerging from his trance, Murphy discovers Endon exploring the permutability of the indicator switch on the hypomanic's pad (247) and returns him to his cell where the final stage of their confrontation is played out in terms, once again, of mirror images. Thus, Murphy on his knees beside the bed, "took Mr. Endon's head in his hands and brought the eyes to bear on his, or rather his on them, across a narrow gulf of air, the merest hand's-breadth of air" (248). So situated, he gazes into Mr. Endon's eyes and sees "horribly reduced, obscured and distorted, his own image" (249). The episode occurs face to face, as Murphy beholds the mirror image of himself, obscured and distorted, and the reader whose ear is attuned to the Bible—as Beckett's was—will hear in such a description 1 Corinthians 13.12: "For now we see through a glass darkly; but then face to face: now I know in part; but then shall I know even as I also am known."

The allusion may seem remote, but the "dark glass" of 1 Corinthians becomes one of the major motifs in Beckett's fiction. Watt, for instance, also undertakes, and then gradually abandons, an effort to discover himself in the Endon-like figure of Mr. Knott: "Little by little Watt abandoned all hope, all fear, of ever seeing Mr Knott face to face. . . . The few glimpses caught of Mr Knott, by Watt, were not clearly caught, but as it were in a glass" (*Watt*, 146–47). In similar fashion, Moran combines the motifs of the font of Narcissus and the dark glass, as he first contemplates his own reflection in a stream ("I dragged myself down to the stream. I lay down and looked at my reflection," *Molloy*, 199) and then scrutinizes a shadow figure who looks suspiciously like himself ("There I was face to face with a dim man, dim of face and dim of body, because of the dark," 205–6).[18]

The encounter with Endon represents, in other words, a moment of self-reflective consciousness, although it simultaneously represents an attempt to transcend self-reflection and enter into the third zone. The contradiction involved here will ultimately prove irresolvable, but Murphy's goal is momentarily glimpsed when he sees himself as a "speck in Mr. Endon's unseen" (250), a clear echo of "a mote in the dark of absolute freedom" (112). Yet to enter into the third zone, to dissolve into radical indeterminacy, means that one cannot be conscious of oneself, and this Murphy most sorrowfully is: "The relation between Mr. Murphy and Mr. Endon could not have been better summed up than by the former's sorrow at seeing himself in the latter's immunity from seeing anything but himself" (250). Murphy has briefly known the space beyond self-consciousness that Endon appears to inhabit, but he has not crossed over and entered into it.

As Murphy goes forth into the dawn, he realizes that he is all played out. He has moved along two paths in an effort to transcend himself, but in both cases he has run into a dead end. Nothing has come of either the Geulincxian-inspired astrology ("He raised his face to a starless sky, abandoned," 251), or the self-willed psychosis ("He saw eyeballs being scraped, first any eyeballs, then Mr. Endon's," 251). He attempts a feeble retreat into his first zone—that mental space where he may summon up and rearrange the stuff of physical reality—but this, too, proves futile: "When he was naked he lay down in a tuft of soaking tuffets and tried to get a picture of Celia. In vain. Of his mother. In vain. Of his father. . . . In vain in all cases" (251).

Murphy returns to his room and his rocking chair, "dimly intending" to resume his old life with Celia and to abandon his psychotic quest for self-dissolution and freedom. The novel's climax ironically explodes this quest when Murphy is delivered up to the third zone by a flush of the cosmic toilet. The heated closet has figuratively and literally overheated and sent the whole Cartesian experiment sky-high.[19] In the end, Murphy enters the "excellent gas, superfine chaos" (253) the only way possible: not through an act of will but by sheer accident—for all along the problem has been that he could not self-consciously seek anti–self-consciousness, that he could not will will-lessness. He finally becomes "the mote in the dark," "the missile without provenance," "the matrix of surds," though not in the way he expected. Murphy has ended as the comic butt of his own epistemological quest.

Of course, the narrator has known from the outset that Murphy's quest for absolute freedom was doomed to failure: "The sun shone, having no alternative, on the nothing new. Murphy sat out of it, *as though he were free*" (1, my emphasis). The mere formulation, "as though he were free," is sufficient to deprive Murphy of any genuine autonomy, since it implies the kind of all-seeing, all-knowing narrator whose characters are determined in advance. This is precisely the case with Murphy: his end has been formulated from the beginning. Thus, although he has used astrology as a way of ironizing his transactions with a deterministic outer world, the horoscope accurately predicts those transactions when it warns against Bright's disease and quadrupeds, thereby anticipating Murphy's unhappy meeting with Rosie Dew and her dachshund. In effect, Murphy's irony is itself ironized, and we see, even as he contemptuously dismisses the outer world, how completely he is circumscribed by it. Murphy had sought to move beyond a world charted along Cartesian coordinates, but he ultimately finds he cannot escape from it; he had sought to move from the cogito to madness, but he discovers how difficult it is to make that transit without bringing the world of the *ratio* with him.

At the same time, there has been considerable narrative criticism, however subtly articulated, of Murphy's major effort to get beyond himself, of his decision that "nothing less than a slap-up psychosis could consummate his life's strike" (184). As a result, those passages that concern the patients at M.M.M. reveal a certain tension between Murphy's rapturously positive view of their situation and the narrator's more skeptical sense of it:

> The issue therefore, *as lovingly simplified and perverted by Murphy*, lay between nothing less fundamental than the big world and the little world. (178)

> The frequent expressions apparently of pain, rage, despair and in fact all the usual, to which some patients gave vent, suggesting a fly somewhere in the ointment of Microcosmos, *Murphy either disregarded or muted to mean what he wanted*. (179)

> Even if the patients did sometimes feel as lousy as they sometimes looked, still no aspersion was necessarily cast on the little world where Murphy *presupposed* them, one and all, to be having a glorious time. (180)

> Stimulated by all those lives immured in mind, as he *insisted on supposing*, he laboured more diligently than ever before at his own little dungeon in Spain. (180)

Murphy is not, then, the one character who moves independently of the narrator-puppeteer, and although we are told that all "the puppets in this book whinge sooner or later, except Murphy, who is not a puppet" (122), we find Murphy himself falling into a puppet-like cry earlier in the novel when he throws "his voice into an infant's whinge" (37). Admittedly, Murphy's whinge is complicated by the fact that in this passage he is consciously parodying the outer world, but this nevertheless means that he is incapable of radically cutting himself off from it. At the same time, Beckett's peculiar procedure here—explicitly telling the reader that Murphy is not a puppet and then going on to suggest ways in which he is—indicates that he, too, is bound by what is generically exterior to his own creation, by a set of narrative conventions that he can deconstruct but cannot transcend. This becomes, as Beckett attempts to negotiate between two conceptions of novelistic form, one of the central problems in *Murphy*.

In a sense, *Murphy* may be understood as simultaneously comprising two different novels: an "outer" novel, which tells the story of Neary and company in pursuit of Murphy, and an "inner" novel, which deals with Murphy's psychotic contraction into himself. The outer novel offers what is, in effect, a caricature of nineteenth-century fiction: its medium is material reality and its motive force appetite, usually directed toward sex and money.[20] Hence, Neary wants Counihan (and later Celia), Wylie wants Counihan and money (and later Celia), Counihan wants Murphy and money (and along the way, Wylie). At the same time, the outer novel takes its subject from that favorite plot device of the nineteenth century, the love triangle, here humorously extended beyond its traditional three sides into a kind of erotic polygon. Thus, at one time or another, Neary loves Dwyer who loves Elliman, Neary loves Counihan who loves Murphy, Neary loves Celia who loves Murphy, Wylie loves Counihan who loves Murphy, Wylie loves Counihan who loves Neary, Wylie loves Celia who loves Murphy, Counihan loves Murphy who loves Celia, Counihan loves Wylie who loves Celia, and so on.

Certainly it is no accident that the main lines of pursuit and desire tend to terminate in Murphy ("Our medians . . . meet in Murphy," 213), for the outer novel is launched in quest of the inner novel. Yet, when Neary and company converge on the flat in Brewery Road and later on the Magdalen Mental Mercyseat, it is not

Murphy they find but something like the sign of his absence, as though the outer novel can only grasp the ungraspability of the inner novel. This is not surprising. On the one hand, if the inner novel finds its model in Murphy's third zone, then it must be radically indeterminate, and if radically indeterminate, it cannot be known; on the other hand, if it can be known, it must be determinate, yet if determinate, it cannot be genuinely inner. Beckett can only express such an aporia in terms of the movement of something present toward something absent, a movement best epitomized by the organization of the novel around its "absent" center, the slightly decentered and hermetically sealed chapter 6, which—plotless, discursive, preoccupied with Murphy's mind—becomes an image for the imageless inner novel.

It is important to understand, however, that Beckett is interested not so much in setting up a simple dualism between the inner and outer novel as in exploring the problems this dualism raises. Principal among these is the form of nineteenth-century fiction and the realist conventions that constitute it, including the treatment of time, summary and scene, verisimilitude, and language. We might begin to consider these conventions by turning to the problem that was of such importance for Proust—narrative temporality. In *Murphy* we are confronted with two forms of time: there is chronometric time, which is associated with the outer novel, and there is durational time, which is associated with the inner novel. Since the latter is contained within the former, the temporal development of the novel is scrupulously plotted, and although the narrative is not sequential, it is possible to reconstruct it, event by event, according to a remarkably precise chronology.[21] Thus, if we wish to fix in time the day on which the novel opens—the day on which Celia has her interview with Mr. Kelly, Cooper discovers Murphy inverted in his chair, and Celia prevails on Murphy to find work—we need only consult pages 2, 17, 42, and 114. Page 2 informs us that on this day the sun was in the Virgin, which means that we are dealing with a time frame running from August 23 to September 22; page 17 indicates that it fell in September, thereby further narrowing the possible days to twenty-two; page 42 situates it a week earlier than Wylie's meeting with Neary in the GPO on September 19; and, for those unable or indisposed to subtract 7 from 19, page 114 tells us, with some exasperation, that "Celia's triumph over Murphy, following her confidence to her grandfather, was gained about the middle of September, Thursday the 12th to be pedantic, a little before the Ember Days, the sun being still in the Virgin."

One of the minor incidents of September 12 involves Celia's near collision with an unidentified man as he is leaving Murphy's apartment building: Celia "raised her hand to knock the knock that he [Murphy] knew, when the door flew open and a man smelling strongly of drink rattled past her down the steps. . . . She entered the house, her mind still tingling with the clash of his leaden face and scarlet muffler, and switched on the light in the passage. In vain, the bulb had been taken away" (26). This incident occurs in chapter 3, and by chapter 4 the alert reader will begin to suspect that the mystery man is Cooper, if the reader connects two bits of information: that Cooper's "only visible humane characteristic was a morbid craving for alcoholic depressant" (54) and that he was "launched in pursuit of Murphy" (54). This hypothesis gains further credibility when we learn that Cooper has alternately found and lost Murphy (57) and that Murphy has left his old flat and taken a new one (63), an eventuality already prepared for on the first page ("Soon [Murphy] would have to make other arrangements, for the mew had been condemned," 1). Finally, some one hundred pages after the incident is first narrated, the reader is given the following account: "After many days [Cooper] picked up Murphy in the Cockpit late one afternoon and tracked him to the mew in West Brompton. . . . Cooper made a mental note of the number and hastened back the way he had come, devising as he went the wire to Neary. At the corner he paused to admire the pub, superior to any he had ever seen" (120). Five hours later he emerges from the pub, smelling, one feels safe in assuming, "strongly of drink" (26), and returns to the mew, where the following scene unfolds:

> The door of the house was ajar, he closed it behind him and stood in the dark hall. He struck a fusee. . . . Two rooms opened off the first-floor landing, one was doorless, a long gasp of despair issued from the other. Cooper entered, found Murphy in the appalling position described in section three, assumed that a murder had been bungled and retreated headlong. As he burst out of the door the most beautiful young woman he had ever seen slipped in. (121)

Another, less elaborate, example of the same kind of cross-referencing occurs in chapter 5, when Murphy meets Ticklepenny and receives the offer of a job at the Magdalen Mental Mercyseat. Earlier that day, as he is about to leave his flat, Murphy notices that his lucky day and lucky number will not coincide "for a full year to come, not until Sunday, October 4, 1936" (75). At this point, the reader possesses two pieces of relevant information: it is October (74), and it is a weekday (otherwise Murphy could not search for employment). If we assume that the "full year to come" is meant as an approximate designation and refers to weekdays on either side of the corresponding Sunday in 1935 (which is October 6), then our candidates for the day in question will include Tuesday, October 1, through Friday, October 4, and Monday, October 7, through Friday, October 11. We may initially incline toward Friday, October 4, since it corresponds exactly to Murphy's lucky day in 1936, but it is by no means a definitive choice, and we find that our circumspection is justified when we turn to the opening of chapter 7 and read: "The encounter, on which so much unhinges, between Murphy and Ticklepenny, took place on Friday, October the 11th" (114).

This consistency of chronology and event is important to the outer novel because it depends on several assumptions that underlie nineteenth-century fiction. First, it suggests that the internal coherence of any sequence is guaranteed by an external standard, one that consists in a stable and objective reality, which exists outside the text even though it is represented within it. Second, it suggests that the narrator can possess the whole of time, that he can play it on fast forward or reverse as necessity dictates ("Let us now take Time that old fornicator, bald though he be behind, by such few sad short hairs as he has, back to Monday, October the 7th," 114).

Opposed to the chronometric time of the outer novel is the durational time of the inner novel. Murphy's chair, a sort of heated closet on rockers, becomes the locus of this durational time, one that finds no analogue in the real world ("Somewhere a cuckoo-clock, having struck between twenty and thirty, became the echo of a street-cry," 2) and that obeys laws entirely of its own devising ("Most things under the moon got slower and slower and then stopped, a rock got faster and faster and then stopped," 9). Murphy's most dramatic accession to durational time occurs after the chess game with Endon, when time spins off its Newtonian axis and Murphy glimpses, if only momentarily, his third zone: "Time did not cease, that would be asking too much, but the wheel of rounds and pauses did" (246).

Perhaps chronometric time cannot, in some final sense, know durational time, but it can lay it out according to a series of calibrations. And for the reader curious to learn just how long Murphy's wheel of rounds and pauses ceased, there is Bom's switchboard, that monument to synoptic authority: "Bom's switchboard the following morning informed him that the hypomanic had been visited at regular intervals of ten minutes from 8 P.M. till shortly after 4 A.M., then for nearly an hour not at all, then six times in the space of one minute, then no more" (247). This means that Murphy's release from time is temporally comprehended, which in turn means that the representational function of the outer novel, at least in this case, has been sustained. And yet, if the outer novel seems inescapable— a kind of gravitational field beyond which Murphy cannot rise—it is also a thoroughly unreliable ground, mined with the collapsing conventions of realist fiction.[22]

One such convention, related to the management of time, is the realist alternation between summary and scene. We first encounter an example of this when Celia describes her meeting with Murphy: "Celia's account, expurgated, accelerated, improved and reduced, of how she came to have to speak of Murphy, gives the following" (12). Much of the comic force of what ensues comes from the fact that time is not managed, that despite its expurgation, acceleration, improvement, and reduction, the account is hopelessly dispersed amid irrelevant details. As Mr. Kelly says, "But I beseech you . . . be less beastly circumstantial" (13). At the same time, because it is meant to manage time invisibly, to create the illusion that the story is told in a natural order and tempo, the convention undermines itself when the narrator steps out from behind the curtain and informs us that Celia's account is a summary.

Another device that erodes the realist intentions of the nineteenth-century novel is the narrative aside designed to break aesthetic distance and remind the reader that the book is a published artifact and not a window on reality. Thus, the novel refers us to almost every stage of its production and consumption. We are reminded that there is a typesetter—"M.M.M. stood suddenly for music, Music, MU-SIC, in brilliant, brevier and canon . . . if the gentle compositor would be so friendly" (236)—and that there is a censor: "This phrase is chosen with care, lest the filthy censors should lack an occasion to commit their filthy synecdoche" (76). And, of course, we are reminded that there is a reader: "That is the end of how Murphy defrauded a vested interest every day for his lunch. . . . Try it sometime, gentle skimmer" (84); "The above passage is carefully calculated to deprave the cultivated reader" (118).

In addition to disrupting aesthetic distance, Beckett builds into the novel a series of narrative fissures, breaks in the coherence and plausibility of representation. We may generally refer to this in *Murphy* as the principle of the missing seventh scarf: "Seven scarves held him in position. Two fastened his shins to the rockers, one his thighs to the seat, two his breast and belly to the back, one his wrists to the strut behind. Only the most local movements were possible" (2). At first glance, this appears to be a perfectly straightforward piece of description, fully particularized and no different (excepting the extraordinary subject matter) from what we might encounter in any nineteenth-century novel. But as Hugh Kenner has pointed out, there is a problem: the narrator has described only six scarves.[23] Where is the seventh? We may also wonder by what Houdini-like trick Murphy has trussed himself up in the first place (tying one's own wrists is no easy matter) and by what equally improbable sleight of hand he intends to free himself. Of course, as the cuckoo clock strikes between twenty and thirty and the rock accelerates toward stasis, we realize that the point is not to provide coherent representation but to render it unthinkable.

The attempt by Murphy and Ticklepenny to set up a portable radiator opens another crack in the solidity and coherence of narrative construction. After some confusion over whether the gas has or has not been turned on, we are presented with the following exchange:

> "Well, that beats all," said Ticklepenny.
> What beat all was how the tap, which he really had turned on, came to be turned off.
> The dismantled jet projected high up in the wall of the W.C. and what Ticklepenny called the tap was one of those double chain and ring arrangements designed for the convenience of dwarfs.
> "As I hope to be saved," said Ticklepenny, "I swear I turned the little b—— on."

"Perhaps a little bird flew in," said Murphy, "and lit on it."
"How could he with the window shut?" said Ticklepenny.
"Perhaps he shut it behind him," said Murphy. (173–74)

The passage gathers to an impossible point the Reason of the outer novel and the Unreason of the inner, as the narrator authoritatively tells us, in the best realist tradition, that Ticklepenny was neither mistaken nor lying ("What beat all was how the tap, which he *really had turned on*, came to be turned off," my emphasis), but then goes on to pose a series of problems and solutions none of which is commensurate with reality ("Perhaps [the bird] shut it behind him"). On the one hand, the narrative fissure opens up only if we are assured there is no natural explanation, and this requires the intervention of the omniscient narrator of realist fiction. On the other hand, the omniscient narrator of realist fiction depends on a world in which there are no narrative fissures, and this requires nothing but natural explanations.

The dilemma of the open gas tap ("What was the etymology of gas? . . . Could it be the same word as chaos?" 175) is in many ways emblematic of the novel's construction as a whole: it at once appears to establish a coherent and objective reality and to dismantle it, to promise a representational function and to deconstruct it. In similar fashion, language for the most part does the yeoman's work of getting the story told, but there are those instances when it goes on holiday, disencumbering itself of any worldly relations and entering into a self-enclosed field of pure play. On such occasions, words begin to generate other words through a kind of verbal sympathy, as when Murphy sits "naked in his rocking-chair of undressed teak, guaranteed not to crack, warp, shrink, corrode, or creak at night" (1). The teak is, obviously, unvarnished (hence—another touch of realism—the need for the guarantee), but the word "undressed" is selected for its affinity with "naked," producing the comic effect of a man without clothes sitting in a chair without clothes. Another example of this sort of verbal sympathy involves Suk's Thema Coeli: "Lucky Colours. Lemon. To avert Calamity the native should have a dash in apparel, also a squeeze in home decorations" (33). Here the semantic value of "lemon" is clearly delineated by the context—bright yellow—but the word breaks free of its context and, again with comic force, generates other words. Suk's prescriptions therefore call for a "dash" and a "squeeze" of lemon, converting decorator and fashion tips into a recipe for right living. To cite a final example, at the Magdalen Mental Mercyseat, a round finished on time was called a "virgin" and "ahead of time, an Irish virgin" (242). A page later this punch line becomes a straight line for yet another punch line: "Never in the history of the M.M.M. had there been such a run of virgins and Irish virgins as on this Murphy's maiden night" (243).

A different, although related, form of linguistic foregrounding occurs when several words find themselves at semantic odds with one another. Thus, when we are told at the beginning of the novel that "the poor old sun [was] in the Virgin again for the billionth time" (1–2), we are forced to conclude that either it's not the billionth time or not the Virgin. In like manner, when we hear of the "virgin Miss Carridge" (134), we must entertain the apparently exclusive notions of chastity and miscarriage. Or when Endon, playing with an indicator switch, makes the hypomanic bounce off the walls of his cell "like a bluebottle in a jar" (247), we struggle against the image—even though we know Beckett is referring to a fly—of a blue bottle fitted into a jar.

Verbal play of this kind has the larger effect of suggesting that there is nothing beyond language, that "there is nothing outside of the text."[24] The Balzacian formulation of the novelist as the secretary to society, and the Stendhalian formulation of the novel as a mirror carried along a highway, both rely on the Cartesian notion that an observing consciousness accurately perceives the world and accurately records it.[25] But if things do not compel words so much as words compel things—indeed, if the whole idea of trying to find the point of correspondence between language and reality is wrongheaded—then the mimetic ambitions of the realist novel will ultimately come to grief.

⌣·

Murphy may finally be understood as an experiment in which the cogito shuts itself away in a lunatic's *poêle* and attempts to doubt its way into madness. Beckett hopes, in the process, to disengage novelistic character and novelistic form from their Cartesian underpinnings, to propel them at higher and higher speeds until they finally lift free of the realist ground. His "missile without provenance" does not, however, enter into an antirealist "beyond" but disintegrates in mid-flight and then slowly drifts back to an earth now scorched and uninhabitable, a kind of novelistic no-man's-land. This is not to say that Beckett attempted to write an experimental novel and failed; rather, he attempted to show what the experiment would look like, where it might take him, what it would involve. One of the things it involved was the explosive deconstruction of its own assumptions, a set of aporias carried to critical mass. Another was a sustained exploration of the problem of novelistic character and novelistic form. *Murphy* does not resolve these problems so much as formulate them, and they continued to exercise Beckett's imagination some seven years later when, having wandered through the literal no-man's-land of occupied France, he sat down to write a second novel. Appropriately, he entitled it *Watt*.

CHAPTER THREE

Beyond the Metaphysics of Presence

'Watt' and the Autobiography of Negation

If *Murphy* offers us a vision of the cogito gone mad, *Watt* offers us a vision of the cogito come to nothing. In Beckett's second novel, subjectivity has grown so enfeebled, so attenuated, that it has finally collapsed into itself, become its own negation—a kind of absence in whose empty but echoing depths we search for a departed presence. The search is in vain. No longer constructed on the foundations of a madhouse, the *poêle* now hangs in midair, floats through space, disperses itself into nonbeing. The cogito becomes, quite simply, what is not: a gap, a nullity, a void. And yet, we must wonder, how is this possible? For while consciousness may doubt its own sanity, surely it cannot doubt its own presence. However profound my skepticism, however rigorous my inquiry, of this much I am certain: that I exist in the here and now, that I am: "The certitude of inner existence . . . has no need to be signified. It is immediately present to itself. It is living consciousness."[1]

Underlying such a claim to apodictic knowledge is the "metaphysics of presence," an idea that starts with the assumption that "being" consists of what is "there," of what can be mentally or physically grasped as a form of presence. This idea begins to acquire metaphysical resonance, however, when we attempt to locate the "deep structure" of being, when we treat it as a kind of noumenal reality that occasionally "bursts forth" into the phenomenal world, manifesting itself as "nature" or "speech" or "self." Derrida's views on this subject are well known: the metaphysics of presence has shaped the entire history of Western philosophy, particularly its conception of truth as correspondence to reality. As a result, the "determination of being in general as *presence*" carries with it a set of

> subdeterminations which depend on this general form and which organize within it their system and their historical sequence (presence of the thing to the sight as *eidos*, presence as substance/essence/existence [*ousia*], temporal presence as point [*stigmè*] of the now or of the moment [*nun*], the self-presence of the cogito, consciousness, subjectivity, the co-presence of the other and of the self, intersubjectivity as the intentional phenomenon of the ego, and so forth).[2]

The modern or Enlightenment tradition develops out of those "subdeterminations" associated with "cogito, consciousness, subjectivity" because the Cartesian self is thought to represent a form of "self-presence" that, placing itself beyond all doubt, provides the "first principle" in a philosophy of certainty. I say "is thought" because postmodern criticism has vigorously disputed the self-presence of the cogito, as well as the Cartesian extrapolation that derives from it. In pursuing this line of inquiry, I want to examine the idea of self-presence in connection with autobiography, the literary form that has been most concerned with bringing forward the self and establishing it as an autonomous presence. I therefore take as my point of departure for what follows the work Paul de Man and Jacques Derrida have done on Jean-Jacques Rousseau, work that specifically relates the metaphysics of presence to problems of autobiography, narration, and negation.[3] I shall consider two pieces of interpretive analysis in particular: de Man's "Self (*Pygmalion*)" in *Allegories of Reading* and Derrida's " . . . That Dangerous Supplement . . . " in *Of Grammatology*.

In "Self (*Pygmalion*)" de Man approaches Rousseau's idea of subjectivity by asking whether we can plausibly speak of "the transparency of the self to its own experience of selfhood, the unmediated presence of the self to itself."[4] He goes on, in discussions of *Narcisse* and *Pygmalion*, to answer this question in the negative, showing how the self becomes imaginable only after it has been transformed into something other than itself, only after it has been displaced into a simulacrum that, by definition, "is and is not the self at the same time" (168). Paradoxically, for the self to begin to "know" itself—to construct its identity and reflectively constitute its being—it must first cease to be itself. What the self cannot do, however, is know itself intuitively, apprehend its inner being as a form of experiential immediacy or primordial presence. Indeed, for de Man, what we call the "self" is not so much discovered through an act of Cartesian meditation as created out of those displacements and substitutions that inevitably occur when the subject attempts to predicate itself, when it attempts to project itself into a condition of exteriority.[5] If, however, we seek to reverse the process of predication, to work our way backward from the simulacrum to the "source," what we discover is not an originary presence but an absence—a "non-being," "the aberrant hypostasis of a 'nothing'" (170), a "nothingness" that has become "a new center of meaning" (174). In other words, de Man does not conceive of the self as a form of "pure" presence or consciousness, existing apart from culture or language, which means that subjectivity is "not a substance but a figure" (170), not "selfhood but . . . a structure of tropes" (186). In the final analysis, then, the self can be known only as a linguistic effect, the words that are generated out of the attempt to look "within." At its "core," the self has no existence—it is nothing.

Derrida's analysis of Rousseau in " . . . That Dangerous Supplement . . . " concentrates more directly on the autobiographical impulse, an impulse that has inspired Rousseau to withdraw from society—literally to "absent" himself from others—so that he may become "present" to himself through his writing. As was the case with de Man, Derrida discovers that the various simulacra of the self—in this case the *Confessions*—lead not to a disclosure of the subject's essential identity but to its dislocation, not to a recovery of presence but to a fall into absence. In particular, Derrida draws a comparison between two different activities that Rousseau describes with the word "supplement": writing and onanism. Standing behind both these "supplemental" activities is the desire to possess an originary presence, whether it is the presence of the self (in the case of autobiographical writing) or the presence of the erotic other (in the case of onanism). However, the supplement leads not to that originary presence—the hypothetical source of all secondary representation—but to an endless cycle of self-duplication, of supplements generating supplements. The more we attempt to know the self by constructing models of it, the more we "adulterate" it, turn it into what it is not, something alien and "other": "In affecting oneself with another presence [a supplement], one *alters* oneself." And yet, Derrida tells us, Rousseau "neither wants to think nor is able to think that this *alteration* does not happen to the self, but is the self's very origin" (my emphasis).[6] Here, Derrida suggests, as de Man does, that the self is not a source, presence, or substance, but a series of substitutions, a "chain of supplements":

> Through this sequence of supplements a necessity is announced: that of an infinite chain, ineluctably multiplying the supplementary mediations that produce the sense of the very thing they defer: the mirage of the thing itself, of immediate presence, of originary perception. Immediacy is derived. That all begins through the intermediary is what is indeed "inconceivable [to reason]."[7]

De Man and Derrida thus identify in Rousseau an aporia basic to Descartes and the entire epistemological tradition: the subject can know itself only by becoming the object of its own consciousness; but in becoming the object of its own consciousness it ceases to be itself, which is to say a subject. What the subject knows, then, is not itself but a representation of the self that is also a displacement, something that at once comprehends identity and difference, inside and outside, self and other. The problem, however, is not simply the difficulty of representing the self; the problem is also that the self is not immediately or directly "present" to itself. For as soon as the subject becomes sufficiently "conscious" to engage in self-reflection, it knows itself not intuitively, but as a being constituted in and through language. As de Man observes, "we do not 'possess' language in the same way that we can be said to possess natural properties. It would be just as proper or improper to say that 'we' are a property of language as the reverse."[8] Or, as Derrida puts it, "the writer writes *in* a language and *in* a logic whose proper system, laws, and life his discourse by definition cannot dominate absolutely. He uses them only by letting himself, after a fashion and up to a point, be governed by the system."[9] Obviously, these claims are of a piece with the postmodern critique of Cartesianism we examined in Chapter 1: consciousness, self-presence, intuitive knowledge—all these "experiences" are mediated through various schemas, whether they are linguistic, cultural, or historic. The self is, as it were, frozen in the amber of language. Our knowledge of it can only be a kind of archaeology, a science of effects rather than causes. And this means that if we attempt to work our way back to some prelinguistic first cause, to know the self as a form of primordial consciousness, what we encounter is not presence but absence, not being but negation.

Watt anticipates the critical approach that de Man and Derrida take toward the self-presence of the cogito. Beckett's novel is structured around an allegorical quest that is best summarized by the novel's central action: a character named Watt pursues a character named Knott. The plot carries us, in other words, from Inquiry to Negation, from Question to Absence. This pattern has led many critics to read *Watt* as a profoundly nihilistic work, a novel in which the defining structures of reality teeter on an epistemological brink and then collapse into themselves, leaving the hero to confront an all-embracing nothingness.[10] But while *Watt* is in many ways Beckett's most epistemologically negative statement, I shall argue that in its larger significance, particularly in Beckett's handling of negation, the novel conveys much more than a simple sense of perceptual alienation or breakdown. Here "nothingness" leads toward what lies beyond the metaphysics of presence, the self that cannot become transparent to itself, that cannot know itself intuitively as a form of primordial consciousness.

In terms of literary genre, the interrogation of the self has most often assumed the form of autobiography. One of my larger claims has been that the pentalogy is animated by, and parodically modeled on, the multivolume autobiographical novels of Proust and Joyce. In *Murphy* the autobiographical impulse expresses itself in the hero's attempt to enter into his third zone where he can "know" himself as a form of anti–self-consciousness. In *Watt* the autobiographical impulse is more directly and immediately related to Beckett. Thus the novel not only offers us two authorial figures—one named Sam and one named Hackett—but it also presents, through the unlikely personage of Larry Nixon, an "episode" from Beckett's life. Admittedly, this is a peculiar form of autobiography, one in which Sam and Hackett do not tell their own stories, one in which Beckett's alter ego, Larry Nixon, never appears. But all of this is very much to Beckett's purpose: he has deliberately marked his novel as autobiographical precisely so that he can dismantle those elements in it that are autobiographical. In this sense we might understand Beckett, as H. Porter Abbott has brilliantly argued, to be engaged in the writing not of "autobiography" but "autography."[11]

Because Beckett is consciously evoking autobiography as a literary form, because he is raising the question of how we write the self, what was largely an epistemological inquiry in *Murphy* becomes largely a narrative inquiry in *Watt*. This shift obviously prepares the way for the trilogy's extended foray into the problem of first-person narration. But if *Watt* looks forward, it also looks back, addressing once again the issue of Cartesian dualism that figured so prominently in *Murphy*. Beckett's second novel accordingly develops a complicated iconography for exploring subject-object relations, an iconography that centers on the figure of the garden.

Like *Murphy*, *Watt* is marked by an internal split, a sense that it simultaneously inhabits two worlds, one modern and one antimodern. This sense of self-division is especially apparent in the novel's approach to subject-object relations, its tendency to construct a series of phenomenological problems, which it then goes on to deconstruct. Most of these problems are implicit in way the novel handles the Romantic revision of the myth of the fall. According to this revision, we begin in an epistemological paradise where the child is so intimately connected with the mother, the subject so fully integrated with the object, that all existence appears as a single and boundless unity. This is the sunlit time in the garden, the time of harmony and plenitude, when the self and the world breathe the same breath and think the same thought. But paradise was not made to last, and when the subject realizes that it is separate from the object, innocence gives way to experience, and man is cast out into the fallen world of Cartesian dialectics.[12]

Proust, whose *Recherche* is full of Edenic gardens and memories of lost childhood, was most likely Beckett's immediate source for this lapsarian epistemology. There are, however, two important differences between Proust and the Romantics. First, in Proust prelapsarian consciousness is never directly presented; paradise is always already lost and can be approached only through the mediating veil of memory. Second, paradise can never be regained; the most one can hope for is to glimpse it in a flash of involuntary memory. These become significant distinctions for Beckett. As we saw in the previous chapter, Murphy can rig up temporary ascensions out of subject-object dialectics, but he is never able to find a highway to paradise. This remains the case in *Watt*. Although characters occasionally experience intimations of epistemological breakthrough, radiant moments when the boundaries between self and world seem to shatter, such moments never involve a recovery of "primordial consciousness," an accession to some more "fundamental" or "authentic" mode of being. In *Watt* paradise drops out of the sky in one instant and vanishes into thin air in the next, but it does not endure.

Arsene's "short statement" provides a useful point of entry into lapsarian epistemology in *Watt*. Arsene begins his statement by talking about the newly arrived servant at the Knott establishment as a kind of phenomenological Christ, one who having suffered in the wilderness of Cartesian dualism, having borne the stigmata of fallen consciousness, now comes to a place of deliverance, even resurrection: "Haw! how it all comes back to me, to be sure. That look! That weary watchful vacancy! The man arrives! The dark ways all behind, all within, the long dark ways, in his head, in his side, in his hands and feet" (39). In terms of the myth of the fall, Christ functions as a second Adam, raising the possibility that humanity will be redeemed and finally restored to a new Eden. In this context, the sojourn at Knott's house is figured as a pilgrimage, one in which Watt will be guided by Erskine, just as Dante was guided by Virgil and Everyman was guided by Knowledge: "Erskine will go by your side, and be your guide, and then for the rest you will travel alone, or with only shades to keep you company" (63).[13] Indeed, the path that has led Watt to Knott takes on the spiraling contours of the Purgatorial Mount, suggesting that what lies beyond, in this case the Knott establishment, is itself a kind of earthly paradise: "All the old ways led to this, all the old windings, the stairs with never a landing that you screw yourself up, clutching the rail, counting the steps, the fever of the shortest ways under the long lids of sky" (40).[14] It is therefore not surprising that the newly arrived servant feels that here he may transcend the fallen world of Cartesian dualism, discovering in its place an Eden of subject-object harmony:

> The sensations, the premonitions of harmony are irrefragable, of imminent harmony, when all outside will be he, the flowers the flowers that he is among him, the sky the sky that he is above him, the earth trodden the earth treading, and all sound his echo. When in a word he will be in his midst at last, after so many tedious years spent clinging to the perimeter. (40–41)

Now, the paradise that Arsene speaks of is momentarily glimpsed when, on a certain Tuesday in October, he experiences something called existence off the ladder:

> I was sitting on the step, in the yard, looking at the light, on the wall. I was in the sun, and the wall was in the sun. I was the sun, need I add, and the wall, and the step, and the yard, and the time of year, and the time of day, to mention only these. To be sitting, at so pleasant a conjuncture of one's courses, in oneself, by oneself, that I think it will freely be admitted is a way no worse than another, and better than some. (42)

Here we have the fulfillment of Arsene's promise of "imminent harmony," that happy coincidence of subject and object, which effectively eliminates the distinction between them: "My personal system was so distended at the period of which I speak that the distinction between what was inside it and what was outside it was not at all easy to draw" (43). The change that has overtaken Arsene is described as an Ovidian metamorphosis ("I felt my breast swell, like a pelican's," 42), which flutters aloft for a brief time and then, Icarus-like, collapses back into itself ("And my breast, on which I could almost feel the feathers stirring, in the charming way breast feathers have, relapsed into the void and bony concavity. . . . This I am happy to inform you is the reversed metamorphosis. The Laurel into the Daphne. The old thing where it always was, back again," 44).

What preceded the reversed metamorphosis was "existence off the ladder"; as Arsene puts it in one of the most commented-on passages in the novel, "What was changed was existence off the ladder. Do not come down the ladder, Ifor, I haf taken it away" (44). In a well-known article, Jacqueline Hoefer reads the ladder as an allusion to the end of Wittgenstein's *Tractatus*, but Beckett himself has indicated that these lines refer to a joke about two Welshmen: "A little 'joke' I heard. 'Did you hear the one about the Welshman?' Then the exhortation. A relief from the usual Scot. Call it folklore."[15] The joke involves one Welshman climbing up a ladder, which a second Welshman then removes; realizing his mistake, the second Welshman looks up at his airborne friend and earnestly warns him against descending the nonexistent ladder.[16] The humor is obviously ethnic, suggesting that Newton has not penetrated the collective intelligence of Wales. Of course, what is important here is not the joke itself but the way it functions within the framework of a lapsarian epistemology, the way it counterpoints an imagery of ascension and suspension with an imagery of fall. Thus, when a character experiences that lighter-than-air condition known as "existence off the ladder," he lifts free, if only momentarily, of subject-object dialectics and glimpses the paradise that lies beyond. Yet, because the "only Paradise that is not the dream of a madman" is the "Paradise that has been lost," Arsene's experience is necessarily fleeting.[17] Once he becomes aware, as did the Welshman without his ladder, that gravity may be defied in leaps and bounds but not as a general principle, he finds himself caught in a kind of phenomenological free-fall: "There I was, warm and bright . . . when suddenly somewhere some little thing slipped. . . . Gliss—iss—iss—STOP!" (42–43).

If Murphy's third zone represents the radical disjunction of subject and object, then existence off the ladder represents their radical conjunction. These conditions are not, however, oppositional or contradictory, since they both produce the same effect: the disruption of Cartesian dualism, which is to say, the disruption of the idea that subject and object are distinct but interdependent, that they at once exclude and define one another. Significantly, we find standing behind Arsene's efforts at transcendence, just as we found standing behind Murphy's, a critique of desire: "The old thing where it always was, back again. As when a man, having found at last what he sought, a woman, for example, or a friend, loses it, or realises what it is" (44). Here are the familiar coordinates of Proustian appetite: to possess a thing means realizing what it is, and realizing what it is means incurring its loss. Disappointment is, consequently, built into the very structure of desire, since the subject and object inhabit time and space and are therefore susceptible to mutation. This means that in the course of moving from desire to possession, both subject and object will tend to undergo change, to be modified, displaced, redefined. As a result, the moment of attainment becomes the moment of disillusionment, the moment when we understand that the thing we most desire is not what we have so long sought and finally obtained, but something altogether different.[18]

In *Proust* and *Murphy*, the solution to this problem is the ablation of desire, but Arsene concedes humanity's fallen condition and so understands that desire can neither be satisfied nor overcome:

"And yet it is useless not to seek, not to want, for when you cease to seek you start to find" (44). It is only in seeking without the hope of finding that those intimations of paradise become possible, whether this involves something as trivial as Marcel learning to appreciate Berma after he has grown indifferent to her or something as momentous as the resurrection of the past through a bit of madeleine. Beckett formulates a similar wisdom, though in terms that are decidedly more pointed:

> The glutton castaway, the drunkard in the desert, the lecher in prison, they are the happy ones. To hunger, thirst, lust, every day afresh and every day in vain, after the old prog, the old booze, the old whores, that's the nearest we'll ever get to felicity, the new porch and the very latest garden. (44)

What we are left with is the vision of an Eden that does not stand immutably outside time but occasionally, if erratically, bursts forth into it. When this happens we glimpse paradise for a passing instant, a paradise in which we recover not the original garden but the "very latest."

꒛•

If the Knott establishment holds out the promise of disrupting stable subject-object relations, it also serves to undermine habitual notions of epistemology and language. Here, what Husserl called the "natural attitude" becomes the flimsiest of constructs. As Watt discovers in his encounter with the piano-tuning Galls, the type of all experience in the Knott household is a kind of antiexperience, a consciousness that something has happened together with a complete ignorance of what that something is:

> [The incident of the Galls] resembled all the incidents of note proposed to Watt during his stay in Mr Knott's house. . . . It resembled them in the vigour with which it developed a purely plastic content, and gradually lost, in the nice processes of its light, its sound, its impacts and its rhythm, all meaning, even the most literal. (72–73)

This lapsing away of meaning from phenomenal reality, this translation of experience into the "purely plastic," constitutes the desired heaven of Murphy's third zone where "there was nothing but commotion and the pure forms of commotion" (112), and we can well imagine the pleasure with which Beckett's earlier hero would embrace an establishment where events are nullified even as they occur. Watt, in contrast, is made "anxious" (75) and feels "vexation" (76) when he confronts phenomena that collapse into a mere play of surfaces, for he wants nothing more than for reality to signify as it habitually has: "This fragility of the outer meaning had a bad effect on Watt, for it caused him to seek for another, for some meaning of what had passed, in the image of how it had passed" (73). This does not mean, however, that we should think of Watt as a foundationalist or representationalist; he is concerned not with how well a given account reflects a given event but with how credible that account is or appears to be. So it is that faced with the incident of the Galls, Watt finds he "did not know what had happened. He did not care, to do him justice, what had happened. But he felt the need to think that such and such a thing had happened then, the need to be able to say, when the scene began to unroll its sequences, Yes, I remember, that is what happened then" (74).

If the incident of the Galls represents the breakdown of the logical and apprehensible sequence, the encounter with the "pot" epitomizes the breakdown of the object and the severing of its customary relations with language:

> Looking at a pot, for example, or thinking of a pot, at one of Mr Knott's pots, of one of Mr Knott's pots, it was in vain that Watt said, Pot, pot. . . . For it was not a pot, the more he looked, the more he reflected, the more he felt sure of that, that it was not a pot at all. It resembled a pot, it was almost a pot, but it was not a pot of which one could say, Pot, pot, and be comforted. (81)

What is important for Watt is not grasping the essence of the pot, but getting words and things to function according to habitual expectations: "Not that Watt desired information. . . . He desired words to be applied to his situation" (81). Here, language serves as a sort of palliative drug ("He could always hope, of a thing of which he had never known the name, that he would learn the name, some day, and so be tranquillized," 81–82), from which Watt asks not for truth but reassurance ("And Watt's need of semantic succour was at times so great that he would set to trying names on things, and on himself, almost as a woman hats," 83).

All of this is to say that the Knott establishment rests, as the novel punningly insists, on a set of "premises" and "grounds" (40, 70) that explode conventional notions of reality, even as they suggest that what sustains that reality is, quite simply, nothing. Hence, in describing the incident of the Galls, that exemplary Knottian event, the narrator tells us "that *nothing* had happened, that a thing that was *nothing* had happened" (76, my emphasis). At the same time, just as the incident of the Galls was the defining event in Watt's experience at Knott's, so the nothingness that stands behind it becomes the peculiarly unstable ground of that experience. Thus, Watt's knowledge is consistently stated in terms of negation:

> The result of this was that Watt *never* knew how he got into Mr Knott's house. He knew that he got in by the back door, but he was *never* to know, *never*, *never* to know, how the back door came to be opened. (37)

> For the day comes when he [the newly arrived servant] says, Am I *not* a little out of sorts, to-day? *Not* that he feels out of sorts, on the contrary, he feels if possible even better disposed than usual . . . and he asks himself if he is *not* perhaps a little seedy. The fool! He has learnt *nothing. Nothing.* (42)

> And Watt made *no* secret of this, in his conversations with me, that many things described as happening, in Mr Knott's house, and of course grounds, perhaps *never* happened at all. (126, my emphasis throughout)

But having acknowledged this linguistic and epistemological negation, having begun to trace, if only in a preliminary fashion, how it breaks down and empties out the most incontestable certainties, we are left with two questions: what is its larger significance—namely, why is the novel constructed around a principle of negation—and how does it relate to Mr. Knott?

＜・

At one point the narrator remarks that "the only way one can speak of nothing is to speak of it as though it were something" (77). We may begin to understand Knott as that something, what cannot be spoken of, what cannot be known. Thus, Watt tells Sam of his term on the ground floor, "But what do I know of Mr Knott? Nothing" (119); and at the end of the first stage of his service: "What had he learnt? Nothing" (148); and finally, before his departure from the

Knott establishment, "Of the nature of Mr Knott himself Watt remained in particular ignorance" (199). One way to think of the
quest for what cannot be spoken of, what cannot be known, is as a
Proustian *recherche* into the self. Watt's pursuit of Knott may be understood as an allegorical expression of this quest, but with one important difference: here subjective or Cartesian inquiry (What) leads
not to self-presence but to its negation or absence (Not). Hence, like
the confrontation between Murphy and Endon, Watt's principal encounter with Knott during his time on the first floor is described in
terms that echo the "dark glass" passage from 1 Corinthians 13.12.
This meeting takes place when Watt accidentally happens upon
Knott in that locus of phenomenological symbolism, the garden:

> One day Watt, coming out from behind a bush, almost ran into Mr
> Knott. . . . Mr Knott's hands were behind his back, and his head
> bowed down, towards the ground. Then Watt in his turn look[ed]
> down. . . . So there for a short time they stood together, the master
> and the servant, the bowed heads almost touching. (145–46)

The encounter, with "bowed heads almost touching," occurs not
quite "face to face," a point the narrator emphasizes when he tells
us, "Watt did not know whether he was glad or sorry that he did
not see Mr Knott more often. . . . And the sense in which he was
sorry was this, that he wished to see Mr Knott face to face, and the
sense in which he was glad was this, that he feared to do so" (146).
Eventually Watt comes to abandon "all hope, all fear, of ever seeing
Mr Knott face to face" (146) and must content himself instead with
a few glimpses of Mr. Knott, glimpses that are "not clearly caught,
but as it were in a glass" (147). Here we have all the constituents of
1 Corinthians 13.12: a fleeting and obscure impression that comes,
"through a glass, darkly," along with the deferral of a "face to face"
encounter. The Biblical passage is, of course, about ways of knowing: "For now we see through a glass, darkly; but then face to face:
now I know in part; but then shall I know even as also I am known."
As was the case in *Murphy*, the "dark glass" motif enables Beckett
to give a narrative shape to an epistemological problem. Thus, while
in 1 Corinthians the "face to face" encounter refers to the way humanity attempts to know God, in Beckett's novels it suggests the way
subjectivity attempts to know itself.[19] As Beckett uses this motif, the
movement from the dark glass to the face-to-face encounter indi-

cates a progression from the partial and fallen knowledge of subject-object dialectics to the ideally reciprocal (and, as we have seen, impossible) knowledge in which the subject apprehends itself as primordial presence. Of course, for Beckett the Biblical language is self-ironizing. To believe that we might achieve a perfectly complementary state of knowledge, a condition of "knowing and being known," is as fanciful as believing that we might recover Paradise or look upon the face of God. As I have suggested, the most one can hope for are intimations of such a condition, flashes of some non-Cartesian beyond. And while we occasionally find such intimations in passages that speak of a "face-to-face" encounter, there is no epistemological breakthrough in the meeting between Watt and Knott, no promise of transcendent knowledge—only a mirrored glimpse that is "not clearly caught, but as it were in a glass."

Now, if the encounter between Watt and Knott may be viewed at some level as self-reflective—if it represents the way in which subjectivity attempts to encounter itself—then we may want further to define how Knott functions as a principle of negation. In a sense, that negation looks very much like the indeterminacy of character that has become a hallmark of much contemporary fiction. The New Novelists in particular have specialized in producing characters that lack the fierce and insistent presence of Balzac's creations, characters that have grown so insubstantial, so rarefied, as to be virtually absent from their own story. Bruce Morrissette, in writing of the peculiarly elusive narrator of Robbe-Grillet's *Jealousy*, has christened this kind of character the *je-néant* or "absent I."[20] In many ways Knott seems to epitomize such indeterminacy, to exist as a character who is unconstrained by any fixed or stable identity. Thus, like Murphy's third zone, the Knott establishment functions as a kind of molecular soup in which forms are constantly rising out of and falling back into one another:

> [Watt was] holding the lamp high above his head, to guide his feet, on the stairs, the stairs that never seemed the same stairs, from one night to another, and now were steep, and now shallow, and now long, and now short, and now broad, and now narrow, and now dangerous, and now safe . . . (115)

Knott's person is similarly protean, taking on, in its various manifestations, a seemingly endless array of traits and types:

> With regard to the so important matter of Mr Knott's physical ap-
> pearance, Watt had unfortunately little or nothing to say. For one day
> Mr Knott would be tall, fat, pale and dark, and the next thin, small,
> flushed and fair, and the next sturdy, middlesized, yellow and ginger,
> and the next small, fat, pale and fair, and the next middlesized,
> flushed, thin and ginger . . . (209)

Of special importance here is the way these descriptions function
as a Beckettian permutation. As we saw in Murphy's experience with
the biscuits, the permutation opens up closed systems, beginning
with a finite group and expanding it toward infinity, much as a
looped program will play itself out interminably, using a limited set
of counters. Yet Knott ultimately represents something more than
the character of indeterminacy, something more than Murphy's permutations or Endon's Unreason. In an effort to distinguish Knott
from the character of indeterminacy, I shall refer to him not as the
je-néant, but as the "not-I." In using this formulation—obviously
borrowed from Beckett[21]—I want to suggest an epistemological
problem: the subject can only become present to itself as the negation of subject-object dialectics; however, such a negation, such an
immersion in "pure" intuition or presence, would not in any mean-
ingful sense constitute knowledge. Hence, Knott functions as the self-
negating logic that is necessarily built into all attempts to predicate
the subject. He is what results from the aporia that lies at the heart
of the cogito, the aporia that leads not to the "I" but to its negation
("not-I").

Murphy also carried its narrative to a point of occlusion, the logical impasse that the hero necessarily encountered when he attempted to will himself into will-lessness, to reason his way into Unreason. With *Watt* we have once again arrived at a logical impasse,
only now it leads not to the dissolution of the plot but to its generation—not to the destruction of character, but to its creation. For
Watt does to aporia what *Murphy* never could: it draws upon it as a
narrative resource, using its incongruities and disparities as a mech-
anism for producing stories. Among the stories it produces two are
of special interest, for they examine how the self narratively constructs itself. One of these stories deals with a character named Sam,
and the other with a character named Hackett.

I have argued that the subject's self-negating attempt to know it-self finds expression in Watt's efforts to encounter Knott. Matters are complicated, however, by the fact that Watt not only pursues Knott but is himself pursued by the novel's narrator, Sam. Indeed, all three of these characters are linked with each other through an imagery of self-reflection or mirroring, which first identifies Watt with Knott, and then identifies Sam with Watt. As a result, the sub-ject's pursuit of itself is no longer presented as merely epistemolog-ical; through the intervention of Sam it has also become narrative.[22]

We may begin to understand how the novel translates its episte-mology into narrative by turning to the novel's third section and ex-amining Sam's relation to Watt.[23] Not surprisingly, this relation is described in terms of a now-familiar lapsarian epistemology. Hence, Sam's first meeting with Watt takes place in a garden and involves a near fall:

> There was a little stream, or brook, never dry, flowing, now slow, now with torrential rapidity, for ever in its narrow ditch. Unsteadily a rustic bridge bestrode its dark waters, a rustic humpbacked bridge, in a state of extreme dilapidation.
>
> It was through the crown of this construction that one day Watt, treading more heavily than was his wont, or picking his steps with less than his usual care, drove his foot, and part of his leg. And he would certainly have *fallen*, and perhaps been carried away by the subfluent flood, had I not been at hand to bear him up. (154, my em-phasis)

Lying prone, each on his side of the bridge, the two men inch toward each other, working to repair the damage: "And when we had lain a little thus, with this exceptional smile, on our faces, then we be-gan to draw ourselves forward, and upward, and persisted in this course until our heads, our noble bulging brows, met, and touched, Watt's noble brow, and my noble brow" (155).

At the center of this tableau, then, is a "face-to-face" encounter—but here it is combined with another motif, for Watt and Sam meet, as Murphy did with Endon, "across a narrow gulf of air, the merest hand's-breadth of air" (*Murphy*, 248). The bridging of the gap de-scribed in this passage occurs as the subject, seeking to know itself, attempts to transcend Cartesian dualism by closing the interval that separates mind from body, inside from outside. We have already seen an example of this in that moment of ecstatic levitation known as existence off the ladder: "So I shall merely state, without enquiring how it came, or how it went, that in my opinion it was not an illusion, as long as it lasted, that presence of what did not exist, that presence without, that presence within, that presence between" (45). The convergence here of the "presence within" and the "presence without" leads to the "presence between," and it is in this liminal space that one discovers the "presence of what did *not* exist" (emphasis added), the presence that we have identified with a self-negating subjectivity, the not-I.

The second meeting between Sam and Watt entails a similar instance of gap-bridging, one that occurs at a threshold, in the space or *couloir* that separates Sam's garden from Watt's.[24] This scene again employs the major motifs of lapsarian epistemology, most particularly those of the encounter in the garden and of the fall: "[Watt's] progress was slow and devious . . . for often he struck against the trunks of trees, or in the tangles of underwood caught his foot, and fell to the ground" (159). The mirror, recalling the dark glass of 1 Corinthians, not only provides another point of reference within the complex of motifs associated with lapsarian epistemology but also serves to frame the whole of Sam's encounter with Knott: "I felt as though I were standing before a great mirror, in which my garden was reflected" (159). Indeed, as Angela Moorjani has pointed out, the entire scene is defined by a mirror logic according to which details are turned round, rearranged back to front, as though reflected in a glass.[25] Thus, Watt's dress ("Then he came, awkwardly buttoning his trousers, which he was wearing back to front," 162), as well as his walk and his talk ("As Watt walked, so now he talked, back to front," 164), all function according to a principle of specular inversion.

The peripatetic dance that follows offers another example of this mirroring, since each partner reproduces the movements of the other, though always in reverse:

> Then I turned him round, until he faced me. Then I placed his hands, on my shoulders, his left hand on my right shoulder, and his right hand on my left shoulder. Then I placed my hands, on his shoulders, on his left shoulder my right hand, and on his right shoulder my left hand. Then I took a single pace forward, with my left leg, and he a

single pace back with his right leg (he could scarcely do otherwise). Then I took a double pace forward with my right leg, and he of course with his left leg a double pace back. And so we paced together between the fences. (163)

It is during this phenomenological *pas de deux*, carried out "face to face" (164), that Watt makes seven brief statements to Sam, each inverting in one way or another conventional linguistic order. These statements—mirror communications as it were—describe Watt's encounter with Knott, which is to say the encounter of the self with the not-I. The obscure and inverted syntax Watt employs is entirely appropriate to an encounter that has, in effect, occurred through a glass darkly. So it is that Knott looms before Watt in the first communication as "dim" (164) and in the second as a "dark bulk" (165). In the third communication he is presented as the principle of negation ("of nought . . . the source," 166) for which Watt is willing to sacrifice whatever he possesses ("abandoned my little to find him [Knott]," 166).

The effort to move beyond subject-object dialectics, to enter into the "source of nought," is related in the most cryptic of all the communications, the sixth: "Lit yad mac, ot og. Ton taw, ton tonk. Ton dob, ton trips. Ton vila, ton deda. Ton kawa, ton pelsa. Ton das, ton yag. Os devil, rof mit" (So lived, for time. Not sad, not gay. Not awake, not asleep. Not alive, not adead. Not body, not spirit. Not Watt, not Knott. Til day came, to go, 167). Here there is a suggestion of epistemological breakthrough, as consciousness appears to move beyond subject and object, mind and body, Knott and Watt ("Not body, not spirit. Not Watt, not Knott"). What emerges as an alternative to this dualism is a condition of radical liminality in which the cogito is represented as neither living nor dead, neither awake nor asleep, a condition that erases, at least momentarily, the distinction between inside and outside.

Such a state of liminality prepares the way for what in the seventh, or final, communication becomes Watt's most sustained confrontation with Knott: "Dis yb dis, nem owt. Yad la, tin fo trap. Skin, skin, skin. Od su did ned taw? On. Taw ot klat tonk? On. Tonk ot klat taw? On. Tonk ta kool taw? On. Taw ta kool tonk? Nilb, mun, mud. Tin fo trap, yad la. Nem owt, dis yb dis" (Side by side, two men. All day, part of night. Dumb, numb, blind. Knott look at Watt? No. Watt look at Knott? No. Watt talk to Knott? No. Knott talk to Watt? No. What then did us do? Niks, niks, niks. Part of night, all day. Two men, side by side, 168). Here, Watt and Knott, in a variation on the face-to-face encounter, come together side by side and enter into a condition that—speechless, sightless, senseless—leads to a consciousness of nothing, a consciousness that is nothing (niks, niks, niks).[26] This experience of liminality carried to the point of self-nullification recalls another such experience, the one Arsene undergoes of that "presence of what did *not* exist, that presence without, that presence within, that presence between" (45, my emphasis). Watt has, in other words, known something akin to existence off the ladder, that momentary eruption into the world of the not-I. Watt's experience is, however, so heavily veiled—enfolded in a language that is difficult in its own right and dependent for its broader meaning on an involved iconography of the fall—that it is quite possible to read through the entire novel without noticing that it has occurred.

Through the mediation of Sam's own "face-to-face" encounter with Watt, we have learned of Watt's "face-to-face" encounter with Knott. But if the phenomenological question remains that of how the individual can know himself as a consciousness that lies beyond subject-object dialectics, and if Watt and Knott function as figurations of the self and the not-I, then Sam's mediation here complicates this formula, since his own encounter with Watt mirrors Watt's encounter with Knott. In other words, what was a simple pairing in *Murphy* (Murphy—>Endon) has been doubled in *Watt* (Sam—>Watt/Watt—>Knott), and this doubling serves, as I have indicated, to transform an epistemological process into a narrative process, one in which Watt relates his story to Sam, who in turn relates it to the reader.

There is, however, another character who must be included in these narrative transactions, and that is the peculiarly marginal Mr. Hackett. In a novel in which the fall is connected with lapsarian epistemology, and "existence off the ladder" suggests a momentary and unstable rising above subject-object dialectics, it is significant that Hackett's deformity is the result precisely of a fall from a ladder (15–16).[27] This means that Hackett bears literally, as Watt does figuratively, the sign of the fall into Cartesian dualism, and it is therefore not surprising that he discovers in Watt, if not the mirror im-

age Sam found, at least a reflection of himself. As Mr. Nixon remarks to Hackett, "The curious thing is, my dear fellow, I tell you
quite frankly, that when I see him [Watt], or think of him, I think
of you, and that when I see you, or think of you, I think of him"
(19).

At the same time, Hackett is associated with Sam, since he functions as an authorial figure, one with a particularly Balzacian cast.
Thus, Watt comes swimming into Hackett's consciousness in much
the way it was popularly imagined that realist novelists conceive
their characters: he appears from nowhere, in a sense out of
nowhere, a flickering shadow, barely perceptible, "scarcely to be dis-
tinguished from the wall behind it" (16). Hackett's curiosity is immediately excited, and he presses Mr. Nixon, one of Watt's casual
acquaintances, for additional information: "But you must know
something, said Mr Hackett. One does not depart with five shillings
to a shadow. Nationality, family, birthplace, confession, occupation,
means of existence, distinctive signs, you cannot be in ignorance of
all this" (21). These are, of course, the kinds of questions that Mr.
Willoughby Kelly asked Celia when confronted with that other bit
of narrative opacity, Murphy, the kinds of question that the realist
novelist puts to himself when he first conceives a character and imagines a story:[28]

> Mr Hackett did not know when he had been more intrigued, nay, he
> did not know when he had been so intrigued. He did not know either
> what it was that so intrigued him. What is it that so intrigues me, he
> said, whom even the extraordinary, even the supernatural, intrigue so
> seldom, and so little. (17)

Intrigue, the word Beckett so insistently repeats, is the French
word for plot, of course, and it is quite literally the appearance of
Watt before Hackett that sets the plot in motion. We might even
treat this opening section as a prologue of sorts in which we witness,
as do the Nixons and Hackett, a character gradually coming into
being. The idea of a narrative "birth" is in fact suggested by a number of details, all of which center on lovemaking and parturition: the
amorous couple who have usurped Hackett's bench (8–9), the passing woman in an advanced stage of pregnancy (12), and Mrs.
Nixon's account of her own heroic accouchement.[29] Significantly, it
is following the prologue, which has taken the reader from love-

making to birth, that Watt is figuratively born when he collides with the porter wheeling the milk can (24).[30]

We should not, however, lose sight of the larger point: that Sam and Hackett, taken together, function as a parodic version of the author himself, of "Beckett the Hack."[31] By providing a narrative frame for Watt's confrontation with Knott, for the subject's confrontation with itself as not-I, Sam/Hackett has made what was an epistemological quest in *Murphy* into a narrative quest in *Watt*. As a result, the exploration of the self has become the exploration of two related genres: the novel and the autobiography.

In both Cartesian epistemology and fictional realism, the way to knowledge is through an observer standing in relation to the world, a subject standing in relation to an object. The idea that the novel is a kind of record of this transaction was best summarized in Balzac's famous secretary metaphor: "French Society was to be the historian, I had only to be the secretary."[32] Glossing this celebrated pronouncement, Stephen Heath writes:

> The novelist is, as it were, a scribe *taking down* his contemporary and immediately pre-contemporary society from a kind of visual dictation. The chronology of the task is clear for Balzac in his role as secretary to Society: observation, *then* expression: "l'auteur pense être d'accord avec toute intelligence, haute ou basse, en composant l'art littéraire de deux parties bien distinctes: *l'observation—l'expression.*"[33]

But, as Heath goes on to remark, the "copy is more than a copy, the novelist must 'surprendre le sens caché dans cet immense assemblage de figures, de passions et d'événements,' must in an act of understanding, seize the significance of the outward circulation of social reality." The "chronology of writing" that Heath proposes for Balzac is, therefore, "observation—expression or reproduction—commentary," a rough equivalence to what in Descartes might be described as observation—representation—examination.[34] What we need to stress here is that the world is not given, in any simple sense, for either the Cartesian or the Balzacian; rather, it presents itself as a series of phenomena, which must be sifted through and placed in some kind of telling order. Perhaps the most characteristic trait of *Watt* is the way it takes this idea and carries it to a point of reductio ad absurdum. Hence, the novel recounts the hero's desire to concatenate events plausibly, to draw out of them a paradigmatic form of the kind he attempted to locate in his account of the Galls or the pot.

Consider, for instance, Watt's explanation of how he gained entry to Knott's house the night of his arrival:

> Watt was surprised to find the back door, so lately locked, now open. Two explanations of this occurred to him. The first was this, that his science of the locked door, so seldom at fault, had been so on this occasion . . . the second was this, that the back door, when he had found it locked, had in effect been locked, but had subsequently been opened. . . . Of these two explanations Watt thought he preferred the latter, as being the more beautiful. For if someone had opened the back door, from within, or without, would not he Watt have seen a light, or heard a sound? Or had the door been unlocked, from within, in the dark, by some person perfectly familiar with the premises, and wearing carpet slippers, or in his stockinged feet? . . . The result of this was that Watt never knew how he got into Mr Knott's house. (36–37)

Such a passage gives us an example of the Cartesian mind at work, sorting data, organizing material, scrutinizing validity. But notice how close this comes to the novelist's task, as the details get filled in, as the person within is suddenly invested with carpet slippers or finds himself moving on stockinged feet. In this case the minute particulars, the hypothetical carpet slippers and the stockinged feet, are subordinate to the analysis and merely help to work out alternative theories. More often than not, however, the analysis so overwhelms its occasion that we lose sight of the hypothetical nature of the discourse and find that the illustrative examples have taken on a life of their own, becoming, in the process, the stuff of fiction.

The dogs kept by the Lynch family provide an example of this tendency. Watt has instructions to dispose of the remains of Knott's daily meals by feeding them to a dog, or more precisely to "the" dog. But this presents a problem since no such animal is to be found on the premises. As Watt proceeds in good Cartesian fashion to a close analysis of the problem, considering and rejecting one proposal after another, the logic grows increasingly elaborate, increasingly baroque, until the solution that finally emerges presents us not with a single dog but an entire kennel, not with a single owner but a family of owners, and not with any family but the inimitable Lynch family. The humor of this shaggy-dog story derives from the grotesque disproportion of the solution to the problem: an army of hounds and four generations of keepers are established to assure that not an atom of food shall be wasted, and all this in the name of economy. Analysis has in this case become so enmeshed in its internal workings, so mesmerized by the concrete particulars it has imaged forth, that it loses sight of both itself and its occasion. As a result, the Lynch family detaches itself from the realist ground and begins to drift into pure fantasy, as though the carpet slippers or the stockinged feet had grown monstrously large and in the process overwhelmed their surroundings.

There are, of course, other examples of the same thing, of the effort to understand an event slowly transmuting itself into a fictionalized account of that event. Watt speculating on how Ann Lynch came to be pregnant (106–9), Hackett and the Nixons wondering why Watt descended from the tram where he did (19–21), Sam asking himself how the holes were made in the asylum fence (160–62)—all of these grow out of a patiently conducted empiricism, which, when carried to its logical extreme, becomes a parody of the realist novel, mocking the attempt to marshal intransigent material into coherent orders, to compel disparate experience into causal sequences.

This means that if the world of the novel is not simply given but must be constructed, then any effort to represent reality will at some level constitute it and so at some level fictionalize it. The story of Erskine's bell illustrates this point. It begins as a straightforward account of what appears to be a common, and in this case habitual, action: "Sometimes in the night Mr Knott pressed a bell that sounded in Erskine's room, and then Erskine got up and went down" (120). Problems begin to appear, however, when the narrator adds, "This Watt knew, for from his bed where he lay not far away he would hear the bell sound ting! and Erskine get up and go down" (120). What has been introduced is a mediating consciousness, a point of view, and from this intervention there arises a whole constellation of doubts, speculations, uncertainties. Among these is the reliability of the consciousness that perceives and records not merely the story of Erskine's bell but also the novel as a whole. Thus, on the one hand we are reassured that the narrator's source is trustworthy: "For all that I know on the subject of Mr Knott . . . came from Watt, and from Watt alone. . . . He assured me at the time, when he began to spin his yarn, that he would tell all, and then again, some years later, when he had spun his yarn, that he had told all" (125). On the other hand, hearing this account called a "yarn" and learning that it took "some years" to relate does little to inspire our confidence. Nor are our hesitations much assuaged when we are informed, a few pages later, that "many things described as happening, in Mr Knott's house, and of course grounds, perhaps never happened at all, or quite differently" (126).

The question of who sounded the bell continues to trouble Watt, and he decides that the only way to solve the mystery is through empirical investigation, which means that he must gain entry to Erskine's room. But this entails a further difficulty, for Erskine keeps his room locked and carries his key in a secret pocket. Having been alerted to the problem of point of view, the reader may now wonder how the narrator knows about a pocket that is, after all, secret: "And if it were asked how it is known that the pocket in which Erskine kept his key was sewn on the front of his underhose, the answer to that would be this, that one day when Erskine was doing his number one against a bush, Watt . . . caught a glimpse . . . of the key, gleaming" (127). Having called into question not only his source but also his own capacity for recording that source, having in other words submitted his narrative to what Edward Said calls "molestation,"[35] Sam now appears to reestablish his authority:

> And so always, when the impossibility of my knowing, of Watt's having known, what I know, what Watt knew, seems absolute, and insurmountable, and undeniable, and uncoercible, it could be shown that I know, because Watt told me, and that Watt knew, because someone told him, or because he found out for himself. (127–28)

The story ends, however, in a moment of pure self-molestation when Watt explains that he got into Erskine's room "ruse a by" only to discover that "There was a bell . . . but it was broken" (128). "Ruse a by" is nothing less than the blithe admission that fiction provides a narrative *passe-partout*—that the narrator can ultimately say and do what he likes, and the mere saying will make it so. The detail of the broken bell makes this point all the more tellingly because it effectively undercuts the entire story; after all, if the bell was broken in the first place, then Watt certainly did not hear it ring. Unless, that is, we choose to play the game at which the novel itself excels and entertain the hypothesis that the bell was working until just before Watt entered Erskine's room, a hypothesis from which we may effortlessly extrapolate a second, a third, and a fourth, filling out the variations, and the pages, as we go.

◆·

We have seen how the attempt to grasp a situation empirically can produce fantastic excrescences of the sort represented by the Lynch family, and how the effect of this Cartesianism run amok is generally to undermine the realist novel's claim to representational fidelity. At a number of crucial moments, *Watt* carries the problem of fictionality to the point of self-reflection, creating a metafictional parable whose critical object becomes its own process of invention. Consider, for instance, the encounter with Mr. Ash. Having described existence off the ladder, Arsene wonders precisely what caused "this sentiment [to] arise . . . and to what forces is the credit for its removal to be attributed" (44–45). He does not, however, pursue these questions, because he has "information of a practical nature to impart" (45), information that he goes on to convey in the form of a story. The story concerns a Mr. Ash, who once buttonholed Arsene on Westminster Bridge for the purpose of telling him that the time was exactly seventeen minutes past five; "A moment later," Arsene explains, "Big Ben (if that is the name?) struck six. This in my opinion is the type of all information whatsoever, be it voluntary or solicited" (46). The investigation into existence off the ladder was passed over so that information might be imparted; the information was imparted in the form of a story; the story was about the uselessness of information. Such is fiction's comment on itself.

In similar fashion, the incident of the Galls is a story preoccupied with its own authority. I say story, because after floundering in the quicksand of theoretical reconstruction, it is conceded that the incident never occurred: "Watt learned towards the end of his stay in Mr Knott's house to accept that nothing happened, that a nothing had happened" (80). Watt, then, or perhaps Sam, has created the story out of nothing; but "to elicit something from nothing requires a certain skill" (77)—the skill of the storyteller. Like the story of Mr. Ash, the incident of the Galls comments on itself by exposing its own lack of credibility, by showing itself to be a piece of trumpery. At the same time, it comments on the novel as a whole by metaphorically describing its creation. Beckett has said of *Watt* that it "was only a game, a means of staying sane, a way of keeping my hand in" and that is precisely how the incident of the Galls may be read.[36] Beckett, the Gaelic writer writing in Gaul, is tuning his piano, keeping his hand in, and wondering all the time whether it is worth it:

> The piano is doomed, in my opinion, said the younger.
> The piano-tuner also, said the elder.
> The pianist also, said the younger. (72)

Of course, once he has cast off the bonds of mimesis, the *auctor ludens* is free to play whatever game he likes, even the most patently useless. One that particularly delights Beckett involves trundling out the worm-eaten machinery of realism and displaying it as a kind of technical curiosity. In this spirit, the novel deftly coordinates two references to Watt's footwear into a well-crafted piece of internal consistency. The first reference comes toward the beginning of the book:

> I met him one day in the street. One of his feet was bare. I forget which. He drew me to one side and said he was in need of five shillings to buy himself a boot. I could not refuse him. (23)

This raises a question: Why would Watt want to buy a single boot? The second reference, which comes toward the end, answers this question with all the circumstantial plausibility we would expect from Balzac:

> Watt wore, on his foot, a boot, brown in colour, and a shoe, happily of a brownish colour also. This boot Watt had bought, for eight pence, from a one-legged man who, having lost his leg, and a fortiori his foot, in an accident, was happy to realize, on his discharge from hospital, for such a sum, his unique remaining marketable asset. (218–19)

The same cross-referencing of detail occurs with the race track, whose relative position is first established as Watt is approaching Mr. Knott's: "The racecourse now appearing, with its beautiful white railing, in the fleeing lights, warned Watt that he was drawing near, and that when the train stopped next, then he must leave it" (29). It is then reconfirmed two hundred pages later from a different, though related, perspective: "Watt's room contained no information. . . . Its one window commanded a very fine view of the race-course" (208). However, as was not the case with *Murphy*, such displays of realist virtuosity are significant because they are the exception rather than the rule in *Watt*, and it is far more common to encounter passages that insist on the novelist's independence from his material, on his right to invent whatever he pleases. Thus, speaking of a certain species of fish that "in order to support the middle depths, are forced to rise and fall, now to the surface of the waves and now to the ocean bed," Sam asks himself whether such fish exist and, having written them into being, triumphantly responds, "Yes, such fish exist, now" (120). Or, having decided that the laws of genetics are unhappily restrictive, he banishes them through an act of authorial fiat: "Haemophilia is, like enlargement of the prostate, an exclusively male disorder. But not in this work" (102).

More generally, *Watt* delights in a concatenation that is willfully implausible. So it is that the novel articulates itself along a series of fault lines, deliberately constructed improbabilities, even impossibilities of narrative. We know, for instance, that *Watt* is the result of two narratives, Watt's to Sam and Sam's to the reader, and we know that neither is reliable:

> Add to this the obscurity of Watt's communications, the rapidity of his utterances and the eccentricities of his syntax, as elsewhere recorded. Add to this the material conditions in which these communications were made. Add to this the scant aptitude to receive of him to whom they were proposed. Add to this the scant aptitude to give of him to whom they were committed. And some idea will perhaps be obtained of the difficulties experienced in formulating, not only such matters as those here in question, but the entire body of Watt's experiences, from the moment of his entering Mr Knott's establishment to the moment of his leaving it. (75)

The effect is a novel teeming with anomalies of the sort that would have horrified a writer like Henry James. For example, Sam confides that "all that I know on the subject of . . . Watt, and of all that touched Watt, came from Watt and Watt alone" (125). Yet Arsene's short statement appears before us full-blown, in spite of the fact that Watt received it in bits and pieces ("For his declaration had entered Watt's ears only by fits, and his understanding, like all that enters the ears only by fits, hardly at all," 80). Is Sam engaging in a bit of playful confabulation when he provides us with Arsene's short statement, so obviously anything but what it advertises itself to be? Or was the short statement in fact much longer, and is the piece we have only a partial account of what Arsene said? These are, as Watt would put it, teasers.

Some narrative impossibilities are, however, just that: they admit of no solution. Obviously, Watt cannot relate what he does not know. Yet Sam's account includes the conversation between Hackett and the Nixons, Lady McCann's story of the medical students, a goat (or ass) that saw Watt but was not seen by him, and the events that transpire at the railway station after Watt has been knocked unconscious. Such narrative impossibilities occur throughout the novel, and the more we encounter them, the more we recognize that they are not so much lapses in construction as openings through which fiction admits its own unlikely creations. The unlikeliest of all these creations is a character named Larry Nixon.

⌒·

I have suggested that *Watt* "narrativizes" the process whereby the subject comes to know itself as not-I. As we have seen, this process involves a series of epistemological transactions in which one figure seeks an image of itself in another figure, which in turn seeks an image of itself in a third. Hence, there is a mirroring or doubling of Watt in Knott, of Sam and Hackett in Watt, and of Beckett in Sam and Hackett. By carrying us back to Beckett, such a sequence identifies the cogito with the *scribo*, the subject with the author. And this means that the metaphoric birth of Watt in the opening section may be understood as the animation not only of a consciousness but also of a character. It is no accident, however, that this metaphoric birth is accompanied by the description of another birth, that of the apparently insignificant Larry Nixon, a character who never makes an appearance in the novel and who is mentioned only once—and then in a narrative aside. Yet in a novel that is preoccupied with the pursuit of the absent self, we may wish to examine with special care a figure who is so conspicuously not there, a figure who, it turns out, is identified with Beckett himself.

This identification is made through the description of Larry Nixon's birth, which parodically reenacts the account Beckett has given of his own birth. As Tetty Nixon relates the event, on the day Larry was born she hosted a dinner party which her husband had arranged: "When Thompson comes into the dining-room, followed by Cream and Berry . . . I was already seated at the table. . . . The first mouthful of duck had barely passed my lips, said Tetty, when Larry leaped in my wom" (13). What is most striking about this episode is the way it repeats, in all its important details, Beckett's celebrated tease about his own birth: "My memories begin on the eve of my birth, under the table, when my father gave a dinner and my mother presided."[37]

Given our discussion of Larry Nixon, we are now in a position to understand how the novel's epistemological and autobiographical trajectories converge. Consider the following diagram:

I	II	III
(narrating self)	(self as simulacrum)	(self as negation)
Sam/Hackett ⟶	Watt ⟶	Knott
Sam Beckett ⟶	*Watt* ⟶	Nixon

At the epistemological level, such a diagram shows how Beckett has deconstructed Descartes on two grounds. First, the figure we have identified with the "inquiry" of the cogito (Watt) does not exist before language but is already defined within the field of writing (Sam/Hackett). Second, the cogito leads not to the revelation of a primordial presence but to its negation or absence (Knott). We may begin to translate this epistemology into an autobiographical scheme by showing how the upper series of terms in the diagram corresponds to the lower series of terms. Thus, Sam/Hackett represents, as we have observed, a parodic version of Sam Beckett, while Watt (the character) functions as Sam/Hackett's simulacrum of the self, just as *Watt* (the novel) functions as Beckett's fictive representation of the process of self-reflection. Of course, this leaves Larry Nixon's function in the diagram unexplained. Is there a sense in which the novel *Watt* can be said to pursue Nixon, as the character Watt pursues Knott? And is there a sense in which Nixon (like Knott) functions as a principle of negation?

We may respond to the first question by observing that insofar as the novel is autobiographical, the story of Nixon's birth (which is to say, Beckett's "description" of his own birth) becomes the novel's generic destination, the point at which it connects with its subject matter. *Watt* is, in other words, in search of Nixon in the same way any piece of autobiographical writing attempts to recover its author's beginnings. In response to the second question, two points are pertinent. First, Larry Nixon's most salient trait as a character is his absence, the fact that he never directly appears in the story. Second, while Nixon is a common Irish surname, Beckett is obsessively attentive to word play, and in this case there is a fairly obvious pun involved: the first syllable indicates a negative (nix)—itself an echo of Watt's description of Knott ("niks, niks, niks," 168)—while the second syllable is the Greek for "being" ("on").[38] In a novel that functions as an extended deconstruction of the metaphysics of presence, it is certainly not insignificant that Nixon's name means "nonbeing." Taken together, these two points suggest that Larry Nixon epitomizes precisely the absence and negation that Knott represents. What all of this means is that Nixon is to Sam Beckett what Knott is to Sam/Hackett: the terminus at the end of the Cartesian line, the point at which self-reflection inevitably becomes self-negation.

More generally, this diagram draws a parallel between the novel's philosophical and generic interests, between the deconstruction of the metaphysics of presence and the deconstruction of autobiography as a literary form. As we have seen, the Sam/Hackett—>Watt —>Knott nexus indicates what happens when the subject attempts to narrate its own self-negating predication—the kind of predication that Descartes undertook in both the *Discourse on Method* and the *Meditations*. At the same time, the Sam Beckett—>*Watt*—>Larry Nixon nexus suggests what happens when this same effort at self-predication is translated into autobiography—a form whose self-consuming moments de Man and Derrida point out in their analyses of Rousseau. Of particular importance in the identification of Beckett and Nixon is the fact that it depends on a description of birth. For all autobiography is, to a greater or lesser degree, based upon a *recherche*, a process of reconstruction that involves working one's way back in time toward the "presence" of the self, particularly a "deep self" (Proust's *moi-permanent*)[39] that stands at the threshold of consciousness and cognition. Hence, Proust begins the *Recherche* with an image of Marcel caught between waking and sleeping, between sentience and nonsentience, just as Joyce begins the *Portrait* with a description of an infantile Stephen constituting his consciousness, faculty by faculty. Beckett, in effect, goes Proust and Joyce one better by carrying the idea of the *recherche* to its logical extreme, by reducing the notion of primordial presence to a caricature of itself, here figured as an impossible prenatal memory.

I should like to conclude this chapter by turning to another apparently minor moment in the novel, a moment near the end of the book when Watt, finding himself at the train station, experiences a kind of double vision. There he catches sight, as Hackett had earlier, of a figure of indeterminate aspect: "Watt was beginning to tire of running his eyes up and down the highway, when a figure, human apparently, advancing along its crown, arrested, and revived, his attention" (225). There can be little doubt who this figure is, for he appears to Watt as "a sheet, or a sack, or a quilt, or a rug" (225), just as Watt appeared to Hackett as a "parcel, a carpet, for example, or a roll of tarpaulin" (16). What is more, he walks before Watt ("The feet, following each other in rapid and impetuous succession, were flung, the right foot to the right, the left foot to the left," 226) just as Watt walked before Lady McCann ("to fling out his right leg as far as possible towards the south, and then again to turn his bust as far as possible towards the south and at the same time to fling out his left leg as far as possible towards the north," 30). About to experience another fall, Watt finally confronts an image of himself—meets himself, so to speak, face to face.

But even this tenuous bit of self-projection is undercut by an intrusive author who, lacking any identity of his own, reminds us that it is all done with mirrors. For when she witnesses Watt's peculiar style of locomotion, Lady McCann privately enjoys a familiar joke:

> She recalled the old story of her girlhood days, the old story of the medical students and the gentleman walking before them with stiff and open stride. Excuse me, sir, said one of the students, raising his cap, when they drew abreast, my friend here says it is piles, and I say it is merely the clap. We have all three then been deceived, replied the gentleman, for I thought it was wind myself. (31)

Some two hundred pages later Watt supplies the joke with its final grace note: "[He] felt them suddenly glow in the dark place, and go out, the words, *The only cure is diet*" (226). This is more than narrative impossibility. It is an admission that all the characters in the novel are effectively emanations of one character, although that one character lacks the self-identity and self-presence that would enable us to refer to him as an individual. And so we call him, for the sake of convenience, Sam Beckett, the fictitious author of an impossible joke whose punch line consists in simultaneously articulating and annihilating himself.

Since we began with Rousseau, it is fitting that we should end with him. Alain Grosrichard has observed that Rousseau's entire *oeuvre* may be understood as an extended effort to name the self, an effort that proved futile because the self turned out to be "unnamable" (*l'innommable*).[40] We might say the same of *Watt*. With this work, Beckett has carried the autobiographical novel to its (il)logical conclusion. The resulting deconstruction treats the self not as a presence but as an absence, not as a being but as a negation. Yet, after so terminal an examination of the cogito, it is difficult to see where Beckett could go next. In looking beyond *Watt*, Beckett continued to be engaged by problems of epistemology, but he was now interested not so much in the nothingness of the self as in the simulacra that are generated out of that nothingness. In particular, he was intrigued by what Derrida was to call the "chain of supplements," the abyssal representation of representation. How better to examine this "chain" than with a trilogy of novels, each of which would "supplement" the other?

CHAPTER FOUR

Beckett's Mirror-Writing

Doubling and 'Différance' in 'Molloy'

The mirror has become our most enduring symbol of literary mimesis, the epitome not of reproduction but of duplication, a simulacrum of the world in which representation corresponds at every point to the thing represented. Cartesianism has also been conceived of on the analogy of a mirror: consciousness functions as a "glassy essence," a window of perception that fixes in its luminous gaze all the shifting shapes and forms of reality.[1] This process of speculation is complicated, however, when the subject and object of consciousness become one and the same, when reflection turns to self-reflection.

Initially it might seem as though self-reflection provides an ideal form of representation, one in which image and essence, appearance and reality, achieve a perfect union. Yet, as we observed in the previous chapter, pure consciousness—consciousness as it might exist before language or history—necessarily eludes our cognitive grasp, and this means that whatever self is projected by the mind's eye is culturally refracted from the beginning. As a result, the original is already a copy; the object is already a mirrored image. We might better explain self-reflection, then, by comparing it not to a mirror but to a mirror-play: two mimes stand face to face and, like a man and his reflection, begin to move in perfect synchrony, just as Watt and Sam do at the asylum. While the mirror-play is clearly meant to be humorous—it is a routine out of vaudeville—it nevertheless raises a number of serious ontological questions. For instance, given the two mimes, how do we determine which represents the man and which the reflection? More generally, what are the criteria, within any perceptual schema, for establishing where reality ends and imitation begins? Finally, to what extent does the mirror-play function as a piece of metacriticism, one that mimes its own mimesis, or stages its own staging?

In addressing these questions, *Molloy*, as it were, moves the reader through the looking glass, eroding those categorical distinctions that have traditionally enabled us to speak of first-order realities and second-order representations. Yet, even though *Molloy* deconstructs the very logic of mimesis, it remains the most binary of all Beckett's novels, a work that organizes itself around two narrators and two narrations. Since each narrator relates his own story, each narrative may be read as an exercise in self-reflection. At the same time, there is a sense in which the narrators are telling each other's story, and this raises—as in the case of the mirror-play—a question of ontological priority. If Molloy and Moran inhabit each other's margins, if each is narrating the other, then where do we locate the antecedent term? Who is the narrator and who is the narrated? Beckett once remarked in a letter that with *Molloy* he hoped to develop a new kind of character, what he called the "narrator/narrated."[2] On the face of it, Beckett's formulation expresses nothing out of the ordinary: he is describing the way a narrator tells his own story. Yet this formulation suggests not only that the narrator narrates himself, but also that he *is narrated* by someone else, that, dispossessed of his own story, he becomes the narrative property of an unidentified third person.

The "narrator/narrated" consequently functions as a dualism that deconstructs itself, one that strikingly anticipates two of Derrida's best-known ideas: supplementarity and *différance*.[3] Supplementarity is especially relevant to our present discussion because it undermines the fundamental assumptions of mimesis. As Derrida argues, any representational image—such as a mirror reflection—necessarily stands in an ambiguous and contradictory relation to its model or archetype. On the one hand, it is a complementary addition, a duplication that repeats and sustains the original, "a plentitude enriching another plentitude, the *fullest measure* of presence." On the other hand, it is a replacement, a stand-in or substitute that "insinuates itself *in-the-place-of*; if it fills, it is as if one fills a void."[4] This leads to what we might call the paradox of hyperrealism: the more a representation succeeds at what it attempts, the greater the likeli-

hood that it will destroy itself.[5] For while the representation is meant
to "supplement" the original, to serve as a repetition of what has
gone before, it accomplishes this by being as "true-to-life" as possible. But if the copy becomes too real, too vivid, too autonomous, it
may take on a life of its own—even begin to displace or replace the
original.

One of the reasons the distinction between origin and copy breaks
down is because of the role *différance* plays in defining the logic of
identity and difference. Of particular interest to Derrida is the way
différance keeps turning up—like a bad penny—within those binary
oppositions that have traditionally characterized Western philosophy (nature/culture, *physis/mimesis*, subject/object, speech/writing,
and so on). The inflationary circulation of *différance* is inevitable
because within any given dualism each term simultaneously defines
itself not only as the other term's opposite (differing) but also as its
substitute (deferring). Hence, culture serves both as the antithesis or
negation of nature and as its surrogate or replacement—what we
have "instead of" nature.[6]

Différance thus functions as a kind of conceptual slippage within
and between terms, "the displaced and equivocal passage of one different thing to another, from one term of an opposition to the
other."[7] Every time we attempt to grasp a term on the left-hand side
of the dichotomy, we find ourselves holding the corresponding term
on the right-hand side of the dichotomy. What we assumed was nature turns out to be a culturally mediated substitute; what we assumed was the self turns out to be a linguistically mediated other.
The difference "between" becomes the difference "within" when a
founding term (nature, subject, origin) breaks apart, and we discover
that it contains within itself its opposite (culture, object, copy). This
is precisely what happens in *Molloy* with regard to the narrator/nar-
rated. A term associated with the subject (narrator) begins to slide
into a term associated with the object (narrated): inside becomes outside; agent becomes recipient.

While Derrida rejects all first principles, *différance* comes perilously close to functioning as the first principle of deconstruction,
the transformational logic according to which an intellectual category can simultaneously be both itself and its opposite.[8] Beckett was
attracted by this kind of thinking and discovered its Renaissance

analogue in Giordano Bruno's notion of the "identified contrary." According to Bruno, when the individual terms within a binary pairing are carried to their logical extreme, they cease to function as terms of opposition and become instead terms of identification. As Beckett explains it:

> The maxima and minima of particular contraries are one and indifferent. Minimal heat equals minimal cold. Consequently transmutations are circular. The principle (minimum) of one contrary takes its movement from the principle (maximum) of one another. . . . Maximal speed is a state of rest. The maximum of corruption and the minimum of generation are identical: in principle, corruption is generation. (*Disjecta*, 21)

While the "identified contrary" and *différance* develop out of different intellectual antecedents, they are remarkably similar in conception and function. Particularly important for our purposes is the fact that both concepts rely on a logic of antithetical equivalence; hence, speed is rest—corruption is generation.[9] It is presumably the identified contrary that Beckett had in mind when, in the mid-1930s, he secured Murphy to a rocking chair in West Brompton and sent him through the circuit of Bruno's transmutation: "The rock got faster and faster, shorter and shorter, the iridescence was gone, the cry in the mew was gone, soon his body would be quiet. Most things under the moon got slower and slower and then stopped, a rock got faster and faster and then stopped" (*Murphy*, 9).

Obviously the idea of the identified contrary continued to exercise Beckett's imagination, and some fifteen years later when he sat down to write *Molloy*, he produced an entire novel about a character who is simultaneously himself and his opposite. I argue in what follows that Beckett constructed this character out of a set of narrative techniques whose function and logic look forward to supplementarity and *différance*. In tracing the development of these techniques and exploring their antimimetic application, I focus on three large issues: the relation of the novel's double plot to the identified contrary or *différance*; the epistemological and narrative functions of Molloy and Moran; and the abyssal use of A and C as examples of textual supplementarity.

Moran and Molloy provide the two terms in Beckett's "narra-
tor/narrated".[10] We may begin to understand how these terms operate, how they represent a convergence of identity and difference,
by considering the openings of the two narratives. Molloy's inhabits a condition of generalized uncertainty. He know that he occupies
his mother's room, but little else. He does not know, for instance,
how he came to be there, when his mother died, even if his mother
died. "The truth is," Molloy confesses, as though it needed con-
fessing, "I don't know much" (7–8). In contrast, Moran appears to
occupy a world about which definite statements can be made, useful information given and received. Here the clockwork of time runs
through its wonted cycles, enabling us to locate ourselves at a particular point, to assert, for example, that "it is midnight" (125).
Here, too, the natural world holds sway, active and expressive,
prompting us, as we "hear the eagle-owl" (125), to situate the story
within a particular space, say the country. What is more, the facts
of this world cohere, so that the eagle-owl nests outside the window
only if the environs are wooded, and the environs are wooded only
if the precipitation is heavy; thus, "the rain is beating on the windows" (125). In brief, Moran's is, or appears to be, a world in which
we may confidently chart the coordinates of time, space, and causal-
ity, a world in which things may be known.

Molloy not only knows imperfectly, but he writes or tries to write
what he imperfectly knows. Although he is certain that he has undertaken a literary work of some kind, its precise character remains
vague ("so many pages, so much money," 7) and his motives for producing it obscure ("I don't work for money. For what then? I don't
know," 7). More important, he considers himself—and so do we—
unequal to the task: "I've forgotten how to spell too, and half the
words" (8). Moran, on the contrary, knows exactly what he is doing: he is assembling a report, one that will be submitted to his superiors and filed—who can doubt it?—according to the author's last
name ("My name is Moran, Jacques," 125). Moran inspires us with
confidence: he works with order and deliberation, trimming his
lamp, sitting at his desk, writing. This, we feel, is a promising sequence. What is more, he has a grasp of his material as a whole,
knowing at the outset that it will be long and even contemplating
the possibility that, despite such tenacity of method, he may not fin-

ish it (125). Here is Moran worrying about an ending, while Molloy can barely manage a beginning.

But if our two narrators diverge entirely in the characters they present and the worlds they project, they converge at the all important level of style, as the openings to their two narratives suggest. Thus Molloy's beginning:

> I am in my mother's room. It's I who live there now. I don't know how I got there. (7)

And Moran's:

> It is midnight. The rain is beating on the windows. I am calm.

Both present themselves as exercises in minimalism, a series of utterances whose construction is so stark, whose substance is so spare, that we almost hear the silence out of which they emerge. And if the language gradually relaxes into something ampler and more fluent, this only reinforces the highly original quality of these two beginnings and so further identifies each with the other.

Of course, this identity of contraries extends far beyond the opening pages of the Molloy-Moran narratives. We may, for instance, distinguish our two heroes by observing that while Molloy is a bum, has few possessions, little will, less appetite, and almost no interest in the world, Moran, at least through the first half of his narrative, is a bourgeois, has many possessions, is willful to the point of tyranny, enjoys appetites both carnal and culinary, and is unmistakably of this world. At the same time, the points of correspondence between the two are remarkable. Both spend time in a garden, set out on a quest, travel by bicycle, meet a shepherd, traverse a wood, have violent encounters with a stranger, lose their bicycles, suffer debility, and fail to reach their objectives.

Other points of convergence/divergence could be indicated. What is important, however, is that a principle of opposition and identity—a principle of *différance*—generally informs these two characters. In the previous two chapters we saw how Beckett associates this principle with the motif of the dark glass from 1 Corinthians 13.12. This association is by no means accidental, for it is in a mirror that we observe ourselves to be identical yet different, since the mirror reproduces what it reflects yet reverses what it reproduces.

The specular image of the self is, in other words, a version of the identified contrary: it is the self and the self turned round; the self made identical and the self made different. Molloy and Moran provide the terms of this particular mirror-play: each is the reflection of the other.[11] Thus both are on a quest, but Molloy is returning home, while Moran is setting forth; both spend time in a garden, but Molloy's retreat occurs in the middle of his story, while it occupies the beginning and end of Moran's; both are concerned with familial relations, but Molloy seeks his mother, while Moran gets rid of his son; both have bicycles, but Molloy's appears in the first half and Moran's in the second half of their respective narratives. As I have indicated, *Molloy* relates such an identification of contraries, such a play of *différance*, to the narrator and the narrated. Yet, standing alongside these two terms, defining their significance and shaping their development, are two other terms that have played a crucial role in Beckett's fiction: the subject and the object.

We might take, as a useful point of entry into the novel's treatment of phenomenological issues, Molloy's fascination with his mother, a fascination that seems incongruous given the contempt and disgust he feels for that "poor old uniparous whore" (23). And yet Molloy calls his efforts to be reunited with his mother "this frenzy of wanting to get to her" (44–45) and regards his maternal obsession as one of the defining characteristics of his life ("All my life, I think I had been going to my mother, with the purpose of establishing our relations on a less precarious footing," 118)—even as the key that will unlock the meaning of who he is and what he wants ("If ever I'm reduced to looking for a meaning to my life, you never can tell, it's in that old mess that I'll stick my nose to begin with," 23). Critics have generally ignored Molloy's fixation with his mother, but we may begin to make sense out of it if we situate it within the context of subject/object dialectics, understanding his obsession as a desire to return to the self-integrated harmony that marked "the only endurable, just endurable, period" (23) of Molloy's life, his time in the womb.[12] According to this reading, Molloy may despise his mother as the agent responsible for expelling him from an intrauterine Eden, but he nevertheless feels compelled to return to her as the source of his prelapsarian bliss.

We have already encountered the topos of the garden as epistemological paradise. In *Murphy* a bit of greenery known as the Cockpit becomes the staging ground for permuting biscuits and consciousness into some dialectical beyond, that point where mind accelerates into the hyperspace of Murphy's third zone, while in *Watt*
the gardens at Knott's house and the asylum provide glimpses of subject-object transcendence, epitomized by Arsene's movement off the
ladder and Sam's passage through the dark glass. The garden Molloy wanders into also promises sustenance for the phenomenological outcast, a kind of nurturing earth where the alienated subject can
slough off the dead skin of self-consciousness and reintegrate itself
into the object-world:

> And there was another noise, that of my life become the life of this
> garden as it rode the earth of deeps and wildernesses. Yes, there were
> times when I forgot not only who I was, but that I was, forgot to be.
> Then I was no longer that sealed jar to which I owed my being so well
> preserved, but a wall gave way and I filled with roots. (65)

Molloy's encounter with Lousse combines the figures of garden
and mother into the promised recovery of a paradisiacal childhood.
Thus, a Molloy recumbent on the grass, much like Murphy in the
Cockpit, is tempted by a maternal Circe who proposes, in effect, that
he abandon the quest for his real mother and adopt her instead:

> And from these propositions, which she enunciated slowly and dis-
> tinctly, repeating each clause several times, I finally elicited the fol-
> lowing, or gist. I could not prevent her having a weakness for me, nei-
> ther could she. I would live in her home, as though it were my own.
> I would have plenty to eat and drink, to smoke too if I smoked, for
> nothing, and my remaining days would glide away without a care. I
> would as it were take the place of the dog I had killed, as it for her
> had taken the place of a child. (63)

Of course, Lousse succeeds only in providing a vague approximation of the experience Molloy seeks, and although there are moments
when Molloy can speak of "my life become the life of this garden,"
he finds such intervals rare and concedes that "mostly I stayed in my
jar which knew neither seasons nor gardens" (65). It is as though in
Lousse's garden Arsene's phenomenological levitation—existence off
the ladder—can only be experienced as a kind of flight without
wings, a momentary suspension of the laws of gravity, which pro-

duces something like a hop or a jump: "For from time to time I caught myself making a little bound in the air, two or three feet off the ground at least, at least, I who never bounded. It looked like levitation" (72). As for Lousse herself, she unmistakably functions as a mother figure for Molloy, but she is a failed mother, one who is incapable of providing any genuine nourishment: "It is useless to drag out this chapter of my, how shall I say, my existence. . . . It is a dug at which I tug in vain, it yields nothing but wind and spatter" (75).

As we know, Molloy does not reach his mother in the course of the narrative, but the vantage from which he relates his story offers a kind of fallen version of what he has sought to achieve. For if he has not regained the privileged and necessarily inaccessible place of his mother's womb, he has come to occupy a structurally and acoustically related enclosure—his mother's room—thereby achieving a limited but significant identification with her: "I sleep in her bed. I piss and shit in her pot. I have taken her place. I must resemble her more and more" (8). The general development of Molloy's character is, then, toward a reintegration with his mother, toward a return to an idealized pre-Cartesian condition, which stands beyond or before subject-object dialectics.

Moran's character moves, at least at the outset, along a very different trajectory, one that carries him toward a set of interconnected and mutually defining subject-object relations. In large measure, he represents Beckett's attempt to create the nineteenth-century character of determinacy, the character who, like Mme Vauquer and her boarding house, both defines his environment and is defined by it. Moran is, in other words, what he has, the "creature of his house, of his garden, of his few poor possessions" (156). Here, the garden takes on a different significance, functioning as a retreat for bourgeois recreation rather than a site for phenomenological re-creation, a pleasure spot in which objects are possessed rather than a paradise in which the self is dispossessed:

> I watched absently the coming and going of *my* bees. I heard on the gravel the scampering steps of *my* son. . . . From *my* neighbors' chimneys the smoke rose straight and blue. None but tranquil sounds, the clicking of the mallet and ball, a rake on pebbles, a distant lawnmower, the bell of *my* beloved church. And birds of course, blackbird and thrush, their song sadly dying, vanquished by the heat, and leav-

ing dawn's high boughs for the bushes' gloom. Contentedly I inhaled
the scent of *my* lemon-verbena. (126–27, my emphasis)

Yet, almost despite himself, Moran finds his garden transformed into
the place of his own fall, the surroundings where his "last moments
of peace and happiness" (127) slip away when Gaber introduces into
its midst the fatal knowledge that is to become the "Molloy affair."
Once this happens, the world that Moran has inhabited, a world of
property, orthodoxy, and complacency, ceases to be sufficient. And
while he continues to call it his "little all" (175) and that "without
which I could not bear being a man" (181), he no longer believes in
it, at least not as he once did, having come to recognize in the very
sanctuary of his bourgeois comfort, his house and garden, a "kind
of nothingness in the midst of which [he] stumbled" (168). This
stumble, a sort of partial fall, is played out alongside Gaber's infec-
tion of Moran's Eden with the satanic knowledge of the Molloy affair: "And yet the poison was already acting on me, the poison I had
just been given. I stirred restlessly in my arm-chair, ran my hands
over my face, crossed and uncrossed my legs, and so on. The colour
and weight of the world were changing already, soon I would have
to admit I was anxious" (131–32).

The color and weight of the world continue to change, so that
when Moran returns to the garden at the novel's close only the birds
remain. The cultivation that functioned as the sign of man, that
made it possible for Moran to consider it *his* garden, has lapsed
away:

> I put my hand in the hive, moved it among the empty trays, felt along
> the bottom. It encountered, in a corner, a dry light ball. It crumbled
> under my fingers. They had clustered together for a little warmth, to
> try and sleep. I took out a handful. It was too dark to see, I put it in
> my pocket. It weighed nothing. . . . My hens were dead too. (239)

Between his departure from the garden and his return to it, that self
defined by status, income, and property disintegrates, crumbles away
like the exposed bees. Moran finds that he is "dispossessed of self"
(204), uprooted from a world that he has defined and that has defined him: "I opened my eyes. I was alone. My hands were full of
grass and earth I had torn up unwittingly, was still tearing up. I was
literally uprooting" (226).

This moment recalls that other moment in Lousse's garden when Molloy "was no longer that sealed jar . . . but a wall gave way and I filled with roots" (65). The language of these two episodes appears, at least initially, to place them in tension with each other: as Moran tears up roots, Molloy lays them down. Yet these episodes may be understood as merely different parts of the same process, consecutive points along a continuous line of development. Moran's effort to disentangle subject from object, to discover a self that is not defined by external conditions, effectively presents itself as an earlier stage of Molloy's more radical efforts to render subject and object continuous with one another. In both instances the movement is toward a dislocation of Cartesian dualism, whether that dislocation is achieved by sundering the terms of the dialectic or collapsing them into each other.

We might take a slightly different approach to Molloy and Moran by considering two pieces of art criticism Beckett wrote at roughly the time he was working on the trilogy, "Le Monde et le pantalon" and "Peintres de l'empêchement."[13] These essays, which have not received sufficient critical attention, treat Bram and Geer van Velde as representatives of two related but opposed developments in an art born out of epistemological crisis: "The painting of the van Veldes . . . emerges from a painting of criticism and refusal, refusal to accept as given the old subject-object relation" (*Disjecta*, 137).[14] Having argued in "Peintres de l'empêchement" that what is distinctive about the van Veldes is their effort to dislocate subject-object dialectics, Beckett goes on to explain their work precisely in terms of that dialectic:

> For what remains to be represented if the essence of the object is to escape representation?
> There remains the conditions of this avoidance. These conditions will take one of two forms, according to the subject.
> One will say: I cannot see the object in order to represent it, because it is what it is. The other: I cannot see the object in order to represent it, because I am what I am.
> There have always been these two kinds of artists, these two kinds of impediment, the object-impediment, the eye-impediment.
> Geer van Velde is an artist of the first kind (in my stumbling opinion), Bram van Velde of the second.
> Their painting is an analysis of a state of privation, an analysis

borrowing in the case of the first term from the outside, light and emptiness, and in the case of the second term from the inside, obscurity, plenum, phosphorescence. (*Disjecta*, 136)

Here, a binary opposition is preserved, indeed insisted upon, as Bram van Velde is treated as a painter of the inside and Geer van Velde as a painter of the outside. We find a further elaboration of this oppositional pairing in Beckett's earlier essay, "Le Monde et le pantalon":

A. van Velde paints extension.
G. van Velde paints succession.

Since before one can see extension, and *a fortiori* before one can represent it, it is necessary to immobilize it, the former turns away from natural extension, that which turns like a top under the whip of the sun. He idealizes it, makes of it an internal sense.

The latter, on the contrary, is turned entirely toward the outside, toward the hub-bub of things in light, toward time. For we only become aware of time in the things which it moves, which it prevents from being seen. It is in giving himself entirely to the outside, in showing the macrocosm shaken by the shudders of time, that he realizes himself. (*Disjecta*, 128)

What is the connection between the van Veldes and *Molloy*? Toward the beginning of the novel, two vestigial characters, denominated simply as A and C, leave an unnamed city, walking in opposed directions (10). This moment bears a striking resemblance to a passage in "Le Monde et le pantalon" involving the van Veldes: "As two men, who having left from the Porte de Chantillon might head out on a road they don't know very well, with frequent stops to fortify themselves, the one toward Rue Champs-de-l'Alouette, the other towards l'Ile des Cygnes" (*Disjecta*, 124). For reasons I shall discuss presently, A and C will converge, while the brothers van Velde diverge, but these passages are connected nonetheless by a departure from a single point and a movement in opposed directions. The metaphor that Beckett elaborates in the van Velde essay is clearly related to the divergence of subject from object, of inside from outside, of Bram van Velde from Geer van Velde. Indeed, in "Peintres de l'empêchement" what leads them apart is precisely the sense that the object, like Nietzsche's God before it, has finally been laid to rest: "The same mourning leads them far from one another, the mourning for the object" (*Disjecta*, 135). Having written elsewhere that the death of the object comes to the same thing as the death of the subject, Beckett here effectively argues that the van Veldes illustrate the coming asunder of this dialectic.[15]

The larger point to be made is not that there is a simple or direct correspondence between the van Veldes on the one hand and Molloy and Moran on the other, but that through these figures Beckett is imaginatively working out variations on the subject/object dichotomy. However, as I indicated above, *Molloy* is increasingly concerned not with the relation between subject and object but with the way this relation expresses itself in narrative terms.

∿·

Molloy and Moran dramatize the problem of the narrator/narrated not only in the sense that each tells his own story but also in the sense that the stories appear to be structurally related, as though one were a variation of the other. Insofar as we think of these two characters as representing an instance of narrative doubling, Moran seems to be the prior term, the "original" on which Molloy is modeled. Not surprisingly, then, critics have generally regarded Molloy as a sort of debased Moran—a Moran who has lost his social standing and fallen on hard times.[16] Yet, as Steven Connor and Thomas Trezise have pointed out, if Moran logically precedes Molloy, he narratively succeeds him. Thus, Moran's story comes *after* Molloy's, despite the fact that he appears to be the "originary" term, and this means that those "moments of *déjà vu* that we encounter in Moran's narrative . . . are both originals *and* repetitions."[17]

In other words, by treating Moran and Molloy as instances of the narrator/narrated, Beckett creates a dichotomy in which the terms of opposition collapse into each other, in which differences resolve into *différance*.[18] Beckett establishes this dichotomy at the beginning of Moran's narrative when the latter retires to his room, indeed to his bed—Proust's preferred writing space—and there contemplates, formulates, and mentally pursues the shadowy figure called Molloy. What Beckett proceeds to give us is a picture of the narrator as novelist (Moran is an anagram for *roman*), one we surprise in the act of creating a character. Yet *différance* has already infected Beckett's narrator before he begins his narration. Hence, Molloy is described as standing outside Moran, inhabiting some real space, an objective and external terrain where Moran pursues him, "in full cry, over hill and dale" (157), as though he were bringing his "quarry" or "prey" (151) to ground. At the same time, Molloy is described as being inside Moran, a "chimera" (156) or "fabulous being" (152), who exists "ready made in [his] head" (152–53). These two accounts of Molloy—he is outside and inside, a thing found and a thing made—remain in tension in Beckett's metaphor of the novelist as detective, a kind of literary bounty hunter who locates missing persons of the imagination:

> I lost interest in my patients, once I had finished with them. I may even truthfully say I never saw one of them again, subsequently, not a single one. No conclusions need be drawn from this. Oh the stories I could tell you, if I were easy. What a rabble in my head, what a gallery of moribunds. Murphy, Watt, Yerk, Mercier and all the others. I would never have believed that willingly. . . . Stories, stories. (188)

While continuing to deconstruct the dichotomy between inside and outside (real world patients become the "rabble in my head") this passage also suggests (with its evocation of Murphy, Watt, and Mercier) that Moran functions in *Molloy* as Sam did in *Watt*— namely, as an authorial figure. As we have observed, in *Watt* that authorial figure sought his mirror image in another, a mirror image that was refracted through the dark glass of 1 Corinthians. This turns out to be the case in *Molloy* as well. Thus, when Moran first retires to his bedroom to contemplate the Molloy affair, he remarks that "all is dark but with that simple darkness that follows like a balm upon the great dismemberings. From their places masses move" (151). And later, when Moran gets his first fix on Molloy, he describes him as "massive and hulking, to the point of misshapenness. And, without being black, of a dark colour" (155). The dark, hulking mass that Moran encounters as he attempts to summon forth some image of Molloy calls to mind Watt's own efforts to meet Knott face to face, efforts that resulted, as Watt told Sam, in "dark bulk."[19] These are, of course, only the barest adumbrations of the dark glass motif, the first in a series of shadows that will move across Moran's narrative. Before we can make sense of this motif, we must first understand it in relation to Moran and Molloy as the narrator/narrated.

Specifying this relation is a difficult matter, because the information we possess is necessarily contradictory. For example, Moran thinks that he is connected with Molloy by means of a sympathetic identity that enables him to share in the latter's emotions and perceptions: "He had only to rise up within me for me to be filled with panting" (154); "my own natural end . . . would it not at the same time be his?" (155). But according to the logic of *différance*, every identity ultimately becomes a difference, which means that Moran may simultaneously experience Molloy as a part of himself, an inner resource that constitutes his identity, and as a disruptive other, an alien agent who threatens to destroy that identity. So it is that Moran describes Molloy as "just the *opposite* of myself" (155, my emphasis) and insists that "if I had to tell the story of *my* life I should not so much as allude to these apparitions, and *least of all* to that of the unfortunate Molloy" (156, my emphasis).

Initially, we are assured that while the terms in the Moran/Molloy relation may be fallible, even false, the relation itself is valid:

> And though this examination prove unprofitable and of no utility for the execution of my orders, I should nevertheless have established a kind of connexion, and one not necessarily false. For the falsity of the terms does not necessarily imply that of the relation, so far as I know. (152)

However, as a representative of both Moran's self and his other, Molloy begins to function as the principle of *différance* itself, introducing a conceptual instability within and between terms that threatens to undermine the entire economy of binary relations. Ultimately, this leads Moran to contemplate the possibility not of one Molloy and one Moran, not even of two Molloys, one imaginary and one real, but of a whole series of Molloys, each related to the others according to the self-generating logic of supplementarity:

> The fact was there were three, no, four Molloys. He that inhabited me, my caricature of same, Gaber's and the man of flesh and blood somewhere awaiting me. To these I would add Youdi's were it not for Gaber's corpse fidelity to the letter of his messages. Bad reasoning. . . . I will therefore add a fifth Molloy, that of Youdi. But would not this fifth Molloy necessarily coincide with the fourth, the real one as the saying is, him dogged by his shadow? I would have given a lot to know. There were others too, of course. But let us leave it at that, if you don't mind, the party is big enough. (157)

The relation between Moran and Molloy becomes, then, an exercise in deconstruction, one in which a number of oppositions—origin and copy, subject and object, narrator and narrated—begin to erode along their conceptual boundaries. And as the terms within the oppositions blur into one another, as they lose their shape and definition, the process of mimesis itself begins to come to pieces. For if there are only copies and no origins, only the narrated and no narrator, then how can representation take place? Indeed, how can Beckett represent this failure of representation?

In "Peintres de l'empêchement," Beckett addresses this problem when he speaks of the artist as painting an image of his prison cell on the stone wall of his prison cell ("cellule peinte sur la pierre de la cellule," *Disjecta*, 136–37). It is through this kind of narrative embedding, what Beckett calls the "art of incarceration" (*Disjecta*, 137), that he deals with the representational difficulties of supplementarity. In *Molloy* the problem of the narrator/narrated is embedded by means of two peripheral figures, who, like Larry Nixon in *Watt*, stand at the margins of Beckett's text. Indeed, we know these figures, who are never named, only as A and C.[20]

᷍

We first encounter A and C in what Molloy describes as the novel's "beginning": "Here's my beginning. It must mean something, or they wouldn't keep it. Here it is" (8). But what "follows" is obviously not the "beginning," which has been unfolding for almost two pages. We have already observed how the question of ontological priority affects the relation of Moran and Molloy, of narrator and narrated. If there is an origin and a copy, then there must be a first term and a second term, a source and an imitation. Yet here the first term, Molloy's so-called beginning, succeeds a page-and-a-half of description and therefore occupies the place of the second term. What is more, A and C appear to be versions of Moran and Molloy—but if they come *after* Molloy, they come *before* Moran, who himself logically precedes Molloy.[21]

However we read the chronology of events, Molloy appears at the outset to be situated somewhere in the hills outside a walled city. From this vantage point, he commands an unobstructed view of a country road, on which he observes the wayfarers, A and C:

> It was two men, unmistakably, one small and one tall. They had left the town, first one, then the other, and then the first, weary or remembering a duty, had retraced his steps. The air was sharp for they wore greatcoats. They looked alike, but no more than others do. (9–10)

Of the two men, Molloy feels a special affinity for C. Like Molloy, C appears to be an "old" and "solitary" tramp (11), moving "with uncertain step" and stopping "to look about him, like someone trying to fix landmarks in his mind" (10). What is more, like Molloy, C is fearful and infirm, relying on a "stout stick" to "thrust himself onward, or as a defence" (11), just as Molloy walks with crutches, which he also uses to ward off the charcoal-burner. Finally, Molloy underscores his sense of identification with C by equating the latter's emotions with his own: "I watched him recede, overtaken (myself) by his anxiety, at least by an anxiety which was not necessarily his, but of which as it were he partook. Who knows if it wasn't my own anxiety overtaking him" (12).

A, in contrast, seems more like Moran. If C appears to be a homeless wanderer, A appears to be a gentleman out for an after-dinner stroll (14). Or, at least, this is what Molloy surmises from the available evidence—namely that A is bareheaded, smokes a cigar, and moves with a "loitering indolence" (13), while his apparently constipated pomeranian trails behind (13–14). Moran is also a proper bourgeois and, like A, he too is followed by a constipated and doglike son. As for the cigar, Moran tells us: "The first day I found the butt of Father Ambrose's cigar . . . I looked at it in astonishment, lit it, took a few puffs, threw it away. This was the outstanding event of the first day" (185).

At one level, it seems that A and C are to Molloy what Molloy is to Moran: a kind of internal resource, the invention of his imagination. Thus, A and C appear out of a mental twilight, in a moment when the distinction between inside and outside, between self and other, has grown especially tenuous: "People pass too, hard to distinguish from yourself. . . . So I saw A and C" (9). Similarly, A and C disappear not as Molloy watches them move out of sight, but as he wills them out of mind: "To watch them out of sight, no, I can't do it. It was in this sense he disappeared. Looking away I thought of him, saying, He is dwindling, dwindling" (15). On another level, however, A and C appear to exist quite independently of Molloy, a "fact" that seems to be demonstrated by their "meetings" with Moran.

The first of these meetings involves C and occurs after Moran has dispatched his son to a nearby town with orders to purchase a bicycle. In his solitude, Moran turns self-reflective:

I tried again to remember what I was to do with Molloy, when I found him. I dragged myself down to the stream. I lay down and looked at my reflection, then I washed my face and hands. I waited for my image to come back, I watched it as it trembled towards an ever increasing likeness. Now and then a drop, falling from my face, shattered it again. (199)

Moran's confrontation here with a mirror image of himself calls to mind the motif of the dark glass. But notice that the clarity of the image has been significantly compromised, first because it is reflected in a stream,[22] which means that its contours are at best tentative, and second because the act of observation further dissipates the image, as the drops falling from Moran's face break it up even more. An unstable ground of reflection is here rendered all the more unstable by the act of observation itself.

What is important in this scene is that a moment of self-reflection, particularly one that is largely undermined, is used to prepare the scene in which Moran encounters C:

But towards evening . . . I saw a man a few paces off, standing motionless. He had his back to me. He wore a coat much too heavy for the time of the year and was leaning on a stick so massive, and so much thicker at the bottom than at the top, that it seemed more like a club. He turned and we looked at each other for some time in silence. (199–200)

Having mentally reflected on Molloy and visually reflected on himself, Moran meets—in the twilight of early evening, as through a glass darkly—Molloy's afterimage, C. The intruder is not named, but like C he is on the road, carries a walking stick that doubles as a club, and, as we shall see, is apparently pursued by a figure who seems to be A. Nothing special comes of this encounter, but toward evening of the following day, Moran meets a second intruder, this time a figure bearing a notable resemblance to Moran himself and therefore recalling that other vestigial self, A. Again, the scene is thoroughly prepared with a moment of self-reflection before the river:

But I also tried to remember what I was to do with Molloy, once I had found him. And on myself too I pored, on me so changed from what I was. And I seemed to see myself ageing as swiftly as a day-fly. But the idea of ageing was not exactly the one which offered itself to

me. And what I saw was more like a crumbling, a frenzied collapsing
of all that had always protected me from all I was always condemned
to be. Or it was like a kind of clawing towards a light and countenance I could not name, that I had once known and long denied. But
what words can describe this sensation at first all darkness and bulk,
with a noise like the grinding of stones, then suddenly as soft as water flowing. And then I saw a little globe swaying up slowly from the
depths, through the quiet water, smooth at first, and scarcely paler
than its escorting ripples, then little by little a face, with holes for the
eyes and mouth and other wounds. . . . But I confess I attended but
absently to these poor figures, in which I suppose my sense of disaster sought to contain itself. And that I did not labour at them more
diligently was a further index of the great changes I had suffered and
of my growing resignation to being dispossessed of self. (203–4)

The components are the same as in the first scene by the river: reflecting upon Molloy, Moran finds himself before a mirroring surface. But the language of the dark glass is now more in evidence, as
the countenance that gradually comes into focus appears as "darkness and bulk," echoing the "dark bulk" that marked Watt's encounter with Knott (*Watt*, 165). What Moran perceives is not his
own reflection—at least not merely his own reflection—but something like the visual equivalent of the not-I, as though the movements
of a self-negating cogito had been rendered palpable. The mental
processes whose traces we are left to decipher involve the apprehension not of the subject but of something like its death's head, here
described as a "dispossession of self." It is under such circumstances
that Moran finally encounters his alter ego, A:

It was evening. I had lit my fire and was watching it take when I heard
myself hailed. The voice, already so near that I started violently, was
that of a man. . . . There I was face to face with a dim man, dim of
face and dim of body, because of the dark. (205–6)

The motif of the dark glass, which Beckett has been hinting at all
along, is at last made explicit. What follows from Moran's halluci-
natory self-reflection is a "face-to-face" confrontation, one that is
darkly perceived ("a dim man"), with a character who is a kind of
double of Moran ("But all this was nothing compared to the face
which I regret to say vaguely resembled my own," 206).

It is especially noteworthy that the face-to-face meeting between
Moran and Molloy is handled through A and C, handled through

two supplemental and embedded versions of Moran and Molloy. What is more, since the confrontation between Moran and Molloy represents an attempt to work through the relation of narrator and narrated, self and simulacrum, it is significant that Moran's most fully developed encounter is with A, that homuncular version of himself. Matters are further complicated, however, when we remember that just as Molloy is in a sense Moran's creation, so A and C are in a sense Molloy's creations. Moran thus says of Molloy "perhaps I had invented him" (152), while Molloy says of A and C "perhaps I'm inventing a little, perhaps embellishing" (9). Indeed, we might regard the rocky perch that Molloy occupies at the outset, his "observation post" (16), as a literalization of narrative point of view, in which event we will not be surprised to hear Molloy remark, as he contemplates reducing his authorial distance from A, "What I need now is stories" (15).[23]

The parallels I have been pursuing may be pushed even further, since Molloy also comes upon a version of his vestigial self (in this case C) in the forest encounter with the charcoal-burner. Here the text is admittedly more ambiguous, but there are compelling reasons for identifying this figure with Molloy, just as A was identified with Moran. For instance, when Molloy imagines himself "seventy years younger," he suggests that the charcoal-burner "would have been younger by as much" (112).[24] And when Molloy asks the charcoal-burner for directions, the latter descends into incoherence (113), just as Molloy did when confronted by the police sergeant (27–28). At the same time, there is a structural parallel between Molloy's meeting with the charcoal-burner and Moran's meeting with A. In both cases, the stranger lays his hand on Moran or Molloy, and in both cases Moran or Molloy react by beating the stranger senseless. Of course, such connections do not directly relate the charcoal-burner to C—not until, that is, Molloy himself begins to wonder if the charcoal-burner might not be someone else, a figure whom he associates with a vaguely familiar memory: "I say charcoal-burner, but I really don't know. I see smoke somewhere" (113). And suddenly, as Molloy reminds us that the charcoal-burner is made up of smoke and sticks, we are recalled through a welter of narrative event to that moment at the novel's beginning when Molloy first constructed his proto-characters, A and C, out of a few constituent parts: "Smoke, sticks, flesh, hair, at evening, afar, flung about the craving for a fellow" (19).

The larger pattern that emerges involves something like a series of mirrored meetings within mirrored meetings, a movement from Moran through Molloy to A and C and back again by way of Molloy and Moran. Such an unfolding describes not merely a narrative whose head is chasing its tail but a narrative in which head and tail have grown increasingly indistinguishable. So it is that the archetypal event out of which the novel spins its impossible thread consists in that dimly perceived meeting between A and C, which occurs in the novel's opening pages:

> But the moment came when together they went down into the same trough and in this trough finally met. To say they knew each other, no, nothing warrants it. But perhaps at the sound of their steps, or warned by some obscure instinct, they raised their heads and observed each other, for a good fifteen paces, before they stopped, breast to breast. Yes, they did not pass each other by, but halted, face to face, as in the country, of an evening, on a deserted road, two wayfaring strangers will, without there being anything extraordinary about it. (10)

Two wayfarers meet "face to face," in the half-light of evening, in the dark glass of Molloy's narrating consciousness, but, we are told, nothing extraordinary has happened. A and C have met, there has been an epistemological transaction of sorts, rendered here as an image of the I contemplating itself as not-I. But rather than move us closer to an originary moment, this quasi-event has merely added another epicycle to the dizzying circle of the subject's movement around its absent center.

Underlying all of this is the idea of narration itself, for Molloy's narrative perspective situates itself atop a slope of "some considerable eminence" (17) among "treacherous hills" (10), a prospect difficult to attain under normal circumstances but impossible to reach on crutches: "And I, what was I doing there, and why come? These are things that we shall try and discover. But these are things we must not take seriously" (17). What makes Molloy's narrative vantage point especially difficult is that it attempts to survey the self from a position where sight is quite literally impossible. Hence, the "treacherous hills" are "cloven with hidden valleys that the eye divines from . . . signs for which there are no words, nor even thoughts" (11); at the same time, these hidden valleys enclose "all that inner space one never sees, the brain and heart and other caverns where thought and feeling dance their sabbath" (11). The novel finally brings us, then, to the recognition that Moran and Molloy, A and C, mother and son, hat, bicycle, stick, and smoke are only so many narrative placeholders designed to make utterance possible in a domain bereft of language and thought. As we are told toward the end of Molloy's narrative, only one event has really occurred in the entire novel: "In reality I said nothing at all, but I heard a murmur, something gone wrong with the silence" (119). It is to this still-point that the novel finally gathers itself.

～•

The simple attempt of the I to utter itself has made for a narrative doubling that has itself doubled into a narrative quadrupling, a proliferation of selves and stories, a mirroring of mirroring. But things do not end here. Moran concludes his narrative with the frank admission that everything he has written is quite simply a lie: "Then I went back into the house and wrote, It is midnight. The rain is beating on the windows. It was not midnight. It was not raining" (241). Invention of this kind becomes a logical necessity in a work in which nothing has happened and nothing has been said, a work in which fiction has articulated itself as a half-mute eruption, "something gone wrong with the silence." Yet, more than simply exposing its own artifice, Moran's conclusion opens up what it seems to close down, for it holds out the possibility of rewriting Moran's story as a mirrored reversal of itself, one in which each assertion would become its own negation, each negation its own assertion. Hence, in a reconstructed version of Moran's narrative, it would *not* be midnight, it would *not* be raining.

Where then does the novel end? Supplementarity and *différance* led to a doubling of self; a doubling of self led to a doubling of narrative; a doubling of narrative led to an embedding of narrative; and an embedding of narrative led to an ending that turned out to be a beginning. Multiplicity of this kind generally appealed to an author who delighted in permutations and indeterminacy, but it also raised the difficult and finally unavoidable problem of how to make an end. As Beckett headed into the second term of the trilogy, this problem was increasingly on his mind.

CHAPTER FIVE

'Malone Dies'

The Death of the Author and the End of the Book

If the subject is no longer present to itself (*Watt*), if *différance* has interrupted self-narration and supplementarity has supplanted origins (*Molloy*), then where do we locate the source or center of textual meaning? By what logic do we reconstruct a genetic first principle, which stands behind or before the written artifact and serves to guarantee its authenticity, coherence, and development? In short, how do we begin to identify and define the increasingly ephemeral figure that we once referred to, with great self-assurance and even a certain cultural fanfare, as the author? These are the questions that dominated literary and philosophical discussion in Paris during the late 1960s. Three texts were of special importance to this discussion: Derrida's "The End of the Book and the Beginning of Writing," which formed the opening chapter in *Of Grammatology* (1967); Barthes's brief but influential essay, "The Death of the Author" (1968); and Foucault's equally important "What Is an Author?" (1969).

We shall consider these texts presently, but before turning to them it will be useful to address the larger issue they raise: how do we read a book about the "end of the book"? How do we discuss an author after the "death of the author"? Certainly, if Derrida, Barthes, and Foucault take their own ideas seriously, then they will want to produce texts that are themselves exercises in *différance* and supplementarity, texts that affirm their own extravagance, their own exorbitance, precisely by refusing to confine themselves to a single authorial origin, texts that deliberately and derivatively cannibalize other writings, no doubt in the full expectation of being cannibalized themselves, texts that ultimately become what Barthes calls an "*irreducible* (and not merely an acceptable) plural," "the text-between of another text".[1] Insofar as such writing functions as a "dissemination," it will intrude itself in the margins within and between texts, taking the form of quotation, citation, allusion. So it is that Barthes opens "The Death of an Author" by quoting a passage from Balzac, a passage of which he asks, "Who is speaking . . . ?" ["Qui parle . . . ?"].[2] At one level, this question and the analysis that accompanies it are meant to impress upon us how ambiguous narrative voice can be, even in the work of a realist writer like Balzac. But at another level, Barthes is playfully introducing an element of ambiguity into his own text, subverting his own authorial origins even as he questions Balzac's. For the reader of contemporary French literature—the reader most likely to be perusing Barthes—hears in the words "Who is speaking" an echo of Samuel Beckett, the sort of self-doubting interrogation we associate with a figure like the Unnamable. What is Barthes doing here? Is this his attempt to unwrite and rewrite the nineteenth-century novel, to insinuate a Beckettian voice into a Balzacian text?

Foucault would seem to think so, since he begins "What Is an Author?" by answering Barthes's question with a quotation, one that he has significantly drawn from Beckett: "What matter who's speaking, someone said what matter who's speaking."[3] Again, where and how do we locate the authorial center of this text? Is Foucault projecting himself into Barthes's essay, seizing narrative control of it, asserting that it is Beckett, not Barthes, who asks the question, "Who is speaking"? If so, does this mean that we should read the "someone" who speaks not as Beckett's unidentified narrator, not even as Beckett himself, but as Michel Foucault, who now winkingly asks of Roland Barthes, "What *matter* who's speaking"? Finally, how are we to interpret Beckett's own statement, one that teases us with the possibility of an authorial vanishing point, constructing itself around a self-consuming utterance, which at once hints at its source (someone) and tells us not to worry about it (what matter)?

Malone Dies is a novel that, in effect, unfolds between Barthes's question and Foucault's quotation, a novel that begins with issues of identity (who is speaking) and ends with an assertion of indifference (what matter who's speaking). Along the way, Beckett describes the death of the author, enacts the end of the book, and anticipates the beginning of writing.[4] In this chapter, I will show not only that Beckett was already experimenting with these textual formulations in the late 1940s but also that he elaborated them in terms remarkably similar to those used by the French poststructuralists twenty years later. Although the relevant texts by Derrida, Barthes, and Foucault are generally well known, it will be helpful here to highlight their principal claims and indicate how they relate to one another.

The opening chapter in *Of Grammatology* is not only the earliest of these three texts but also the most comprehensive, the place where ideas relating to the end of the book and the death of the author find their fullest exploration. One of Derrida's most familiar claims in *Of Grammatology* is that speech (*parole*) and writing (*écriture*) have acquired over time a set of mythic associations.[5] Hence, speech has come to be understood as a form of pure meaning, a semantic incarnation that requires no intercessor or substitute, while writing has been treated as a form of debased meaning, an imitation of the thing itself, existing as a second- or even third-order representation. However, once we give up on the idea that "true" language is grounded in the metaphysics of presence (whether this refers to the world or the cogito), once we start to think of language as a human creation that is conventional rather than natural, then the opposition between an "originary" speech and a "secondary" writing disappears. Or, to put the matter differently, once we abandon philosophical foundationalism, we may begin to understand all language as a form of "writing" insofar as all language is man-made, a historical construct that is contingent through and through.

For Derrida the "beginning of writing," or what he calls "grammatology," coincides with the "end of the book." The "book" is a totality, a self-contained and self-identical whole, whose autonomy and coherence are guaranteed by the fact that it refers to another self-contained and self-identical whole, which we variously describe as Nature or the Self or the World. The "book" depends, then, on the adequacy of words to things, on the correspondence of the signifier to the signified:

> The idea of the book is the idea of a totality, finite or infinite, of the signifier; this totality of the signifier cannot be a totality, unless a totality constituted by the signified preexists it, supervises its inscriptions and its signs, and is independent of it in its ideality. The

idea of the book, which always refers to a natural totality, is profoundly alien to the sense of writing.[6]

The same year Derrida published *Of Grammatology*, he elaborated on the idea of the "book" in an interview with Henri Ronse. Derrida particularly emphasized the notion that the "book" is classically ordered, a shaped and coherent whole, and that his own writing represents an attempt to disrupt or unsettle that classical ordering:

> In what you call my books, what is first of all put in question is the unity of the book and the unity "book" considered as a perfect totality, with all the implications of such a concept. . . . Under these titles [Derrida's "books"] it is solely a question of a unique and differentiated textual "operation," if you will, whose unfinished movement assigns itself no absolute beginning, and which, although it is entirely consumed by the reading of other texts, in a certain fashion refers only to its own writing. . . . Therefore it would be impossible to provide a linear, deductive representation of these works that would correspond to some "logical order."[7]

Here Derrida suggests a broad opposition between the "book" and the "text," not unlike the one Barthes was later to draw between the "work" and the "text."[8] As Derrida develops this opposition, the book is unified and linear, moving from a clearly defined beginning to a clearly defined end, fully contained within its own textual boundaries and referring to a reality that stands beyond itself. The text, in contrast, is multiple and nonlinear, without beginning or end, constantly crossing textual boundaries and incessantly preoccupied with its own generation. Whereas the book represents the "encyclopedic protection of theology and of logocentrism," the text represents, in all its "aphoristic energy," the "disruption of writing."[9]

Developing alongside and in parallel relation to the end of the book is the death of the author. If what we once called the "book" has ceased to function as a "natural totality," that is because it is no longer grounded either in the presence of nature—what Derrida refers to as the "totality of the signified"—or in the self-presence of the cogito, in this case the controlling consciousness of the author. What follows from this second point is the death of the author. As Barthes puts it in his essay of that title, "Writing is the destruction of every voice, of every point of origin. Writing is that neutral, com-

posite, oblique space where our subject slips away."[10] This means
that the mere act of narration itself alienates the utterance from the
author, thrusts it into a realm of the purely symbolic where it exists
on a new ontological plain: "As soon as a fact is *narrated* no longer
with a view to acting directly on reality but intransitively, that is to
say, finally outside of any function other than that of the very practice of the symbol itself, this disconnection occurs, the voice loses its
origin, the author enters into his own death, writing begins."[11] Barthes concludes, with a nod toward Derrida, by situating the death
of the author in terms of the speech/writing dichotomy; hence, *écriture* means the end of expression, a moving hand that has liberated
itself from a speaking voice:

> Having buried the Author, the modern scriptor can thus no longer be-
> lieve, as according to the pathetic view of his predecessors, that this
> hand is too slow for his thought or passion and that consequently,
> making a law of necessity, he must emphasize this delay and indefi-
> nitely "polish" his form. For him, on the contrary, the hand, cut off
> from any voice, borne by a pure gesture of inscription (and not of ex-
> pression), traces a field without origin—or which, at least, has no
> other origin than language itself.[12]

Foucault is of importance to our discussion because he gives special emphasis to two ideas—one articulated by Derrida, the other
by Barthes. The first of these ideas involves the notion of writing as
play:

> Today's writing has freed itself from the dimension of expression. Re-
> ferring only to itself, but without being restricted to the confines of
> its interiority, writing is identified with its own unfolded exteriority.
> This means that it is an interplay of signs arranged less according to
> its signified content than according to the very nature of the signifier.
> Writing unfolds like a game (*jeu*) that invariably goes beyond its own
> rules and transgresses its limits.[13]

This passage picks up on the Saussurian claim—developed both in
"Structure, Sign, and Play" and *Of Grammatology*—that linguistic
meaning is generated not through reference to the world but by the
"play" or movement of signifiers within a given system.[14] Of course,
if words are no longer fixed by a nonverbal reality, then they themselves will be subject to "play" in the sense of semantic slippage.
Hence, for the poststructuralist, language is shot through with a

polysemy that compels it, as Foucault says, to "go beyond its own rules and to transgress its limits."

Foucault's second idea develops Barthes's notion that the writer does not express himself through his writing but, on the contrary, effaces himself. The author's death, then, is a matter not simply of the narrated material cutting itself off from the author but also of the author, in effect, consuming or destroying himself in the very act of narration:

> Writing has become linked to sacrifice, even to the sacrifice of life: it is now a voluntary effacement which does not need to be represented in books, since it is brought about in the writer's very existence. . . . That is not all, however: this relationship between writing and death is also manifested in the effacement of the writing subject's individual characteristics. Using all the contrivances that he sets up between himself and what he writes, the writing subject cancels out the signs of his particular individuality.[15]

Foucault memorably distills these two ideas into a single sentence: "As a result, the mark of the writer is reduced to nothing more than the singularity of his absence; he must assume the role of the dead man [*du mort*] in the game [*le jeu*] of writing."[16]

The dead man in the game of writing. Foucault's formulation perfectly describes *Malone Dies*, a novel that begins by announcing the prospective demise of its author ("I shall soon be quite dead at last in spite of all," 1), while promising to play games in the meantime ("Now it is a game, I am going to play," 2).[17] Beckett's moribunds are, however, notoriously tenacious of life, and this presents a problem—for the game of writing cannot be played until the author is dead, but the author can only be dispatched by playing the game. At the same time, the book cannot be brought to an end until writing begins, but writing cannot begin until the book ends. Hence, *Malone Dies* generates itself out of a set of impossible conditions, developing according to a logic of displacement and replacement, of oppositions erected, deconstructed, resurrected. The penultimate term in Beckett's pentalogy, *Malone Dies* stands at the threshold of its own dissolution, forever advancing toward and retreating from an authorless abyss of *écriture*. Yet here the boundary between "book" and "text," between author and writing, is not crossed so much as sighted, erased, recovered, approached, and then erased again. Every time the novel takes two steps forward, it takes one step back, and while it doggedly pursues its particular "ends," it never decisively achieves them, since one of the things it wants to end is precisely the idea of "ends."

Four large points will emerge from the analysis that follows. First, while *Malone Dies* insists that it is different from Beckett's earlier novels, preferring the game of writing to the work of self-examination, it continuously slides from the former into the latter, even as it deconstructs the opposition whereby these terms are defined. Second, the novel thrusts into the foreground as never before the act of narration, at once reaffirming the dichotomy between narrator and narrated and reminding us that these terms are entirely artificial, the creations of fiction. Third, as Beckett further shifts the trilogy away from phenomenology and toward grammatology, he starts to dismantle various subject-object paradigms, most notably the lapsarian epistemology that figured so prominently in the earlier works. Finally, as the novel lurches toward *écriture*, we are simultaneously confronted with the death of the author and the end of the book. Yet *Malone Dies*, whose very title promises to make an end, is in a sense all middle, neither the beginning of the trilogy nor its finale— a text that, as we shall see, reconstitutes in itself all of Beckett's previous works, thereby opening itself up to the pantextuality that lies beyond both the death of the author and the end of the book.

If writing is a game, one in which signs are constantly being run through various combinations and transformations, undergoing the kind of permutations that defined Murphy's biscuits and Molloy's sucking stones, then *Malone Dies* plays the game as no other Beckett work before it. Nevertheless, the metaphysics of presence will continue to cling to the novel as long as the author remains alive, and this means that *Malone Dies* is forever vacillating between the work of introspection and the game of narration, between an *auctor sapiens*, who struggles to know himself, and an *auctor ludens*, who wants only to play. As Malone remarks at the outset, apparently signaling a shift from introspection to diversion, "This time I know where I am going, it is no longer the ancient night, the recent night. Now it is a game" (2). The opposition that Beckett draws here is, however, complicated, disrupted, and finally annulled, in three passages that are worth examining at some length. The first begins with the words quoted above:

> Now it is a game, I am going to play. I never knew how to play, till now. I longed to, but I knew it was impossible. And yet I often tried. I turned on all the lights, I took a good look all round, I began to play with what I saw. People and things ask nothing better than to play, certain animals too. All went well at first, they all came to me, pleased that someone should want to play with them. If I said, Now I need a hunchback, immediately one came running, proud as punch of his fine hunch that was going to perform. It did not occur to him that I might have to ask him to undress. But it was not long before I found myself alone, in the dark. That is why I gave up trying to play and took to myself for ever shapelessness and speechlessness, incurious wondering, darkness, long stumbling with outstretched arms, hiding. Such is the earnestness from which, for nearly a century now, I have never been able to depart. From now on it will be different. (2)

In its larger terms, this passage relates how Malone tried and failed to play in the past, how he threw himself into a form of diversion ("I often tried. I turned on all the lights, I took a good look all round, I began to play with what I saw") only to see it collapse back into introspection ("It was not long before I found myself alone, in the dark"). What caused the game to come to grief? What brought Malone back to himself?

We may begin to answer these questions by observing that the game Malone plays is narrative, one that involves summoning up characters and getting them to "perform." In this particular case, the character who "came running" is a hunchback, the very type, as we know from our acquaintance with Mr. Hackett, of the authorial figure, the stand-in for Beckett the "hack."[18] And this means that by conjuring the hunchback, Malone is not so much turning away from the authorial self as evoking it in one of its earlier manifestations. Hence, the suggestion that the hunchback undress, that he expose his true identity, necessarily leads to his departure, since the game remains a game only so long as the narrator is engaged in diversion rather than introspection, only so long as he turns away from himself and toward play. Once it becomes evident that the toy with which he plays is an image of the self, the game is up. In another sense, however, the hunchback has not taken flight but agreed to bare himself, for what results from this characterological disrobing is "myself alone" or, more simply, "M-alone." Terms that seemed to exist in binary opposition—introspection and diversion, self and story, author and game—have effectively collapsed into one another, but even as they come together they come apart. For if the self that Malone confronts appears to stand at the limits of apprehension ("myself for ever shapelessness and speechlessness, incurious wondering, darkness, long stumbling with outstretched arms, hiding"), then this M-alone is quite simply inenarrable, a self that cannot be rendered in the form of a story, indeed a self that is at odds with the very idea of story.

What *Malone Dies* claims as its innovation, its insistence that "from now on it will be different . . . I shall play a great part of the time, from now on, the greater part" (2–3), depends precisely on keeping the work of introspection separate from the game of narration—depends, that is, on treating self and story as terms of opposition. When, however, Malone contemplates the possibility that his plan for narrative reform might fail ("But perhaps I shall not succeed any better than hitherto. Perhaps as hitherto, I shall find myself abandoned, in the dark, without anything to play with," 3), he proposes making himself the object of his game ("Then I shall play with myself," 3). And yet if playing and the self, if telling stories and interrogating consciousness, are at odds with each other, then what does it mean to play with the self? It means that the characters who came running were, like the hunchback, simulacra of the author's self. But it also means that as simulacra, as supplements, they were not that self but displacements of it.

If the first passage we have considered seems to erode the straightforward opposition between self and story, another passage further blurs their categorical boundaries. Here is Malone breaking off his narration of the Sapo story:

> What tedium. And I call that playing. I wonder if I am not talking yet again about myself. Shall I be incapable, to the end, of lying on any other subject? I feel the old dark gathering, the solitude preparing, by which I know myself, and the call of that ignorance which might be noble and is mere poltroonery. Already I forget what I have said. That is not how to play. Soon I shall not know where Sapo comes from, nor what he hopes. Perhaps I had better abandon this story and go on to the second, or even the third, the one about the stone. No it would be the same thing. I must simply be on my guard, reflecting on

what I have said before I go on and stopping, each time disaster
threatens, to look at myself as I am. That is just what I wanted to
avoid. But there seems to be no other solution. (12)

This passage appears once again to mark out the two sides of a dichotomy between self and story: on the one hand, there is the narrative of Sapo ("I call that playing") and, on the other, there is the
turn toward the self ("I feel the old dark gathering, the solitude
preparing, by which I know myself"). Yet here the telling of stories—
in this case Sapo's—is not a game but a form of "tedium," which
Malone rejects precisely because it is *not* playing but what is "called"
playing. Indeed, Malone begins to suspect that, despite his best efforts, what looked like a playful diversion has again yielded to an
onerous introspection, that once more the toy has become the self
("I wonder if I am not talking yet again about myself").[19]

Malone considers forsaking the story of Sapo ("Perhaps I had better abandon this story and go on to the second," 12) but decides it
will make no difference: "I must simply be on my guard, reflecting
on what I have said before I go on and stopping, each time disaster
threatens, to look at myself as I am. That is just what I wanted to
avoid. But there seems to be no other solution" (12). This passage
appears to insist on maintaining the opposition between storytelling
and self-reflection (he will tell the story, and when disaster threatens
he will stop and reflect on himself), but he has told us, "That is just
what I wanted to avoid," and while he proclaims that there is "no
other solution," it becomes increasingly evident that this, too, is a
nonsolution, one that permits the self constantly to intrude upon the
story ("talking yet again about myself").

This series of aporetic collisions is brought to something like critical mass in a third passage:

> Live and invent. I have tried. I must have tried. Invent. It is not the
> word. Neither is live. No matter. I have tried. While within me the
> wild beast of earnestness padded up and down, roaring, ravening,
> rending. I have done that. And all alone, well hidden, played the
> clown, all alone, hour after hour, motionless, often standing, spell-
> bound, groaning. That's right, groan. I couldn't play. (18)

Live and invent. This describes the peculiarly divided situation that
Malone occupies, a kind of parafictional status according to which
he functions as a character who must himself come alive ("live") and

yet who must at the same time create other characters ("invent"). In
both instances, however, this narrative ventriloquism is at odds with
the promise of some more "authentic" being, a self that is here suggested by the "wild beast of earnestness," "well hidden" and "all
alone." Again, the constantly shifting opposition between self and
story is at work, since this figure—what we might call "M-alone"—
is opposed to the Malone who must "live and invent." This other
M-alone, that inarticulable creature whose absence is typographi-
cally inscribed in his very name, continues to exert himself as an invisible force throughout the rest of this passage:

> And gravely I struggled to be grave no more, to live, to invent, I know
> what I mean. But at each fresh attempt I lost my head, fled to my
> shadows as to sanctuary, to his lap who can neither live nor suffer the
> sight of others living. . . . After the fiasco, the solace, the repose, I be-
> gan again, to try and live, cause to live, be another, in myself, in an-
> other. (18–19)

The dutiful determination to play ("gravely struggled to be grave no
more") is again connected with storytelling—here represented as the
attempt to bring Malone to life ("to try and live")—and with Malone's effort to bring his creations to life ("cause to live").[20] In contrast to the narrator's efforts to vivify himself and his characters is
the loss of the self that these efforts bring about, punningly referred
to when Malone tells us that "at each fresh attempt I lost my head."
The result is a glimpse of what lies beyond the metaphysics of presence, the not-I now figured as an authorial corpse: "Who can neither
live nor suffer the sight of others living." The aporetics of the whole
project is neatly summed up in "be another, in myself, in another."

⌣·

Nowhere are the tensions and contradictions involved in introspection more evident than in the relation of narrator to narrated.
That relation is complicated in *Malone Dies* by the fact that Malone is himself a writer who invents two fictitious characters, Sapo
and Macmann. Whereas in *Watt* and *Molloy*, the narrators write
about characters who are purportedly real, in *Malone Dies* the narrator forthrightly admits that he has invented his characters. It may
be that we are meant to *interpret* Molloy as a figment of Moran's
imagination or Watt as Sam/Hackett's invention, but within the lit-

eral terms of their stories they are not fictitious characters, at least not in the sense that Sapo and Macmann are. This means that *Malone Dies* widens the space between narrator and narrated by stressing the artificiality of self-fashioning: Malone's attempt to narrate the self produces two patently "unreal" versions of it. At the same time, the novel seems—at least initially—to narrow this space, suggesting that the alternative to surrogates like Sapo and Macmann is indeed an authentic self-consciousness: the "real" Malone in whom narrator and narrated hypothetically converge.

In *Malone Dies* the relation of narrator and narrated is largely developed through what, in *The Unnamable* (37), Beckett will call a "vice-exister," or an authorial surrogate. In their very different ways, both Sapo and Macmann serve as vice-existers for Malone. Saposcat is one of Beckett's early minimalist characters, a sort of fleshed out version of A and C. His name appears to combine variants of the Latin *sapio* (I know) and the Greek *skor, skatós* (dung), suggesting that he functions as a kind of sensorium for the exclusively physical, a locus of material apprehension. Such a view is generally consistent with the little we learn of his character: "Sapo's phlegm, his silent ways, were not of a nature to please. In the midst of tumult, at school and at home, he remained motionless in his place, often standing, and gazed straight before him with eyes as pale and unwavering as a gull's" (15). The image is of an observer who shows no signs of an interior life, who records the scene before him without interest and without emotion ("gazed straight before him"), who stands fixed within his own point of view and in apparent indifference to those around him ("in the midst of tumult . . . motionless"). Disengaged observation of this sort becomes Sapo's chief activity at the Lamberts' farm, where he "had his place, by the window" (26), as though his surveillance required nothing more than a situating frame. Indeed, we would probably do better to understand Sapo not as a character at all but as a distillation of novelistic point of view, purified of all psychology and reduced to its simplest terms.

With the figure of Sapo, Beckett has in a sense desophisticated point of view, cleared away in a single sweep the whole complex of interrelations that implicate narrators in their narratives and call into question the reliability of what they do and say. He has not, however, delivered us into the provenance of some hypothetical "innocent eye,"[21] some utopia where the limitations of perspective are transcended and reality is finally seen clear and seen whole; on the contrary, objective vision is here parodically reduced to the mechanical status of a tape recorder or a video camera. Hence, Sapo is described as a kind of doll or mannequin, the very type in Beckettian iconography of narrative mechanization:

> Assembled in the farmyard they watched him depart, on stumbling, wavering feet, as though they scarcely felt the ground. Often he stopped, stood tottering a moment, then suddenly was off again, in a new direction. So he went, limp, drifting, as though tossed by the earth. And when, after a halt, he started off again, it was like a big thistledown plucked by the wind from the place where it had settled. (19–20)

The image of a figure that hangs limp as it is tossed along or stands tottering and unsure as it ceases moving recalls the puppets and stringed dolls, which in *Murphy* were associated with the "outer novel." This idea is driven home in another passage where we learn that Sapo's stops and starts are dictated to him by a controlling voice, that this character is not autonomous but governed by an external authority: "And when he halted it was not the better to think, or the closer to pore upon his dream, but simply because the voice had ceased that told him to go on" (30). In this reading, Sapo stands to Malone as a mere opening onto narrative description, the machinery of novelistic point of view that enables Malone to hold together the odd little story that comprises the first half of the novel. Sapo is identified with Malone, then, not as a kindred soul but as a technical convenience: he is what helps Malone tell his tale.

Macmann, in contrast, seems to present a much clearer analogue to Malone, and his story largely recapitulates his creator's own life. Generally speaking, both men begin as tramps, making their way on the open road, and both end in what appear to be institutions, cared for by others. The two sides of their lives—the road and the room—are more specifically represented by the accoutrements they either possess or have lost. Thus, both have owned at one time a hat, a greatcoat and a pair of boots, and both find themselves at another time in a bed and without their clothes:[22]

> No trace left of any clothes for example, apart from the boot, the hat and three socks, I [Malone] counted them. Where have my clothes

disappeared, my greatcoat, my trousers and the flannel that Mr. Quin gave me, with the remark that he did not need it any more? Perhaps they were burnt. (79–80)

He [Macmann] at once began to clamour loudly for his clothes, including probably the contents of his pockets, for he cried, My things! My things! over and over again, tossing about in the bed and beating the blanket with his palms. Then Moll sat down on the edge of the bed and . . . told him that his clothes had certainly ceased to exist. (87)

Another parallel is drawn between Malone and Macmann in their living situations. Both men are attended by women who take care of them, and in each case this attention involves a well-regulated circulation of feed bowls and chamber pots:

The door half opens, a hand puts a dish on the little table. . . . It is soup. . . . When my chamber-pot is full I [Malone] put it on the table, beside the dish. . . . What matters is to eat and excrete. Dish and pot, dish and pot, these are the poles. (7)

She brought him [Macmann] food (one large dish daily, to eat first hot, then cold), emptied his chamber-pot every morning first thing and showed him how to wash himself. (86)

Finally and most significantly, both men meet their ends (or what appear to be their ends) following an actual or contemplated blow to the head. This is delivered in Malone's case by an unnamed visitor to his room: "I felt a violent blow on the head. . . . The light has been queer ever since, oh I insinuate nothing, dim and at the same time radiant, perhaps I have a concussion" (99). In Macmann's case it is threatened by the apparently insane Lemuel: "Lemuel is in charge, he raises his hatchet on which the blood will never dry, but not to hit anyone, he will not hit anyone" (119).

To a lesser or greater extent, then, Sapo and Macmann function as vice-existers for Malone, and the relation of these creations to their creator raises again the problem of how we should connect self and story, narrator and narrated. But notice that Beckett is raising a question, not pursuing an equation; for if *Malone Dies* appears, particularly in the account I have given, to establish a simple correspondence between Malone and his vice-existers, this is only so that the correspondence may be interrogated, scrutinized, rejected. Thus, Malone will say, speaking of Sapo, "Nothing is less like me than this

patient, reasonable child" (17); and, speaking of Macmann, "I had
forgotten myself, lost myself" (97). The larger effect of this taking
away with one hand what has been given with the other, this ad-
ducing of relations that are then denied, is to throw open, even to
throw over, not only binary oppositions like self and story, author
and game, narrator and narrated, but also the entire economy of
subject-object thinking. *Malone Dies* thus initiates what *The Unnamable* will conclude: Beckett's final and decisive assault on phenomenology. This assault includes, of course, Beckett's own phenomenological constructions, particularly the one we have called
lapsarian epistemology.

～・

Just as for Hamm and Clov there are no more bicycle wheels, for
Malone there are no more gardens. Paradise has largely retreated
from this novel, and Malone comes to us as something like the last
survivor of a postlapsarian world, one who does not know how he
has gotten where he is but who dimly remembers some other, some
better, time:

> One day I found myself here, in the bed. Having probably lost con-
> sciousness somewhere, I benefit by a hiatus in my recollections, not
> to be resumed until I recovered my senses, in this bed. As to the events
> that led up to my fainting and to which I can hardly have been obliv-
> ious, at the time, they have left no discernible trace, on my mind. . . .
> I was walking certainly . . . perhaps I was stunned with a blow, on
> the head. (5–6)

If there was a blow to the head and a loss of consciousness, then presumably somewhere between these two events there was an icono-
graphically crucial fall, a fall that is not explicitly recounted but narratively passed over, as though to suggest that the very conditions of
paradisiacal expulsion somehow render its own telling unimagin-
able. Yet, despite a general amnesia toward all that is prelapsarian,
Malone retains a vague sense of the paradise he has left behind.

Of particular importance is his experience of existence off the ladder, an experience that (given the context of the passage) arises out
of the tension between self and story, narrator and narrated, author
and game: "What I sought, when I struggled out of my hole, then
aloft through the stinging air towards an inaccessible boon, was the

rapture of vertigo, the letting go, the fall, the gulf, the relapse to darkness, to nothingness, to earnestness, to home" (19). The language explicitly suggests a lighter-than-air condition (aloft, rapture, vertigo), followed by its gravity-bound opposite (letting go, fall, gulf)—a cycle of ascension and fall, which we have come to associate with the transcendence, or at least dislocation, of Cartesian dualism. In earlier works, however, the fall explicitly marked the termination of existence off the ladder, whereas now it seems to constitute its desired climax, precisely the "letting go" of the self into the "gulf," elsewhere described as "interdit à nos sondes,"[23] and here connected with the "darkness" and "nothingness" that stand beyond the metaphysics of presence. Beckett has effectively unwritten his own phenomenological iconography by overturning the significance of the fall: rather than a debasement into the subject-object dialectic, it has become an elevation above and beyond it.

But things are not so simple, for what has been described is not merely a fall but a "relapse," a falling again and a falling back, away from the diversion of storytelling and toward the "earnestness" of introspection. The Malone who has declared himself an *auctor ludens* ("I am going to play," 2) finds himself, despite his best intentions, reverting to his old ways. Fall in this second sense of a "relapse" means at one level nothing more than a departure from the original plan to play. But at another level it again raises the issue of phenomenology, since it involves slipping back into a metaphysics of presence, here suggested by that unnamed other, described as "waiting for me always, who needed me and whom I needed, who took me in his arms and told me to stay with him always, who gave me his place and watched over me, who suffered every time I left him, whom I have often made suffer and seldom contented, whom I have never seen" (19). This other vaguely hovers along the descriptive horizon, the barest wraith in Balzacian terms but for Beckett sufficiently well individualized to represent a comedown from Arsenian levitation, although he is also sufficiently close to some radical indeterminacy that, occupying "darkness" and "nothingness," he is "never seen." The mere effort, however, to situate narratively this avatar of the self, to describe him even in the most rudimentary way, effectively dissipates him: "There I am forgetting myself again" (19).

If the other who was waiting for Malone and took him in his arms momentarily suspends himself beyond determinacy, if for an instant he approaches the conditions of the not-I, then that second other far beneath Malone, of whom he now speaks, is a patently artificial construction, one who has, in the Sartrean sense of the word, *aventures*:

> My concern is not with me, but with another, far beneath me and whom I try to envy, of whose crass adventures I can now tell at last, I don't know how. Of myself I could never tell, any more than live or tell of others. How could I have, who never tried? To show myself now, on the point of vanishing, at the same time as the stranger, and by the same grace, that would be no ordinary last straw. Then live, long enough to feel, behind my closed eyes, other eyes close. What an end. (19)

Yet despite Malone's efforts to "envy" this other character of Balzacian determinacy, he nevertheless turns back to the "self," attempting once again to apprehend it ("show myself") even as it fades away ("on the point of vanishing"). The final image in this passage—the eyes of the other closing behind Malone's eyes—suggests that the effort to mediate between self and story has fallen into the interval between these terms, that the speaking voice has been caught within, even lost between, the space separating narrator from narrated. Existence off the ladder, rewritten and unwritten, has produced our first glimpse of that no-man's-land that will become *The Unnamable*.

I have been discussing Malone's function within the iconography of a lapsarian epistemology, but Sapo and Macmann, as we might anticipate, also play important roles in this regard. As is true of so much connected with Sapo, his story offers only the most elementary hint of how these themes might be elaborated. There is a garden, but it is not that locus of phenomenological destruction and creation we have come to expect so much as the horticultural equivalent of bourgeois self-sufficiency: "The life of the Saposcats was full of axioms, of which one at least established the criminal absurdity of a garden without roses and with its paths and lawns uncared for" (10). There is a retreat to the countryside, but unlike Molloy and Moran, Sapo enters no forests overgrown with the symbols of quest romance, undertakes no spiritual journeys that redefine the ground of his being.[24] There is even the now-inevitable bowl of milk, but it is merely the simple refreshment of the Lamberts' board ("Sapo remained alone, by the window, the bowl of goat's milk on the table before him," 27), not the sign of a redemptive mother offering subject-object unity. What we finally confront with Sapo is something like a lapsarian epistemology in suspension: all the necessary elements have been assembled, but, purged of their significance, they now fail to cohere.

Macmann presents a similar if more difficult case. We have already seen how Beckett treated Watt as a kind of second Adam, a character who, having suffered the fall into Cartesian dualism, came to the Knott establishment seeking deliverance and transcendence. Macmann's very name, which literally means "Son of Man," suggests that he, too, functions as a Christ figure, an idea that is underscored when he is caught in the rain far from shelter:

> His hands at the ends of the long outstretched arms clutched the grass, each hand a tuft. . . . The idea of punishment came to his mind, addicted it is true to that chimera and probably impressed by the posture of the body and the fingers clenched as though in torment. And without knowing exactly what his sin was he felt full well that living was not a sufficient atonement for it or that his atonement was in itself a sin, calling for more atonement, and so on, as if there could be anything but life, for the living. (66–67)

> And just as an hour before he had pulled up his sleeves the better to clutch the grass, so now he pulled them up again the better to feel the rain pelting down on his palms, also called the hollows of the hands, or the flats. (69)

Here purgation (cleansing water) and crucifixion (the spread-eagle position) converge in the imagery of the passion, but it is a mock-passion, played out by a hobo-Christ who has lost his umbrella, a messiah who is literally all wet.

Macmann's arrival at the asylum is handled with the same kind of parodic undercutting. The model is Watt's entry into Knott's house, which mythologized, in phenomenological terms, Christ's emergence from the wilderness as a potential return to Eden. Here, the symbolically crucified Macmann ends his own wanderings at Saint John of God's (a name resonant with possibility), discovering in its enclosed park an image of Dante's earthly paradise.[25] Yet, this "little Paradise" (108) appears, under closer examination, to be less a reclamation of prelapsarian bliss than a caricature of it—Eden as a week in the country with room and board included: "Macmann sometimes wondered what was lacking to his happiness. The right to be abroad in all weathers morning, noon and night . . . food and lodging such as they were free of all charge, superb views on every hand" (108).

The ground of phenomenological transformation has effectively been displaced from the garden to what lies beyond it, the "way out into the desolation of having nobody and nothing, the wilds of the hunted, the scant bread and the scant shelter and the black joy of the solitary way, in helplessness and will-lessness" (108). If Watt sought deliverance from the "dark ways" (*Watt*, 39), Macmann seeks deliverance into "the solitary way"; if Watt sought "nobody and nothing" in Mr. Knott's house and garden, Macmann seeks them in the wilderness. The result is a complete inversion of lapsarian epistemology. Now the sign of Knottian indeterminacy, of what lies beyond the metaphysics of presence, is situated not within the garden but without ("Beyond the gate, on the road, shapes passed that Macmann could not understand," 109); now the effort to overcome Cartesian dualism is figured not as ascension but as collapse ("the earth enjoining him to fall," 109).

Yet lapsarian epistemology has been more than merely inverted: it has been subverted as well. Hence, Macmann never experiences a breakthrough, never penetrates into a beyond of helpless, will-less, ataraxic bliss. We have observed in the preceding novels moments that approached transcendence, but here there is none, and that is perhaps because the announced goal of the narrative is not to enter into a condition of indeterminacy but to achieve a decisive shape, one that clearly delineates its boundaries, one that finally, that mercifully, makes an end.

～•

Toward the beginning of his story, Malone describes himself as "for ever shapelessness and speechlessness" (2). There is nothing new here. Ever since *Murphy* the narrative parlor trick has consisted in at once evoking the self as indeterminately boundless (inaccessible and inexpressible) and nevertheless seeking to contain it within determinate boundaries, seeking to scale it down to the finite level of beginnings and ends. Somehow the stories always got told—there was a first word where the reader started and a last word where the reader stopped—but amid all this business-as-usual, the self remained elusive right up to, or more precisely beyond, the end. What appears to be new about *Malone Dies* is precisely its announced willingness to bring the self to term.

And yet, in a novel that presumably tells the story of its author's death, there is throughout an imagery of nativity, which identifies Malone's room with the womb and suggests that the vigil through which we are sitting is a difficult birth rather than a protracted death. Malone speaks of a world that "parts at last its labia and lets me go" (12), of the window through which he watches his "umbilicus" (49); he speaks of his own body swelling to the proportions of a womblike enclosure ("There I am, who always thought I would shrivel . . . swelling," 62), and even of the rhythmic contractions of birth itself ("The ceiling rises and falls, rises and falls, rhythmically, as when I was a foetus," 114). But this is a peculiar sort of birth, one that is consistently equated with death. Malone punningly makes this point when he speaks of himself as having been "born grave" (18) or remarks that the "end of life is always vivifying" (37). He is, in his own words, "an old foetus . . . hoar and impotent" (51), whose birth will be a kind of death: "I am being given, if I may venture the expression, birth to into death" (114).

But if the nexus is clear—womb, room, tomb—its significance is less so. One way to understand why Beckett draws a connection between birth and death is to approach this problem generically. According to the logic of the nineteenth-century novelist's *faire vivre*, only those characters can be conjured into life who are fully formed and clearly outlined, whose personality projects a species or kind about which we may usefully generalize (Grandet is a miser) and whose actions are reducible to a series of anecdotes, neatly tied off at their beginnings and ends. However, for a writer like Beckett, it is precisely this Balzacian process of *faire vivre* that fixes characters in formaldehyde. Thus, in the climactic scene of a novel like Sarraute's *Portrait d'un inconnu*, if the father adheres to the Balzacian genre of miser, if he proves to be little more than a plot formula or a character type, then he will rigidify into mere puppetry. The determinism that animates the characters of Balzac undermines the characters of Beckett.

We may carry this argument a step further by suggesting that here Beckett is engaging in a kind of *askesis*, ritualistically emptying out even the most debilitated and anemic of Balzac's character types, entering the sickroom of some pale descendant of *La Comédie humaine* and, after a certain show of professional courtesy, applying the leeches.[26] If, however, Malone seems to be an unlikely offshoot, no matter how etiolated, of that robust growth we call the Balzacian family tree, we may locate his more immediate antecedents elsewhere, in a character who is also sickly, also bedridden, also given to writing, a character named Marcel. Admittedly, *A la recherche du temps perdu* is, seen from one perspective, an unrelenting assault upon the idea of the character of determinacy: time and again we hear of the multiple selves that comprise characters and render them literally unrecognizable—and this, no doubt, is one of the reasons Proust exercised so powerful an influence on Beckett. Nevertheless, Proust represents, by Beckettian standards, not the subversion of the nineteenth-century novel but its final efflorescence, and Marcel remains, however multilayered, however densely textured, of a piece with the Balzacian tradition.[27] Indeed, even Malone is too heavily demarcated, too inertly substantial, to achieve the kind of airy indeterminacy that would move the self beyond the metaphysics of presence. This means, in turn, that if Beckett wants his novel to function as a piece of *écriture*, he will ultimately have to destroy Malone, which is to say, destroy the entire logic of narrator and narrated, of author and book.

Yet this is easier said than done. For if Beckett's vice-existers are haunted by the presence of Malone, Malone is himself haunted by another authorial presence, one that is not easily eliminated, one that goes by the name of Samuel Beckett. Of course, the connection between Malone and Beckett is, at one level, generic: both are writers who tell semiautobiographical stories. But at another level, this connection is specifically autobiographical, elaborated through a series of details that connect Malone and his creations to Beckett.[28] Thus, Malone's surrogate, Sapo, possesses those signature Beckettian eyes, "unwavering as a gull's" (15) and of the "palest blue" (14).[29] As for Malone, he describes two experiences that Beckett has often related from his early childhood: witnessing one of the first loopings of the loop and asking his mother how far the sky was from the earth (98).[30] More significant for our purposes, Malone also relates Beckett's outrageous account of his own birth. The immediate source for this third autobiographical item is a letter that Beckett wrote to Arland Ussher ("My memories begin on the eve of my birth, under the table, when my father gave a dinner and my mother presided") and that, as we have seen, he recast as the story of Larry Nixon's birth in *Watt* (13–15).[31] By referring to the prenatal dinner party, Beckett works this well-known anecdote into Malone's own account of his birth-as-death: "Yes, an old foetus, that's what I am now, hoar and impotent, mother is done for, I've rotted her, she'll drop me with the help of gangrene, perhaps papa is at the party too" (51). Indeed, the identification of Malone's death with Beckett's birth is underscored when we realize that Malone consistently predicts that he will die in April or May, the two months variously given for Beckett's birth:[32]

> I shall soon be quite dead at last in spite of all. Perhaps next month. Then it will be the month of April or of May. (1)

> I feel it's coming . . . sure of feeling that my hour is at hand. . . . All I have to do is go on as though doomed to see the midsummer moon. For I believe I have now reached what is called the month of May. (60)

It is as though Malone's projected demise has been caught up in a cycle of death and birth, one in which the death of one author (Malone) leads to the (re)birth of another (Beckett). Hence, Malone's death is consistently described in terms of resurrection:

> The sun was dragging itself up, dispatching on its way what perhaps would be, thanks to it, a glorious May or April day, April more likely, it is doubtless the Easter week-end, spent by Jesus in hell. (111)

> Can it be Easter Week? Thus with the year the Seasons return. If it can, could not this song I have just heard, and which quite frankly is not yet quite stilled within me, could not this song have simply been to the honour and glory of him who was the first to rise from the dead . . . ? (33)

Insofar as *Malone Dies* can be said to progress, it is according to a logic of assertion and contradiction, so that just when it seems that we have been delivered from the self, just when it seems that the au-

thor has been laid to rest, he is rejuvenated, here in the form of that
Ur-author, Samuel Beckett.[33] Admittedly, all of this is obliquely handled, as it was in the case of Larry Nixon in *Watt*, or A and C in
Molloy. But whereas these earlier novels acknowledged their own
supplementarity, ruefully conceding that their vice-existers had failed
to return us to some first principle, some authorial source, *Malone
Dies* presents an entirely different situation, one in which we discover that the difficulty now consists not in recovering the self but
in escaping from its various manifestations. It is as though every time
one version of the self is dispatched, it is replaced by another. As we
shall see, *Malone Dies* is a novel that will ultimately leave unresolved
the question of whether or not the author has died. Certainly, there
is strong presumptive evidence to suggest that we are witnessing
Malone's end, but the evidence is by no means definitive. For this is
a novel in which definitive statements are increasingly difficult to
imagine, much less to make. And that is because this is a novel that
seeks to level all definitional boundaries, to blur the outlines of the
literary oeuvre, to throw itself open to a form of pantextuality.

Malone Dies advertises itself as a novel that has finally come to
grips with the difficulties of narrative shaping, a novel that we know
will make an end because, as the title tells us, the hero dies. And yet,
as an effort to achieve closure, to provide the final term in a sequence, it obviously fails—otherwise *The Unnamable* would not
have been written. Indeed, I shall argue that closure is precisely what
Malone Dies most deliberately subverts. More than any other writing in Beckett's canon, it is a studied effort at opening up the boundaries between texts, at resolving itself and everything around it into
a kind of pantextuality. In this sense, just as the novel is struggling
to move beyond the author, it is also struggling to move beyond the
"book."

At one point, as he contemplates ending his story, Malone speaks
of pebbles functioning as narrative constituents: "This may well be
my last journey, down the long familiar galleries, with my little suns
and moons that I hang aloft and my pockets full of pebbles to stand
for men and their seasons" (63). The image of a Beckettian derelict,
his pocket full of pebbles, inevitably calls to mind Molloy and his

sucking stones. The connection is instructive. *Malone Dies* does to the narrative constituents of the preceding novels what Molloy sought to do with his pebbles: it runs them through a series of combinations; it achieves a Beckettian permutation. The result is a novel that, incorporating in itself elements of *Murphy*, *Watt*, and *Molloy*, erodes all textual boundaries, a piece of writing that is, as Derrida puts it, "consumed by reading other texts."[34]

Consider the way *Malone Dies* opens. Having offered itself as a fresh start, a new departure, a break with the past, the novel folds back on itself like a narrative Möbius strip, locating its own beginnings ("This room seems to be mine. . . . I do not remember how I got here. In an ambulance perhaps, a vehicle of some kind certainly," 5) in that other, antecedent text, *Molloy* ("I am in my mother's room. . . . I don't know how I got there. Perhaps in an ambulance, certainly a vehicle of some kind," 7). Indeed, Malone's narrative appears to take up precisely where Molloy's left off: "Perhaps I was stunned with a blow, on the head," Malone tells us, "in a forest perhaps, yes, now that I speak of a forest I vaguely remember a forest" (6). What is more, both novels share a binary structure that organizes itself around two stories, one concerning a bourgeois (Moran/Sapo) and one concerning a bum (Molloy/Macmann), thereby suggesting that in its larger contours, *Molloy* has provided a kind of blueprint for *Malone Dies*.

At the same time, Malone is a reworked Molloy, a former tramp who is confined to his sickbed and passes his days writing. Molloy's "What I'd like now is to speak of the things that are left, say my good-byes, finish dying" (*Molloy*, 7) has become Malone's "I shall soon be quite dead at last in spite of all" (*Malone Dies*, 1). These connections are elaborated by Malone's vice-exister, Macmann, whose refuge at Saint John's recalls Molloy's sanctuary at Lousse's. Hence, both characters discover at a certain point that, along with their clothing, their hats have been removed, and both prove unyielding in their demands that the missing headgear be returned:

> But as Macmann continued passionately to clamour for his things, and notably for his hat, she [Moll] left him, saying he was not reasonable. And she came back a little later, holding with the tips of her fingers the hat in question, retrieved perhaps from the rubbish-heap. (*Malone Dies*, 87)

> But the valet having brought my clothes, in a paper which he un-
> wrapped in front of me, I saw that my hat was not among them, so
> that I said, My hat. And when he finally understood what I wanted
> he went away and came back a little later with my hat. (*Molloy*, 59)

Even more striking is the reappearance in the second novel of a
knife-rest, which Molloy pilfered in the first novel: "I had stolen
from Lousse a little silver . . . small objects whose utility I did not
grasp. . . . Among these latter there was one which haunts me still,
from time to time. It consisted of two crosses joined, at their points
of intersection, by a bar, and resembled a tiny sawing-horse" (*Molloy*, 85). This object later turns up at Saint John's, now identified
and in the possession of Macmann: "With regard to the objects
found in [his] pockets, they had been assessed as quite worthless and
fit only to be thrown away with the exception of a little silver knife-
rest" (*Malone Dies*, 87).

Although less fully developed, the affiliations between *Malone
Dies* and *Watt* are also worth remarking. These are most evident in
the Macmann section of the novel, which, like *Watt*, involves the
now familiar figure of a derelict traveling to an asylum. Once there
he meets a certain Lemuel (a variation on Samuel) who turns out to
be (like his namesake in *Watt*) another author figure. Of course, since
Watt itself permuted *Murphy* in its story about a bum who ends up
at a mental institution, *Malone Dies* offers something like a double
exposure of these two novels. At the same time, it incorporates a
number of specific references to *Murphy*. Thus, Malone recalls Murphy through his earlier interests in astrology ("I have studied the
stars a little here. But I cannot find my way among them. Gazing at
them one night I suddenly saw myself in London. Is it possible I got
as far as London?" 7), his description of Sapo's gull-like eyes ("I
don't like those gull's eyes. They remind me of an old shipwreck, I
forget which," 16), his efforts to embrace the insane ("With the insane too I failed, by a hair's-breadth," 44),[35] and finally his suicidal
musings ("Be born, that's the brainwave now, that is to say live long
enough to get acquainted with free carbonic gas, then say thanks for
the nice time and go," 51).

If, however, all of this suggests that the novel is textually opening
itself up to its antecedents, breaking down boundaries and moving
toward *écriture*, it nevertheless remains obsessed with at least one
kind of closure, the closure that comes with the death of the author.

Hence, Beckett rounds up various vice-existers from earlier novels and then prepares to kill them as a prelude to killing the author. The idea of making a clean sweep of all these narrative inventions, past and present, is first broached when Malone contemplates his own death and those of his creations:

> But let us leave these morbid matters and get on with that of my demise, in two or three days if I remember rightly. Then it will be all over with the Murphys, Merciers, Molloys, Morans and Malones, un-less it goes on beyond the grave. But sufficient unto the day, let us first defunge, then we'll see. How many have I killed, hitting them on the head or setting fire to them? Off-hand I can think of four, all un-knowns, I never knew anyone. . . . There was the old butler too, in London I think, there's London again, I cut his throat with his razor, that makes five. (63)

The five characters Malone mentions appear to include Murphy and the butler from *Murphy*, the police officer from *Mercier and Camier*, and A and C from *Molloy*. The outing that occurs at the end of *Malone Dies* may be read as a deadly reprise of these other killings, one in which Malone-Beckett now makes an end, as he had promised, of the heroes of his earlier works. Thus, the character in the first cell—described as "a young man, dead young, seated in an old rock-ing-chair, his shirt rolled up and his hands on his thighs, would have seemed asleep had not his eyes been wide open" (112)—recalls Mur-phy rocking himself into a state of ataraxic bliss and, as the pun has it, "dead young." The second cell contains

> one whose only really striking features were his stature, his stiffness and his air of perpetually looking for something while at the same time wondering *what* that something could possibly be. *Nothing* in his person gave any indication of his age, whether he was marvel-lously well preserved or on the contrary prematurely decayed. He was called the Saxon. (113, my emphasis)

Here we may detect echoes of Watt in the stiffness (Watt's gait strikes Lady McCann as "stiff and open," *Watt*, 31), the large stature (Watt has grown to huge proportions in *Mercier and Camier*), the em-phasized play on *what* and *nothing*, and—given the French context of the trilogy—Watt's characterization as a Saxon.[36] The third char-acter suggests Moran, here presented as "a small thin man . . . pac-ing up and down, his cloak folded over his arm, an umbrella in his

hand. Fine head of white flossy hair. He was asking himself questions in a low voice, reflecting, replying" (113–14). Moran is described as compact of build (small and thin) and as a proper bourgeois (he carries an umbrella and a folded cloak), and he appears to
be engaged in a dialogue with himself, as, allegorically speaking,
Moran is with Molloy. In the fourth cell is "a misshapen giant,
bearded, occupied to the exclusion of all else in scratching himself,
intermittently" (114). This character seems to be a version of Molloy, who is also bearded and is described as "massive and hulking,
to the point of misshapenness" (*Molloy*, 155).[37]

Of course, these figures are not meant to be precise reconstitu-
tions of Beckett's earlier characters so much as suggestive points of
reference, and their pairings with Murphy, Watt, Moran, and Molloy are by no means exact. Rather, what is important is to see that
Beckett is inviting us to make these equations, to recognize these figures as a gallery of past moribunds who are now going to be decisively done away with, finished once and for all in a way that they
never were before. Thus, Lemuel, the analogue to Samuel of *Watt*
and therefore a substitute for Beckett himself, takes these vice-existers on a fatal outing. This authorial bloodletting is, however, complicated by the way in which Malone himself dies (or appears to die)
through an act of narrative embedding. The embedding consists first
in Malone receiving a blow on the head, which fails to kill him but
which injures him, perhaps critically:

> The visit. I felt a violent blow on the head. . . . I don't doubt he gave
> me due warning, before he hit me. I don't know what he wanted. He's
> gone now. What an idea, all the same, to hit me on the head. The light
> has been queer ever since, oh I insinuate nothing, dim and at the same
> time radiant, perhaps I have a concussion. (99)

Lemuel, as the intermediary between frame and story, narrator and
narrated, inflicts upon himself the kind of injury that Malone has already suffered and that Lemuel will presently inflict upon his own
victims: "Lemuel produced a hatchet from under his cloak and dealt
himself a few smart blows on the skull, with the heel, for safety"
(117). In the final scene of the novel this hatchet is transmuted into
a pencil (119), as if to insist that the writer's instrument is synonymous with the instrument of death, that Lemuel's mass homicide
should be read as an act of authorial intervention.[38]

Intervention of this sort (the author steps from behind the curtain) destroys any effort at illusion. It forthrightly concedes that when it is time to make an end, the character does not die naturalistically but is killed, deus ex machina, by the narrator: "Moll. I'm going to kill her" (94). Such an ending is artificial in the sense that it lacks *vraisemblance*, but it is also artificial in the sense that we do not know whether or not to read it as "real." For one thing, the novel has come full circle, "ending" where it began, with Malone receiving a blow to the head. Is this, we must then ask, a conclusion, a genuine completion of action, or is it simply a point of leaving off before we begin again? Indeed, there is a genuine question of whether the author has died at the end of the novel, since at various points the narrative raises the possibility that he is already dead:

> The truth is, if I did not feel myself dying, I could well believe myself dead, expiating my sins. (6)

> There is naturally another possibility that does not escape me, though it would be a great disappointment to have it confirmed, and that is that I am dead already and that all continues more or less as when I was not. Perhaps I expired in the forest, or even earlier. (45)

> If at dawn I am still there I shall take a decision. I am half asleep. But I dare not sleep. Rectifications in extremis, in extremissimis, are always possible after all. But have I not perhaps just passed away? (79)

What is more, even if we assume that Malone is not dead, there is little reason to think that the last blow succeeded in killing him where the first blow failed. As Malone expostulates in the final pages, "My story ended, I'll be living yet" (115).

⌣·

Malone Dies represents a tour de force in aporetic transformation: a work that effaces the differences between narrator and narrated even as it marks them out, that throws open its textual boundaries even as it insists on closing them down. In a sense the self-permutation that *Molloy* contemplates at its end—the story will be retold (it is midnight) but in negative terms (it was not midnight)—is realized in the way *Malone Dies* inverts whatever project it avows. But it is precisely in this novel, which appears to resist an ending, that Beckett brings to term both the author and the book. At the same time, he finishes with the *askesis* or systematic emptying out of the novelistic form he has pursued since *Murphy*. Instead of working within an aesthetic of failure, an aesthetic that acknowledges, depends on, and even celebrates its representational insufficiencies, Beckett will go on to invent a way of naming that which has heretofore remained unnamable, of carrying the afterimage of the not-I into a new domain, one where the hero can confidently proclaim: "My story ended, I'll be living yet."

CHAPTER SIX

'The Unnamable'

The End of Man and the Beginning of Writing

"As the archaeology of our thought easily shows," Michel Foucault famously wrote in *The Order of Things*, "man is an invention of recent date. And one perhaps nearing its end." Sounding a decidedly apocalyptic note, he went on to conclude: "If those arrangements [which define man] were to disappear as they appeared, if some event . . . were to cause them to crumble, as the ground of Classical thought did, at the end of the eighteenth century, then one can certainly wager [*parier*] that man would be erased, like a face drawn in sand at the edge of the sea."[1]

Foucault's final image recalls Pascal's celebrated wager, only that wager has here been recast in a Beckettian universe, one long since abandoned by God and now inhabited not by man but by the effigy of his former self, a pale and spectral being that the tides of time gradually wash away. What Foucault describes—the now-familiar "end of man"—is part of the larger discourse associated with the "end of modernity." Standing behind this discourse and helping to motivate it is an anti-Enlightenment critique of humanism that rejects the idea that the cogito provides the ground of all knowledge, that "truth" is exclusively a function of human perception. As we have seen, Nietzsche provides the source for this critique: "What then is truth? A movable host of metaphors, metonymies, and anthropomorphisms. . . . At bottom, what the investigator of such truths is seeking is only the metamorphosis of the world into man."[2] Foucault not only acknowledges the Nietzschean legacy in the "end of man" discourse, but he insists as well on carrying that legacy forward, indeed on making it the test for what is philosophically new:

Perhaps we should see the first attempt at this uprooting of Anthropology—to which, no doubt, contemporary thought is dedicated—in the Nietzschean experience: by means of a philological critique, by means of a certain form of biologism, Nietzsche rediscovered the point at which man and God belong to one another, at which the death of the second is synonymous with the disappearance of the first, and at which the promise of the superman signifies first and foremost the imminence of the death of man. In this, Nietzsche . . . marks the threshold beyond which contemporary philosophy can begin thinking again.[3]

Yet in his enthusiasm for answering Nietzsche's challenge, for crossing the philosophical threshold and moving beyond the end of man, Foucault comes perilously close to constructing an alternative metaphysics, one represented by a new master code (a combination of psychoanalysis, ethnography, and linguistics) that is meant to place Foucault outside his subject, to secure for him a privileged point of view.[4]

Jacques Derrida's "The Ends of Man," an essay that clearly responds to Foucault, addresses this problem by asking whether man can take as his end precisely his own transcendence:

The thinking of the end of man, therefore, is always already prescribed in metaphysics, in the thinking of the truth of man. What is difficult to think today is an end of man which would not be organized by a dialectics of truth and negativity, an end of man which would not be a teleology in the first person plural.[5]

This returns us to the central problem posed by the discourse of postmodernity: how to "overcome" a modernity that is itself based on a logic of critical "overcoming." As we observed in Chapter 1, Derrida does not offer a definitive solution to this problem, but he does indicate that, given our position within the metaphysical tradition, we are faced with two choices: on the one hand, a deconstruction of existing terms that, undertaken from the "inside," assaults founding concepts, "without changing terrain"; and, on the other, an effort to place "oneself outside," to affirm "an absolute break," a real change of terrain, while recognizing that this effort presents nothing more than "a *trompe-l'oeil* perspective."[6] Yet for Derrida these choices, and the procedures they imply, are by no means exclusive. He therefore recommends a form of "plural" writing, which comprehends both these approaches without attempting to reconcile their differences or resolve their contradictions: "It also goes without saying that the choice between these two forms of deconstruction cannot be simple and unique. A new writing must weave and interlace these two motifs of deconstruction. Which amounts to saying that one must speak several languages and produce several texts at once."[7] I would like to suggest that *The Unnamable* can be read as just such a "plural" text: a sustained meditation on how we might move beyond the end of man, which nevertheless acknowledges that no absolute transcendence is possible.

We might best approach the novel and its interest in negative limits (un-namable) by way of Derrida's question: How can we think "an end of man which would not be organized by a dialectics of truth and negativity"? Of course, the very term *end*, by touching an outer bound, the place of its own cessation, necessarily defines itself as a negative limit. Derrida is presumably aware of this point and wants us to feel the way his own logic recoils in a moment of deconstructive arrest, as he strives to think his way beyond ends in an essay about ends. The resulting aporia illustrates the double movement proposed at the conclusion of his essay, a movement at once covering the same ground and changing the terrain, attempting to subvert from "within" and assault from "without." We may understand the larger project here as involving a transition or passage that carries us from the idea of man to some negative beyond. I shall represent this in Beckett's pentalogy as the general movement from the "M" word (Murphy, Molloy, Moran, Macmann, Mahood, and, of course, Man) to the "Un" word (the unnamable, *l'innommable*, *l'inhomme-able*).[8]

Beckett himself anticipated this development as early as the 1930s when, in the so-called German Letter, he imagined a kind of irruptive writing that would effectively dislocate what had been conceived, within the humanist tradition, as the mimetic function of language. The literary alternative Beckett proposed involved following music and painting into an aesthetic of antirepresentation:

> Let us hope the time will come, thank God that in certain circles it has already come, when language is most efficiently used where it is being efficiently misused. As we cannot eliminate language all at once, we should at least leave nothing undone that might contribute to its

falling into disrepute. . . . I cannot imagine a higher goal for a writer today. Or is literature alone to remain behind in the old lazy ways that have been so long ago abandoned by music and painting?[9]

Beckett went on to speak of the linguistic assault this would involve as holding out the promise of a radically new kind of literature, what he called, in a memorable phrase, the "literature of the unword" (*Disjecta*, 173). Both Foucault and Derrida have had recourse to various forms of the "unword" in their own attempts to develop a language that undermines the metaphysical and humanist traditions. In a subsection of *The Order of Things* entitled "The 'Cogito' and the Unthought," Foucault speaks of trying to think beyond the outer limits of Cartesian dualism in ways that strikingly recall *The Unnamable*: "The question is no longer: How can experience of nature give rise to necessary judgements? But rather: How can man think what he does not think, inhabit as though by a mute occupation something that eludes him, animate with a kind of frozen movement that figure of himself that takes the form of a stubborn exteriority?"[10] The same year *The Order of Things* appeared, Derrida published "Structure, Sign, and Play," an essay that also contemplates the problem of transcending, or at least displacing, metaphysics by reverting to a language of the unword: "By orienting and organizing the coherence of the system, the center of a structure permits the play of its elements inside the total form. And even today the notion of a structure lacking any center represents the *unthinkable* itself."[11]

Yet Derrida—who has acknowledged Beckett's importance to his own work—carried the notion of the "unword" even farther, developing what has become an extended metaphor of unnamability.[12] One of the earliest and most dramatic uses of this figure occurs at the end of "Structure, Sign, and Play," when Derrida finds himself in the now all-too-familiar position of the postmodern philosopher, who can no longer work within the Western metaphysical tradition yet is unable to move beyond it. What remains, he tells us, is to explore both the "common ground" that joins these alternatives and the "irreducible difference" that separates them. Derrida refers to this intellectual no-man's-land as *différance*, and he compares its strange eruption to a monstrous and "unnamable" birth:

Here there is a kind of question, let us call it historical, whose *conception, formation, gestation,* and *labor* we are only catching a glimpse of today. I employ these words, I admit, with a glance toward the operations of childbearing—but also with a glance toward those who, in a society from which I do not exclude myself, turn their eyes away when faced by the as yet *unnamable* [my emphasis] which is proclaiming itself and which can do so, as is necessary whenever a birth is in the offing, only under the species of the nonspecies, in the formless, mute, infant, and terrifying form of monstrosity.[13]

"Structure, Sign, and Play" is not the only place where Derrida evokes the "unnamable." Again and again in his work, the struggle to gain a position outside the Western philosophical tradition has the same effect: it points toward, opens onto, or glimpses at what cannot be named. Thus, in *Speech and Phenomena*, the effort to move beyond voice as self-presence leads "across the inherited concepts [of the West], toward the unnamable"; in "White Mythology," the Nietzschean acknowledgment of philosophy as metaphor is identified with an "*unnamable* articulation" [Derrida's emphasis]; in "Plato's Pharmacy," the deconstruction of the "pharmaceutical system" of "Platonism" prompts the question, "Into what general, unnamable necessity are we thrown?"; in "La Parole soufflée," the attempt to project oneself "beyond man, beyond the metaphysics of Western theater" looks toward the "unnamable Divine"; and in *Of Grammatology*, the assault on Saussure and "the age of the sign" discloses the "crevice through which the yet unnameable glimmer beyond . . . can be glimpsed."[14] Derrida provides what we might take as a summary view of the "unnamable" in *Positions*:

To "deconstruct" philosophy, thus, would be to think—in the most faithful, interior way—the structured genealogy of philosophy's concepts, but at the same time to determine—from a certain exterior that is unqualifiable or unnameable by philosophy—what this history has been able to dissimulate or forbid.[15]

As this catalogue of citations makes clear, the *unnamable* functions as one of Derrida's key terms, something on the order of *supplement, tympan, trace,* or *hymen.* It is worth pointing out, however, that a certain grammatical slippage occurs as we move between Beckett's use of the "unnamable" as a noun and Derrida's use of it as both noun and adjective. This slippage is already present in Beckett, since *l'innommable* is by definition whatever resists nominalization, a noun (*nom*) that denies its own power to name, a noun that, like the "unword," negates itself (*in-nom*). Indeed, even at the level of grammar, the "unnamable" appears to be a kind of *faux substantif*, an adjective that, by virtue of a definite article, has reinvented itself as a noun.[16]

Given the semantic and grammatical instability of the "unnamable," it is not surprising that Derrida consistently associates it with that other master trope of linguistic dislocation, *différance*. For what makes possible the emergence of the "unnamable" in Derrida, what elicits its transitory and fugitive appearance, is precisely the discovery within Western philosophy of its own deconstructive potential, the discovery at bottom of a *différance* that threatens to unsettle the very foundations of metaphysics.[17] Hence, the connection between *différance* and the "unnamable" becomes necessary, even inevitable, since *différance* is "literally neither a word nor a concept" and is, therefore, unwritable, unspeakable, and unnamable:

> *Différance* has no name in our language. But we "already know" that if it is unnameable [*innommable*], it is not provisionally so, not because our language has not yet found or received this *name*, or because we would have to seek it in another language. . . . It is rather because there is no *name* for it at all.[18]

Indeed so intimate is the relation between *différance* and the "unnamable" that Derrida concludes his title essay on the subject by treating these terms as virtually interchangeable: "This unnameable [*cet innomable*] is the play which makes possible nominal effects, the relatively unitary and atomic structures that are called names, the chains of substitutions of names in which, for example, the nominal effect *différance* is itself *enmeshed*, carried off, reinscribed."[19]

Obviously there is a decisive connection to be drawn between Derrida's *différance* and Beckett's "unnamable." Because the relevant scholarship has generally overlooked this connection—even failed to recognize Derrida's insistent references to the "unnamable"—my purpose here is to sketch out an approach to the subject that attempts to understand how *différance* and the "unnamable" are related to each other.[20] My attention therefore focuses, at least in part, on how Beckett takes up the philosophical problems and procedures associated with *différance* and then reconfigures them in ways that are essentially narrative—how he, in effect, narrates *différance*. More generally, I shall suggest the ways *The Unnamable* has attempted to think beyond the ends of man, ways that do not involve simply replacing one metaphysical system with another negative or "antimetaphysical" system. Here again the connection between *différance* and the "unnamable" becomes especially important. For the persistent problem in Beckett's novels, beginning with *Murphy* and extending through *Malone Dies*, has been how to "overcome" modernity without falling back into its logic of origins and endings, of teleology and transcendence. In an effort to avoid this problem, much postmodern discourse has turned away from the categorical and oppositional thinking characteristic of the Enlightenment tradition, preferring instead an *écriture* that seeks to operate both "inside" and "outside" the tradition. It is through such a *différantial* discourse that Beckett and Derrida have sought to explore what lies beyond the end of man, a figure that resists definition, a figure whom they both call "unnamable."

With this in mind, I focus in this chapter on three issues: first, I examine how Beckett dismantles the narrator/narrated dialectic by submitting it to the operations of *différance*; second, I chart the final deconstruction of the cogito and relate its demise to the "end of man"; third, I trace the development of what Derrida calls the "beginning of writing," a mode of discourse that dislocates traditional metaphysical categories, while projecting itself into something approaching pure textuality, a place where word and unword contest for dominion.

～・

If *Malone Dies* carries us to the end of the book, *The Unnamable* offers us our first glimpse of what lies beyond: the beginning of writing. In moving toward a condition of pure textuality, toward a literature that seeks to free itself from representation and expression, Beckett takes up once again the problem of the narrator/narrated. As we have seen, in *Malone Dies* the narrator/narrated opposition functions like a Gestalt image in which the viewer has transposed figure and ground so often that they have become interchangeable, if not indistinguishable. Yet however volatile these terms may be, however eroded the opposition they imply, the larger dialectic that defines them remains in force: in *Malone Dies* we may still speak meaningfully of a narrator (Malone) and a narrated (Sapo and Macmann), even if this serves only to prepare those moments when the one engulfs the other. In *The Unnamable* this is no longer the case. Here, Beckett succeeds in collapsing the narrator/narrated into an undifferentiated third term, the mediating slash that formerly stood as the sign of demarcation but now disperses itself into an interstitial zone, the space of an in-between that not only refuses to resolve itself into either of these two terms but renders impossible their very articulation.

Certainly there are moments in *The Unnamable* that recall what by comparison must strike us as the balmy days of the earlier novels, moments in which the narrator draws lines of distinction between himself and the narrated, despite the complications and involutions this necessarily implies. A passage like the following is unusual but not extraordinary:

> Perhaps it is time I paid a little attention to myself, for a change. I shall be reduced to it sooner or later. At first sight it seems impossible. Me utter me, in the same foul breath as my creatures. . . . Yes, I will say it, and of *me alone*. Impassive, still and mute, Malone revolves, a stranger forever to my infirmities, one who is not as I can never not be. (15–16, my emphasis)

Such a passage, insisting on a recognizable boundary between narrator and narrated, might well have been drawn from *Malone Dies*. Admittedly, a linguistic pinhole has opened up in the wall that separates these terms, and the "me alone" has begun to seep into the "Malone," but while this compromises the binary opposition, it does not destroy the dialectical relation. Indeed, all of the effects described here depend entirely on treating these terms as contraries. We may find other examples of this sort of interplay between narrator and narrated,[21] but the dialectic it implies generally does not operate in *The Unnamable* for the simple reason that the larger framework within which these terms gained an oppositional force has ceased to be available. What results is an absolutely new kind of novel, one without narrator or narrated.

Of course, these two terms already contain within themselves the logic of their own dissolution. It will be remembered that Beckett uses "narrator/narrated" to describe what he saw as a newly emergent character in the trilogy, but it is important to notice that this phrase leaves the relation between these two terms teasingly ambiguous.[22] If we associate the first term with the subject or agent of narration and the second with the object or recipient of narration, then this phrase represents a simple opposition: the narrator versus the narrated. If, however, we understand the second term as modifying the first, as descriptively filling it out, then this phrase represents not an opposition but an identity; not narrator versus narrated, but narrator as narrated. Such a reading of the narrator/narrated— it represents an opposition, it represents an identity—recalls the aporetic play of *différance*. For Beckett this play is also present in, and indeed helps to constitute, what we might call the Cartesian moment, that point in time when the subject attempts to predicate itself, when it attempts to project itself into some external or objective form. Take, for example, the simple assertion, "I say I." In one sense, the two "I"s in this sentence are identical, referring, as they presumably do, to a single and unitary subject. Yet in another sense, these two "I"s are not merely different but antithetical, since one functions as a subject and the other as an object—or, to shift our frame of reference, since one functions as a narrator and the other as a narrated.

Now it so happens that Beckett actually uses this hypothetical sentence in the opening paragraph of *The Unnamable*, but, crucially, he adds a comma between "I" and "say," so that the sentence becomes: "I, say I" (3). The effect of this comma is to reconfigure entirely the dynamic patterning of *différance* in the sentence. Rather than moving back and forth in a simple bipolar fashion between the two I's, *différance* now circulates around, through, even within each of these terms. Thus, depending on how the sentence is construed, subject-object functions may be distributed in any number of ways. Consider, for instance, the first "I." There is a strong predisposition among English readers to treat it as a subject, since it occupies the initial position in the sentence and is followed by a conjugated verb. Obviously, the comma interrupts and reverses such a reading, but this reading is nevertheless implied by the norms of English usage, and that means that Beckett's sentence (with the comma) begins by referring us to a more standard form in which the first "I" functions as a subject.

Once we move beyond this standard form to Beckett's actual sentence, matters become more complicated still. There are at least three different ways of making sense out of the first "I" as it appears in Beckett's text. First, we may read it as an intensifier, an anticipatory repetition that emphasizes the second "I" and is therefore grammatically linked to it, in which event it functions as the implied object of the verb "say." Second, we may read the first "I" as a simple exhibition or representation of the self, a kind of ostensive gesture that is syntactically unrelated to the rest of the sentence, in which event it functions either as an implied subject, which has no verb or object attached to it, or—perhaps more plausibly—as a fragment without any real grammatical function. Finally, we may treat the first "I" (and for that matter the second) as part of a citational form, reading "I, say I" on the analogy of "cheese, say, cheese" or "no, say, no," in which event what little grammatical determinacy it retained in the second reading is lost, and it ends up functioning neither as subject nor as object.[23]

If I have lingered over this little sentence, it is because it demonstrates in miniature how *différance* generally functions at the level of narrative in *The Unnamable*. We may approach this larger narrative function by considering a passage that occurs early on in the novel:

> Decidedly Basil is becoming important, I'll call him Mahood instead, I prefer that, I'm queer. It was he told me stories about me, lived in my stead, issued forth from me, came back to me, entered back into me, heaped stories on my head. I don't know how it was done. . . . It is his voice which has often, always, mingled with mine, and sometimes drowned it completely. Until he left me for good, or refused to leave me any more, I don't know. (29)

It is difficult to know where, or even how, to begin analyzing such a statement. A "character" called Mahood told stories about someone we suppose to be the "narrator." This Mahood lived in the place of the "narrator," issued forth from the "narrator," and entered into the "narrator." Yet it is not at all clear how we can make sense out of these different assertions. For if Mahood issued forth from the narrator, if he was the narrator's creation, then Mahood was acting as his representative, and the stories are finally about the narrator himself. But if Mahood entered into the narrator, if he in effect took possession of him, then the narrator was acting as Mahood's representative, and the stories are finally about Mahood. Amid these competing claims, this play of *différance*, who is the narrator and who is the narrated? It is ultimately impossible to say. As the very awkwardness of my own language reveals—an awkwardness that has led me to speak within quotation marks—the real difficulty here consists in attempting to enforce traditional categories like "narrator" and "narrated" on a text that systematically denies such categories, on a text that fundamentally challenges the concepts of agency, action, and reflexivity.

Another way of putting this: narrator and narrated no longer function as useful descriptive categories for approaching a novel like *The Unnamable*. In their place, I would like to propose two new terms: *locutor* and *dislocution*. With the first term, I hope to dispel those assumptions we normally associate with the word "narrator"—namely, that narrative utterance is unitary (consisting of a single voice throughout), that it is originary (behind it there is an identifiable source), and that it is authoritative (it commands a privileged position of knowledge). The locutor should not, in other words, be thought of as a character so much as a depersonalized function, a locus or site from which discourse emanates. With the second term, I mean to suggest that the locutor has no fixed residence, that it carries on a kind of itinerant discourse, a locution without a location. Dislocution means that the "identity" of the locutor is shifting and inconstant: unlike a narrator, a locutor may speak with Basil's voice in one breath and Mahood's in the next.[24]

We may begin to observe how dislocution—or *différantial* play within the narrative voice—functions in *The Unnamable* by focusing on the early part of the novel, which deals with the so-called stories of Mahood.

⌣·

The first of these stories tells of the efforts of the debilitated Mahood to return to his family, which is now housed in a rotunda. The story begins by positing a contingent identity between the speaker and Mahood: "At the particular moment I am referring to, I mean when I took myself for Mahood" (40). This identity is sustained for several pages during which Mahood appears to speak in the first person, but it is interrupted when a sudden telescoping of personal pronouns dislocates the narrative center: "According to Mahood *I* never reached them [his family]. . . . But not so fast, otherwise *we'll* never arrive. It's no longer *I* in any case. *He'll* never reach us if he doesn't get a move on. He looks as if he had slowed down, since last year"

(42, my emphasis). Within the space of a few sentences, the narrative refers to locutor/Mahood in the first-person singular, the first-person plural, and the third-person singular. One way to read this passage and make traditional narrative sense out of it is to assume that there has been a simple shift in focalization: we initially see from locutor/Mahood's perspective (hence he refers to himself as "I" and "we"), but then the point of view changes to the parents in the rotunda, and we see from their perspective (hence Mahood is referred to as "he"). There is, however, another, equally plausible explanation. From time to time, a group called the "committee," or simply "they," obtrudes its voice upon the narrative, usually to complain that if the locutor does not get moving, he'll never arrive. Perhaps, then, this shift in focalization means that we are seeing through the eyes not of the parents but of the mysterious committee. Both readings are feasible, and there is no ultimately compelling reason for preferring one to the other. The larger point to be made is that whichever interpretation we choose, the result remains the same: a speaking voice has dispersed itself across a field of grammatical and referential possibilities; a speaking voice has, in effect, dislocuted itself.

If it is never clear where we should situate Mahood with respect to his narrative, it is equally unclear what that narrative is. A story of return is conventionally teleological, building toward the moment when the wanderer achieves his homecoming. Beckett exploits this basic narrative pattern by deriving—however parodically—all the suspense of his narration from the simple question, Will Mahood arrive?

> In a word I was returning to the fold, admittedly reduced, and doubtless fated to be even more so, before I could be restored to my wife and parents. . . . I kept saying to myself, Yonder is the nest you should never have left, there your dear absent ones are awaiting your return, patiently, and you must be patient. It was swarming with them, grandpa, grandma, little mother and the eight or nine brats. With their eyes glued to the slits and their hearts going out to me they surveyed my efforts. (41)

The question of Mahood's return is, however, never answered, or more precisely, it is simultaneously answered "yes" and "no." Thus, according to one version of the story, Mahood turns back after he learns that his family has been wiped out by ptomaine poisoning:

"The misfortune experienced by my family and brought to my notice first by the noise of their agony, then by the smell of their corpses, had caused me to turn back" (47). Yet, according to another version, one that insists upon its own authenticity ("Let us consider now what really occurred," 49), Mahood not only reaches the rotunda but, in a bit of Gothic extravagance, also tramples under foot the decomposed remains of his family (49–50). In the end, however, the locutor rejects both these accounts of Mahood's homecoming, suggesting a third possibility that is entirely unrelated to the first two: "But enough of this nonsense. I was never anywhere but here, no one ever got me out of here" (50). One of the most fundamental of all plot types, the *nostos*, has generated three different formulations: the hero did not return, the hero did return, the hero never left. *Différance* has, yet again, entered into the narrative, transforming a situation from either/or to both/and.

The second Mahood story concerns an armless, legless, speechless creature who inhabits an urn in the meat-packing district of an unnamed city. Once more, the reader is given to understand that the story is related by Mahood but that it is about the locutor: "I might as well tell another of Mahood's stories and no more about it, to be understood in the way I was given to understand it, namely as being about me" (53). And, once more, the locutor is caught up by, propelled through, and finally lost within a sequence of shifting pronouns: "It's usually with sticks *they* put *me* out of *their* agony, the idea being to demonstrate, to the backers, and bystanders, that *I* had a beginning, and an end" (64, my emphasis). Of course, beginnings and ends, those definitional thresholds that make binary oppositions possible, are precisely what *différance* and dislocution break down. Mahood's second story is concerned with just such a threshold, the boundary where issues of identity and difference, presence and absence are most acutely felt, the boundary separating life from death. The locutor appears to approach this boundary, perhaps even to cross it, when suddenly and unaccountably he ceases to attract attention. The people who pass before his urn fail to notice him; the woman who has ministered to his needs stops attending him. It is as though he no longer exists: "That the jar is really standing where they say, all right, I wouldn't dream of denying it. . . . No, I merely doubt that I am in it" (78). Under the circumstances, the reader is reduced to asking that most embarrassing of all questions: What, literally, has happened? As was the case in the first Mahood story, several explanations are presented that, given the logic of traditional narrative, attempt to make sense out of this strange turn of events. Perhaps Mahood has suffered a stroke but tenaciously lives on; or perhaps (less plausibly) he has died but miraculously speaks on.

There is, however, another way of reading Mahood's second story: dislocation, carried to its logical extreme, has dissolved not merely the idea of a stable identity but of any identity at all. As a result, the locutor now simultaneously experiences himself as same and other, as present and absent:

> For this feeling of being entirely enclosed, and yet nothing touching me, is new. The sawdust no longer presses against my stumps, I don't know where I end. I left it yesterday, Mahood's world, the street, the chophouse, the slaughter. . . . There will never be another woman wanting me in vain to live, my shadow at evening will not darken the ground. The stories of Mahood are ended. (80)

This is an entirely new incarnation for the locutor, one in which the body is marked out as a contained and yet boundless space, a network of mobile and shifting surfaces that recede even as they enclose. But dislocation has here leveled not only the defining structures of the Cartesian inheritance—of subject and object, of inside and outside—it has also swept away the narrative framework that helped sustain those structures, the framework of narrator and narrated. "The stories of Mahood are ended" is as terminal as Prospero's farewell to magic. What lies beyond, or at least elsewhere, is an austere and impossible geometry shorn of the accidents of time and place, presence and absence, identity and difference—an unimagined limit that itself transgresses all limits and, in the process, admits locutor/Mahood to "that peace where he neither is, nor is not, and where the language dies that permits of such expressions. Two falsehoods, two trappings, to be borne to the end, before I can be let loose, alone, in the unthinkable unspeakable" (65–66). In what we were once content to call the "end," locutor/Mahood does not die or even fade away, but undergoes a transfiguration of sorts, a kind of encounter at Colonus, which has the effect of dislocating him within the contours of the human, of redefining him according to some radically new order of things.

‿·

And yet, to paraphrase Beckett, the danger is in the neatness of the *différance*. For if in moving toward the "unnamable" what Beckett proposes to eliminate are precisely limits, borders, margins, then he will not want to mark out the passage beyond them in too insistent or decisive a fashion—to indicate, for example, the frontier that transcends frontiers or the outer boundary of boundaries. The end of Mahood, cannot, in other words, stand in any simple or direct relation to what we might hypothesize as the beginning of the "unnamable." As Derrida's own language suggests, *différance* does not produce the "unnamable" so much as generate the conditions under which it might appear. Thus, the post-Mahood section of Beckett's novel presents itself not as an unambiguous movement from one thing to another, a simple accession to unnamability, but rather as a series of dissolving images, fade-ins and fade-outs, which have the effect of gradually, almost imperceptibly, shifting our frame of reference, of carrying us away from whatever residual identity Mahood commanded and delivering us into the murky regions that lie beyond. It is there that we discover the proto-character, Worm.

Of course, Worm is not the "unnamable"—if he were, he would not be named—and, as we have seen, the transition to what lies beyond Mahood is necessarily vague and ambiguous. Still, as difficult as it is to fix a boundary between Mahood and Worm, they are separated by one crucial distinction—the distinction between the human and the nonhuman. For while Mahood is both literally and figuratively reduced as a man—bereft of family, of senses, even of body parts—his character nonetheless continues to function within a system of classification that is identifiably human. Indeed, as Mahood's name suggests,[25] the one attribute he retains amid the otherwise complete collapse of his identity is a measure of humanity—a humanity that ultimately makes possible the very dislocations and dislocutions we have observed. Worm, on the other hand, occupies an evolutionary order that is essentially different from Mahood's. If Mahood is only minimally human, then Worm, as his name suggests, is barely protoplasmic: "His senses tell him nothing, nothing about himself, nothing about the rest, and this distinction is beyond him. Feeling nothing, knowing nothing, he exists nevertheless" (82).

The larger point to be made here is that while Mahood represents a terminal moment in the humanist tradition, Worm represents some unspecified *jenseits*. As we have seen, "The Ends of Man" contemplates the same question that *The Unnamable* struggles to answer: How can man decisively move beyond the philosophical and narrative conventions of the West, when the whole notion of such transcendence—of the establishment of a point of reference outside or beyond discourse—is itself intimately bound up with the Western tradition? As I indicated earlier, Derrida responds by calling for a kind of "plural" writing based on *différance*, a writing that simultaneously deconstructs metaphysics from "within" and assaults it from "without."

The Unnamable may be read precisely as an example of this new kind of writing, one that brings together Derrida's two modes of deconstruction through the stories of Mahood and Worm, stories that are at once complementary and oppositional. Thus, Mahood's stories deconstruct from the inside: they come to us before the end of man, and while they seek to undermine the humanist tradition, they do so from a position within that tradition. Worm's stories—if we may call them that—assault from the outside: they attempt to project themselves beyond the end of man, and while they can only present what Derrida calls a "*trompe-l'oeil* perspective," they glance back at the humanist tradition from an external vantage point. The kind of contrast I wish to draw between Mahood and Worm becomes more explicit when we consider the changes these characters undergo during their stories, the divergent paths along which their narratives move. In the case of Mahood, this movement involves a shift from restricted mobility to absolute fixity, from limited human interaction to radical solipsism, from diminished sensory being to an almost extinguished consciousness. In other words, while Mahood begins as a human figure, that humanity is relentlessly stripped away, emptied out, reduced, and dispersed. Worm, in contrast, seems always already beyond the end of man, and insofar as there is any narrative movement in his story, it consists of an effort to "reclaim" him, to return him to the humanist fold, to bring him back across the great poststructural divide and make him a "man" once more.

Hence, the post-Mahood section of the novel presents itself as a kind of narrative siege in which Worm inhabits a "den" (99), and "they" try to lure him to the wall (97), "where they have made other holes through which to pass their arms and seize him" (98). By drawing him out of his enclosure, Worm's "prompters" hope to return him to a recognizably human condition and, in the process, to "bring him alive" as a character. To this end, they invest Worm with a rudimentary sensorium, consisting of an embryonic ear (90, 93, 95–96) and eye (97, 101). It soon appears, however, that in his evolutionary drift toward sentience, Worm is "getting humanized" (101), that from that ear and eye, a head may grow ("These millions of different sounds . . . are all one requires to sprout a head," 93), that on that head, a face may blossom ("A face, how encouraging that would be, if it could be a face," 105). Provided with a human attribute or two, Worm threatens to return from the great beyond, a sort of Mahood redux, mannequinized and propped up in a novelistic display window:

> It might even pause, open its mouth, raise its eyebrows, bless its soul, stutter, mutter, howl, groan and finally shut up. . . . And even should the notion of time dawn on his darkness, at this punctual image of the countenance everlasting, who could blame him? Involving very naturally that of space, they have taken to going hand in hand, in certain quarters, it's safer. And the game would be won, lost and won, he'd be somehow suddenly among us, among the rendez-vous, and people saying, Look at old Worm, waiting for his sweetheart, and the flowers, look at the flowers, you'd think he was asleep, you know old Worm, waiting for his love, and the daisies, look at the daisies.[26] (105–6)

But in Worm country all assertions are made in the subjunctive, so that if the scandalous appearance of an eye and an ear threatens to humanize the locutor, he can sweep it aside through a simple act of negative fiat: "I don't believe in the eye either, there's nothing here, nothing to see, nothing to see with" (123); "Do I feel an ear, frankly now, do I feel an ear, well frankly now I don't" (134). Certainly there are moments when it seems as though Worm can wade through the epistemological clutter to some naturally ordered space, a philosophical high ground on which he might erect his Cartesian closet, from which he might systematically doubt his way to apodictic knowledge. Hence, the occasional effort to wrest a hard-edged chunk of certainty from the empirical mess:

> Assume notably henceforward that the thing said and the thing heard have a common source, resisting for this purpose the temptation to call in question the possibility of assuming anything whatever. Situate this source in me, without specifying where exactly, no finicking, anything is preferable to the consciousness of third parties and, more

generally speaking, of an outer world. Carry if necessary this process of compression to the point of abandoning all other postulates than that of a deaf half-wit, hearing nothing of what he says and understanding even less. Evoke at painful junctures, when discouragement threatens to raise its head, the image of a vast cretinous mouth, red, blubber and slobbering, in solitary confinement. . . . Better, ascribe to me a body. Better still, arrogate to me a mind. Speak of a world of my own, sometimes referred to as the inner, without choking. Doubt no more.[27] (144–45)

The naturalized explanation of the kind we saw a fading Mahood employ ("Did I have a stroke, while I was meditating?" 80) is here used as a desperation measure by a speaker who can make plausible sense of his situation only by imagining himself a deaf half-wit. Nothing is, however, definitively established by locutor/Worm, and no sooner has this admirably Cartesian model been advanced than it is superseded by a new and, as it turns out, contradictory model: "Yes, in my life, since we must call it so, there were three things, the inability to speak, the inability to be silent, and solitude" (153).

This last instance of *différance*—the inability to speak together with the inability to be silent—recalls the two narratives we have been examining: that of the aphasic Mahood who somehow manages to speak and that of the mouthless Worm who cannot manage to keep silent.[28] What emerges from the interplay between these two narratives is a third term, one that belongs to neither of the preceding terms and yet is identified with both. Having associated this third term with the operations of *différance*, I want to suggest how Beckett uses it to approach the "unnamable." But before we can begin to follow Beckett toward this third term, we must consider two points: how the novel depicts itself as a radically depersonalized form of *écriture*, and how it dislocates the idea of the structured and centered whole.

⌣･

We have observed various instances in *The Unnamable* where a speaking voice loses its center, carrying on a kind of errant or itinerant discourse. This dislocution grows even more confused as we begin to discern, amid all the jostling words of locutor/Mahood/Worm, an occasional verbal trace of "they" or "the master." The last two figures function, along with locutor/Mahood/Worm, as part

of an elaborate "writing-machine" in which dictation is given and
a report prepared. Initially, this involves nothing more than an act
of audition followed as faithfully as possible by an act of iteration:

> But let us proceed with method. . . . I shall transmit the words as re-
> ceived, by the ear, or roared through a trumpet into the arsehole, in
> all their purity, and in the same order, as far as possible. This infini-
> tesimal lag, between arrival and departure, this trifling delay in evac-
> uation, is all I have to worry about. (86)

Sometimes the locutor hears all the dictation, sometimes only part:
"I hear everything, every word they say, it's the only sound, as if I
were speaking, to myself, out loud in the end you don't know any
more, a voice that never stops, where it's coming from" (114); "I
must doze off from time to time, with open eyes, and yet nothing
changes, ever. Gaps, there have always been gaps, it's the voice stopping, it's the voice failing to carry me, what can it matter" (114).[29]
Nevertheless, it is assumed that what will emerge from this, as it did
in the case of *Molloy* and *Malone Dies*, is a piece of writing, a kind
of secretary's "report of the proceedings":

> When all goes silent, and comes to an end, it will be because the
> words have been said, those it behoved to say. . . . They have to be
> ratified by the proper authority, that takes time, he's far from here,
> they bring him the verbatim report of the proceedings, once in a way,
> he knows the words that count, it's he who chose them, in the mean-
> time the voice continues, while the messenger goes towards the mas-
> ter, and while the master examines the report, and while the messen-
> ger comes back with the verdict, the words continue. (115)

The famous Balzacian formulation of the novelist as secretary to society has here been reduced to an almost imperceptible afterimage
of itself, as the Cartesian ground that rendered it possible by opposing subject to object, self to society, is now cut away, leaving the
voice as origin and presence suspended somewhere beyond narrative accessibility. To put the matter differently, it is as though Beckett had seized upon Balzac's falsely modest description of himself as
a mere recorder and insisted upon construing it in a rigorously lit-
eralistic fashion, with the result that the novelist, on Balzac's own
account, ceases to be the source of his work. Into the void left by
this absent authority there rush, or seem to rush, "they" and "the
master."

The sense of dislocution in *The Unnamable* becomes all the more
acute as we attempt to plot the ever-receding series of terms that
appear to stabilize and identify the speaking voice. We have already
observed that Basil is Mahood, Mahood is related to Worm, and
all three have at one time or another spoken through or been spoken by the locutor. Various terms that seem to stand outside these
three characters are nonetheless connected with them, as we learn
when it is revealed that Basil-Mahood is one of the delegates or
"they":

> There were four or five of them at me, they called that presenting their
> report. One in particular, Basil I think he was called, filled me with
> hatred. Without opening his mouth, fastening on me his eyes like cin-
> ders with all their seeing, he changed me a little more each time into
> what he wanted me to be. Is he still glaring at me, from the shadows.
> Is he still usurping my name, the one they foisted on me, up there in
> their world, patiently, from season to season. (13)

In the course of this passage, Basil shifts from being one of "them,"
part of the authority that manipulates the likes of the locutor, to being a mere agent who is himself "foisted" on the locutor, who himself becomes the locutor. This kind of dislocution continues as "they"
at once appear to be the source of authority that controls characters, as well as the object of authority that is itself controlled:

> [These voices] make me say that I can't be Worm, the inexpungable.
> Who make me say that I am he perhaps, as they are. Who make me
> say that since I can't be he I must be he. That since I couldn't be Ma-
> hood, as I might have been, I must be Worm, as I cannot be. But is it
> still they who say that when I have failed to be Worm I'll be Mahood,
> automatically, on the rebound? (84)

> But for them there would be nothing, not even Worm, he's an idea
> they have, a word they use, when speaking of them. (111)

> They say they, speaking of them, to make me think it is I who am
> speaking. Or I say they, speaking of God knows what, to make me
> think it is not I who am speaking. (115)

If it is not clear whether "they" manipulate other characters or
are themselves manipulated, there nevertheless stands beyond them
the possibility of a more coherent authority: "the master." We have
already sketched out Worm's situation: he occupies a den or lair and
is encircled by "them," who as a group attempt to lure him out into

the light of day. They, in turn, are acting on the orders of the master to whom they are ultimately answerable: "Yes, they'll go . . . towards their master, who will punish them, or who will spare them" (108). The locutor even considers the possibility that the master will force them to return to Worm and try once more to extricate him from his nonexistence: "For they may come back, long after the lights are spent, having pleaded for years in vain before the master and failed to convince him there is nothing to be done, with Worm, for Worm. Then all will start over again" (109).

The master exercises his prerogatives like a god. Thus, while it is "they" who brandish the rod of punishment over Worm, exacting from him a limited cooperation "under pain of supplementary thunderbolts" (110), this Jovian authority originates in the master who has conferred it upon his delegates ("They know how to cause suffering, the master explained [it] to them," 110) but who continues to exhibit the vanity and imperiousness of an Old Testament deity ("He is there, says the master, somewhere, do as I tell you, bring him before me, he's lacking to my glory," 113). It is, however, no more possible to locate authority in the master than it was to locate it in Basil, Mahood, Worm, or the delegates, for this master is susceptible to the same kind of dispersion through multiplication that affects all the characters in *The Unnamable*. Just as Basil becomes Mahood and Mahood becomes Worm, just as "he" becomes "they," the master finally becomes a whole board of masters:

> But before I forget, there may be more than one, a whole college of tyrants, differing in their views as to what should be done with me, in conclave since time began or a little later, listening to me from time to time, then breaking up for a meal or a game of cards. (31)

And because he may not be alone, because his power may be shared among others, he cannot be held responsible for what he creates, nor can he be said to exercise authority over his work:

> But perhaps I malign him unjustly, my good master, perhaps he is not solitary like me, not free like me, but associated with others, equally good, equally concerned with my welfare, but differing as to its nature. Every day, up above, I mean up above me, from one set hour to another set hour, everything there being set and settled except what is to be done with me, they assemble to discuss me. Or perhaps it's a meeting of deputies, with instructions to elaborate a tentative agreement. (35)

Authority is, in the final analysis, completely dislocuted; "I," "they," "the master" are all relieved of narrative responsibility: "We've been told a lot of lies, he's been told a lot of lies, who he, the master, by whom, no one knows, the everlasting third party, he's the one to blame, for this state of affairs, the master's not to blame, neither are they, neither am I . . . I them, the master, myself, we are all innocent" (123–24). In the world of the writing-machine, authority loses its force, its definition, its center.

⌣•

In "Structure, Sign, and Play" the emergence of the "unnamable" is associated, as we have seen, with the double bind of postmodernity: its inability either to work within the metaphysical tradition or to move beyond it. Derrida's essay is important, however, not only for its treatment of the "unnamable" but also for a number of other tropes that are present in Beckett's work as well. Indeed, in many ways, "Structure, Sign, and Play" can be read as a kind of extended commentary on *The Unnamable*, one that is all the more valuable for not naming its subject, or, more precisely, for referring to it only obliquely and belatedly. While Derrida's essay takes up a number of themes and motifs that are significant to Beckett, I would like to focus on one in particular: the centered circle as an image of authority and control.[30]

A quick survey will show the larger importance of this conceit to *The Unnamable* as a whole. At the novel's outset, the locutor appears to have entered into a kind of celestial machinery, one whose precise operation remains obscure but which appears to function on the model of planetary revolution: "I too am in perpetual motion, accompanied by Malone, as the earth by its moon" (9). A similar circling motif informs the two Mahood stories: after returning from his "adventures" abroad, locutor/Mahood finds himself "in a kind of vast yard or campus. . . . At the centre of this enclosure stood a small rotunda. . . . It was swarming with [my family]. . . . So we turned, in our respective orbits, I without, they within" (41). And even after being confined to his urn, locutor/Mahood still rests within a circular container, as though the rotunda that housed his family had shrunken to the proportions of his body: "Stuck like a sheaf of flowers in a deep jar . . . I am at rest at last" (55). Finally, although Worm's abode resists precise description, we are told that he is surrounded by the delegates or "they," who wheel about him in a circle: "Let them stay . . . where they are, turning in a ring" (100).

At one level, Beckett appears to be exploiting the idea, as old as Plato's *Timaeus*, that because divinity is perfect it manifests itself as a circle and that because it is omniscient and omnipotent it occupies the center of the circle.[31] Within this context, the traditional narrator is figured as a god or first mover about whom all creatures turn in obedient adoration. No doubt with this in mind, the locutor we encounter at the beginning of the novel is anxious to establish himself at the center of his narrative universe, and he therefore devotes a good deal of his soliloquy to worrying about his position relative to Malone:

> I like to think I occupy the centre, but nothing is less certain. In a sense I would be better off at the circumference, since my eyes are always fixed in the same direction. But I am certainly not at the circumference. For if I were it would follow that Malone, wheeling about me as he does, would issue from the enceinte at every revolution, which is manifestly impossible. But does he in fact wheel, does he not perhaps simply pass before me in a straight line? No, he wheels, I feel it, and about me, like a planet about its sun. (8–9)

Unable to deliver himself to any point outside his own frame of reference, he cannot, on the one hand, satisfactorily describe the larger pattern of movement within it, except by way of conjecture: "From centre to circumference in any case it is a far cry and I may well be situated somewhere between the two" (9). On the other hand, if occupying the center functions as the narrative sign of divine authority, then the locutor is, by his own admission, all too human: "Impassive, still and mute, Malone revolves, a stranger forever to my infirmities, one who is not as I can never not be. I am motionless in vain, he is the god. . . . I alone am man and all the rest divine" (16).

In the first of the Mahood stories, the locutor is once more swept through the circuit of something like a planetary motion, but there is no longer any question of his occupying the center, that privileged position having now been staked out by his family. Indeed, as we have already remarked, one of the issues that arise in this section of the novel is precisely the location of authority, and in a passage I quoted earlier, the narrative center shifts from the locutor, to locutor/Mahood, to Mahood's family. But if the family has established itself at the center, it becomes quite literally a dead center, a point of convergence where nothing converges. That the family should through a kind of ironic prank predecease locutor/Mahood, thereby undoing his *nostos*, is itself sufficient to argue against their own centrality to his story. But beyond this, the question remains open as to whether he ever arrives at this increasingly vague and receding center, whether he ever left it, whether it even exists.

The second Mahood story presents a minimalist version of the locutor gazing upon an orbiting Malone:

> Stuck like a sheaf of flowers in a deep jar, its neck flush with my mouth, on the side of a quiet street near the shambles, I am at rest at last. If I turn, I shall not say my head, but my eyes, free to roll where they list, I can see the statue of the apostle of horse's meat, a bust. His pupilless eyes of stone are fixed upon me. That makes four, with those of my creator, omnipresent, do not imagine I flatter myself I am privileged. (55)

The locutor is "at rest," he "turns," he "rolls" his eyes. Within his cylindrical enclosure, he has contracted and reduced Mahood's rotations, localized them to a few bodily movements. In addition to the idea of a shrunken and fixed orbit, the image of a higher authority is again evoked. In the first case, the locutor was centered but mortal and therefore presumably without omniscient authority; in the second, he was at the circumference, and authority appeared centerless; in the third, it is impossible to say where the center is, and the image of authority ("the creator") finds its earthly counterpart in the parodic "apostle of horse's meat" that looks upon locutor/Mahood with unseeing eyes.

Two patterns are discernible in these three scenes. One involves a general undermining of the notion of centered authority: an assault on the idea that the center can be located, that it is the place of authority, that there is any authority to be centered. The other pattern is one of diminishment and contraction, the scope of the circle gradually shrinking from the planetary movements of the locutor at the novel's beginning, to Mahood spiralling in on his family, to Mahood's confinement in his jar.

These three instances have their final elaboration in the case of the encircled Worm. Here, the idea of centered authority is inverted, as Worm occupies the center (97) while "they" move about him, "turning in a ring" (100), despite the fact that authority would seem to rest with the delegates. What we confront here, however, is more than a simple inversion of classic relations between center and circumference, since, as we saw earlier, authority finally locates itself not with the delegates, not with the master, not with anyone or anything. It has been dispersed beyond itself and its system. What results, then, is the deconstruction of the center as a concept, a deconstruction that, as "Structure, Sign, and Play" suggests, necessarily follows from the logic of what the center means and how it operates:

> Thus it has always been thought that the center, which is by definition unique, constituted that very thing within a structure which while governing the structure, escapes structurality. This is why classical thought concerning structure could say that the center is, paradoxically, *within* the structure and *outside it*. The center is at the center of the totality, and yet, since the center does not belong to the totality (is not part of the totality), the totality *has its center elsewhere*. The center is not the center.[32]

For Derrida the history of the metaphysics of presence, the metaphysics that depends on ideas like subject and object, finds its imagistic expression in forms like center and circumference: "It could be shown that all the names related to fundamentals, to principles, or to the center have always designated an invariable presence—*eidos, archē, telos, energia, ousia* (essence, existence, substance, subject) *alētheia*, transcendentality, consciousness, God, man, and so forth."[33] Beckett is particularly interested in exploring one of the associations Derrida adduces, that which imagines the phenomenological subject as occupying the center of a circular field of consciousness. At several points, *The Unnamable* solidifies the circle into a sphere and identifies it with a speaking voice: "It is a great smooth ball I carry on my shoulders, featureless" (23); "I'm a big talking ball. . . . And after all why a ball, rather than something else, and why big? . . . All that matters is that I am round and hard" (24). The ball, solid and round, serves to evoke, as a number of related passages show, the head as seat of consciousness, seat of voice, seat of narration: "I shall begin to know something, just enough for it to turn out to be the same place as always . . . which is perhaps merely the inside of my distant skull where once I wandered, now am fixed" (19–20). This point is made all the more emphatically when the idea of the sphere as head is directly connected with the motif of the orbiting satellite: "I on whom all dangles, better still, about whom, much better, all turns, dizzily, yes yes, don't protest, all spins, it's a head, I'm in a head" (119).

But if these circles, spheres, and orbits all seem to suggest that the novel has located itself within the head and that narration and consciousness are somehow identical, this is simply so that Beckett can dismantle what is, after all, a "central" part of the modernist tradition. Thus, the locutor's claim that he is fixed inside his distant skull begins to unravel when he describes himself as "lost for tininess, or straining against the walls, with my head, my hands, my feet, my back" (20). The image, evoking what Beckett has elsewhere called "the art of incarceration,"[34] offers the spectacle of a human figure struggling to find some impossible point of purchase as he presses against the inside of his own head, using not only his four limbs but also his own head. Other passages also serve to deconstruct the idea that we should locate the speaking voice within the head by offering a series of alternate explanations that effectively undermine any simple identification between narration and consciousness:

> And sometimes I say to myself I am in a head, it's terror makes me say it, and the longing to be in safety, surrounded on all sides by massive bone. (88)

> If I speak of a head, referring to me, it's because I hear it being spoken of. (92)

> No, no, no head either, anything you like, but not a head, in his head he doesn't go anywhere either, I've tried, lashed to the stake, blindfold[ed], gagged to the gullet, you take the air, under the elms in se, murmuring Shelley, impervious to the shafts. Yes, a head, but solid, solid bone, and you imbedded in it, like a fossil in the rock. (148)

We have been following the way in which Beckett has delivered himself into something approaching a pure textuality, a language of the unword that stands beyond or in-between those organizing concepts that have traditionally ordered the world: concepts like subject and object, inside and outside, narrator and narrated, center and circumference. *The Unnamable*, however, moves beyond the mere deconstruction of nineteenth-century fiction, a deconstruction we have followed from *Murphy* through *Malone Dies*. What is genuinely revolutionary about this novel is the way it does more than simply dramatize its failure to enter into something approximating Murphy's third zone. At last, with this final term in the trilogy, itself a kind of third zone, we gain access to the "big blooming buzzing confusion."

⌣·

One way to understand *The Unnamable*'s movement toward a third term is to examine the larger structure of the novel, a structure that appears to be predominantly ternary, involving an opening section devoted to Mahood's stories, a middle section devoted to Worm's stories, and a concluding section that is plotless and characterless.[35] The development of this third section is especially important within the larger context of the trilogy, since the two previous novels in the series were clearly binary in their organization, which consisted in the case of *Molloy* of a double narrative (Molloy's and Moran's) and in the case of *Malone Dies* of a double story line (Sapo's and Macmann's). Obviously, the very idea of a trilogy of novels—and therefore of a third term—points toward the end of a simple binarism, but that end is handled with great complexity in *The Unnamable*. Although the novel begins with what appears to be a binary structure, involving the two Mahood stories, this structure is almost immediately disrupted by the development of a third story involving Worm.

It might be argued, of course, that the two Mahood stories constitute a single unit designed to stand in opposition to the Worm story, in which event the novel's binarism is preserved. Yet the fact that we are presented with two interpretive options indicates that *The Unnamable* is neither merely binary nor ternary, but alternates between these systems, as though to suggest that the novel is, like *différance* itself, struggling to move beyond the dualisms of Descartes. Still, a breakthrough of sorts does occur, for if the Mahood story makes up the first third of the novel and the Worm story the second third, the novel's final third nevertheless remains to be accounted for. It is here that Beckett launches himself into the verbal play most often associated with Derridean *écriture*, a brilliant exercise in *différance*, conducted at a purely stylistic level, without plot and without character.

I have spoken above of how *The Unnamable* collapses the narrator/narrated or the subject/object into their mediating slash, how it drives these terms into some interstitial space where the dialectic that rendered them significant ceases to function. This place in-between, this third term that is not a term, represents Beckett's update of what in classical philosophy was referred to as the *tertium quid*, that intermediate component that partakes of two mutually exclusive categories without being an instance of either. One of the most often cited examples of the *tertium quid* is God, who (significantly for Beckett) represents an instance of both body and soul without being one or the other.[36]

The idea of the *tertium quid* is alluded to in a passage in which the locutor makes one of his many attempts to identify the source of his own voice, to connect it with narrator or narrated, Worm/Mahood or Mahood/Worm:

> Is it not the fault of one [Worm or Mahood] that I cannot be the other [Mahood or Worm]? Accomplices therefore. That's the way to reason, warmly. Or is one to postulate a *tertius gaudens*, meaning myself, responsible for the double failure? Shall I come upon my true countenance at last, bathing in a smile? I have the feeling I shall be spared this spectacle. At no moment do I know what I'm talking about, nor of whom, nor of where, nor how, nor why, but I could employ fifty wretches for this sinister operation and still be short a fifty-first, to close the circuit, that I know, without knowing what it means. (70–71, my emphasis)

Here the locutor attempts to make sense out of his relation to Mahood and Worm by postulating a version of the *tertium quid*: a transcendent third term, identified as the self ("meaning myself"), which is related to both Mahood and Worm, both subject and object, without being either one or the other. Yet in this passage the *tertium quid* has been ironically transformed into the *tertius gaudens*, as though to indicate Beckett's own wry incredulity: were this higher third term actually to exist, it would be no less an occasion for praise and celebration—*gaudeamus!*—than the Second Coming. But, it turns out, the *tertium quid* is as much a myth as God or man.

Still, if the transcendence of the *tertium quid* is not available to Beckett, he nonetheless continues to seek a third term that might serve as an alternative to the dualism he has been struggling to work beyond. He finds that alternative not so much beyond the binary terms of the Western tradition as within and between them, in that space of *différance* that separates—and ultimately subverts—subject and object, narrator and narrated. In the novel's last section, the figure for that third term, that space in-between, is the "tympanum":

> I'll have said it, I'll have said it inside me, then in the same breath outside me, perhaps that's what I feel, an outside and an inside and me in the middle, perhaps that's what I am, the thing that divides the world in two, on the one side the outside, on the other the inside, that can be as thin as foil, I'm neither one side nor the other, I'm in the middle, I'm the partition, I've two surfaces and no thickness, perhaps that's what I feel, myself vibrating, I'm the tympanum, on the one hand the mind, on the other the world, I don't belong to either. (134)

To be neither inside nor outside, but a partition that is related to both these conditions and belongs to neither—this is what follows from the strange conjunction of Mahood and Worm, what emerges as the third term in their particular series. Of course, as an intermediary term that simultaneously presents itself as identity and difference, the tympanum is closely connected to *différance*, a point Derrida himself makes in an essay entitled, appropriately enough, "Tympan."[37]

Derrida's essay is of special interest because the figure of the tympanum so perfectly evokes the peculiarly self-divided character of postmodernity. Hence, Derrida begins by arguing that philosophy has traditionally legitimated itself as a foundational discourse by fixing its own limits, by determining at the outset what lies inside its system of discourse and what lies outside.[38] Yet to "tympanize," or to philosophize in Derrida's specifically Nietzschean sense, involves breaking down those limits by positioning oneself on both sides of the tympanum: "Thus, one will have said nothing, or in any event done nothing, in declaring 'against' philosophy that its margin is within or without, within and without, simultaneously the inequality of its internal spacings and the regularity of its borders."[39] To occupy the interspace described here, the "without" that is also the "within," is to acknowledge that one never definitively moves beyond the limits of one's own discourse, that one never arrives at a point of absolute or final transcendence: "Beyond the philosophical text there is not a blank, virgin, empty margin, but another text, a weave of differences of forces without any present center of reference."[40] Certainly, the idea that the philosophical text includes what stands beyond it and that this consists of a "weave of differences" is by now familiar: it recalls the passage from "The Ends of Man" in which Derrida proposes a new kind of writing, one that "must weave and interlace" a deconstruction practiced from the inside (which I have associated with the Mahood narrative) and a deconstruction practiced from the outside (which I have associated with the Worm narrative).[41] In "Tympan" such a double-weave or tympanic philosophy leads to another instance of the "unword," not the "unnamable" but a related figure. This Derrida calls the "unthought" (*l'impensé*) (xxviii), a condition he explains as "a new play of opposition, of articulation, of difference" (xxviii). In summing up the "unthought" he uses a single word, one he has repeatedly associated with the "unnamable": *différance* (xxviii).

The "tympanum" as used by both Beckett and Derrida represents another assault on binary opposition. To formulate it as a third term suggests, however, just the kind of demarcation the "tympanum" seeks to avoid. We therefore might better describe it not as a term but as a region or zone, intending to recall that third part of Murphy's mind where he was "caught up in a tumult of non-Newtonian motion (*Murphy*, 112–13). Thus, immediately following the passage in which the locutor postulates the failed *tertium quid*, he goes on to remark: "The essential is never to arrive anywhere, never to be anywhere, neither where Mahood is, nor where Worm is, nor where I am, it little matters thanks to what dispensation" (71). This is, fairly speaking, Murphy's "matrix of surds," where he imagines himself a "missile without provenance" (*Murphy*, 112), an idea that is again recalled following the locutor's assertion that he is the only one absent from the world: "All that is needed is to wander and let wander, be this slow boundless whirlwind and every particle of its dust" (161).

It is worth remarking that after contemplating the pleasures of entropic self-consumption, the locutor adds, "It's impossible" (161). For reasons we have already discussed, the "tympanum" stands beyond the resources of language: it is unnamable or, even more, unspeakable.[42] Hence, "*De nobis ipsis silemus*, decidedly that should have been my motto" (58), and "It's a lot to expect of one creature, it's a lot to ask, that he should first behave as if he were not, then as if he were, before being admitted to that peace where he neither is, nor is not, and where the language dies that permits of such expressions . . . [where I] can be let loose, alone, in the unthinkable unspeakable" (65). Of course, this inability to move beyond dualism would seem to return the reader to the beginning of the pentalogy, to that point of narrative deadlock where language stopped, where words failed, where storytelling ceased.

ᵕ·

In *Murphy* the unspeakable nature of the third zone, its inaccessibility to language, understanding, and experience, presented the novel with its irresolvable problematic. Murphy attempted to enter into the third zone by willing himself into will-lessness, by self-consciously seeking anti–self-consciousness, but this brought the novel to a logical impasse from which it could not deliver itself. There resulted a kind of mental overheating that led figuratively and literally to Murphy's explosion. The next three novels warily circled around this problem, gradually sketching out an aesthetic response to it, one that increasingly took as its model the Beckettian permutation.

The Unnamable carries this new aesthetic right up to the threshold of the unword from which *Murphy* could only avert its gaze, and it accomplishes this precisely by submitting itself to the logical impasse rather than attempting to surmount it, by converting the aporetics of introspection into the very stuff of the third zone. We have already discussed the deconstructive movement of the novel, the fact that assertion and denial are the logical engine that drives the "plot" forward and that might be summarized by the novel's famous "I can't go on, I must go on." Consider for a moment one of the richer aporias in the novel: "I'm like Worm, without voice or reason, I'm Worm, no, if I were Worm I wouldn't know it, I wouldn't say it, I wouldn't say anything, I'd be Worm. But I don't say anything, I don't know anything, these voices are not mine, nor these thoughts" (83). We might chart the logical movement of this passage in the following way:

(A) It begins with affirmation and negation. Thus, because the locutor knows he is Worm and says he is Worm, he cannot be Worm, who by definition is without voice or reason. Here, we have the classic aporia: an assertion that is swallowed up by its own contradiction.

(B) Cancel A: "No, I don't know it and say it, because these voices are not mine." This delivers the locutor from the first aporia since the voice and reasoning are not his own, meaning that he can still be the unspeaking, unreasoning Worm.

(C) Restore A: "I don't know anything; I know that these thoughts and words are not mine." This means that the locutor is aware that the voice he speaks with is not Worm's, which is something Worm (unspeaking, unreasoning) would not know or say.

We may consequently conclude that the aporia opened up at C reaffirms A. Hence:

(i) aporetic discourse is self-consistent;

(ii) but aporetic discourse is, by definition, not self-consistent but self-contradictory;

(iii) but in this case, aporetic discourse has been both self-contradictory and self-consistent, which means that at the level of metadiscourse it moves simultaneously in opposing directions and consequently is true to its own nature.

(iv) Yet to be true to its own nature it would have to be untrue to its own nature, etc., etc.

All of this is merely an elaborate way of saying that in the universe of *différance* everything and its opposite are true: It was midnight, the rain was beating on the windows . . . it was not midnight, it was not raining. We have already seen in *Molloy* how aporetic discourse functioned as a Beckettian permutation, how its combinatory resources posited an almost infinite self-generation. *Malone Dies* opened itself up to the interminable textuality *Molloy* only contemplated, exploring the possibilities of *écriture* in the sense of free play. In *The Unnamable* this serves as the central principle of novelistic construction, one that yields whole sections along the lines of assertion, qualification, denial, counterassertion. The idea is to play out variations on a series of largely binary formulas: "It is I, it is not I" would be one example; "I am speaking, I am not speaking" would be another. Now if we begin to permute these constituent parts we get something like: "I'm speaking, no someone is speaking, but it is not I, I'm in speech, no, I'm in silence, no, I'm not anywhere, hell, I've contradicted myself again."

At a more general level, this leads to the story line equivalent of dislocution, a kind of contingent ramification that involves the elaboration of mutually exclusive actions.[43] Yet whether this technique is applied at the local level of argument and description (see the various and conflicting accounts of Worm's appearance) or at the larger level of story line (did Mahood arrive at the rotunda, did he die in the urn?), the reader experiences the sensation of having entered into a "churn of words" (31), a kind of liquified verbiage in which waves of signification rub out what they have written almost as soon as their figures are traced in the sand. In a sense, if the novel has any progression, it is most aptly described through a series of acoustic identities—a passage that moves from "return" to "urn," from "urn" to "worm," and from "worm" to "churn."

Another way of sketching out the larger movement of the pentalogy from beginning to end is to indicate how *The Unnamable* has effectively turned *Murphy* inside out. As we have seen, the earlier novel divided itself into a massive parody of nineteenth-century fiction (what I called the "outer" plot) and a tentative exploration of a postmodern alternative (what I called the "inner" plot). The outer plot focused on Neary-Wylie-Counihan and their pursuit of the hero, while the inner plot, confined to chapter 6, offered a description of Murphy's mind. In *The Unnamable* those ratios are reversed. For a brief two pages, toward its end, the novel presents us with a hilarious parody of mainstream realism, a kind of crazy quilt of *Anna Karenina* and *War and Peace*. The parody begins abruptly, without preparation:

> They love each other, marry, in order to love each other better, more conveniently, he goes to the wars, he dies at the wars, she weeps, with emotion, at having loved him, at having lost him, yep, marries again, in order to love again, more conveniently again, they love each other, you love as many times as necessary, as necessary in order to be happy, he comes back, the other comes back, from the wars, he didn't die at the wars after all, she goes to the station, to meet him, he dies in the train, of emotion, at the thought of seeing her again, having her again, she weeps, weeps again, with emotion again, at having lost him again, yep, goes back to the house, he's dead, the other is dead, the mother-in-law takes him down, he hanged himself, with emotion, at the thought of losing her, she weeps, weeps louder, at having loved him, at having lost him, there's a story for you. (167–68)

What is described here is precisely the kind of mechanistic determinism that Murphy sought to escape, a plot that by repeating a tiresomely familiar story (hence the proliferating "again") has reduced its characters to the status of puppets. For Beckett the old stories have died with Mahood, and any effort to resurrect them will necessarily strike us as stunted, even a trifle ridiculous—as though the grandeur of Tolstoy had been reduced to the proportions of a comic strip or soap opera. It is important to remember, however, that this particular story, this antediluvian deposit that ironizes the old way of speaking, is the exception rather than the rule and that the rest of *The Unnamable* represents the kind of *écriture* whereby the reader is launched into that "matrix of surds" *Murphy* could only imagine. With this last novel, the pentalogy has delivered itself from the impasse of the first novel precisely by dwelling in that impasse, by making of it a resource, by reinventing it as a medium, by transforming it into the endlessly permuting, self-contesting indeterminacy of the "tympanum" or "third zone."

Or almost. Murphy's third zone, existence off the ladder, the dark glass—all represent in Beckett experiences that, like Proust's involuntary memory, cannot be summoned up on demand but fall instead from the heavens according to some arbitrary and inscrutable logic. In a sublunary world that can never decisively and conclusively transcend itself, the closest voluntary approach we can make to what lies beyond all the binary oppositions—indeed, what lies beyond man as we have traditionally conceived him—consists of entering into a pure verbal play, a literature of the unword. This is in many respects reminiscent of the "voluntary" solution Proust was to propose in the last volume of the *Recherche*, a solution that consisted precisely in the writing of literature. Yet, as we have seen, the differences between Proust and Beckett are finally more telling than the similarities. The larger project of the *Recherche* depends on the myth of depth; it depends on discovering continuities between past and present, inside and outside, narrator and narrated. As Jean Rousset has observed:

> One can discern still more reasons for the importance attached by Proust to this circular form of a novel whose end returns to its beginning. In the final pages one sees the hero and the narrator unite too, after a long march during which each sought after the other, sometimes very close to each other, sometimes very far apart; they coincide at the moment of resolution, which is the instant when the hero becomes the narrator, that is, the author of his own history.[44]

In a sense, the resolution of the pentalogy turns on its lack of resolution, on the fact that narrator and narrated are not united but displaced and that the metaphysics that informed nineteenth-century fiction, and with it the novels of Proust and Joyce, is transformed if not transcended. For Proust and Joyce, the truth of art ultimately consists in an act of finding, whether that involves Marcel finding himself and his past (*le temps perdu*) at the Princesse de Guermantes's reception, or Stephen finding himself and his past (his spiritual father) in Leopold Bloom's kitchen. But for Beckett art is generative rather than recuperative. *The Unnamable* delivers us, in a way no previous novel ever has, into a new literary domain where we explore a world not of transcendence but of contingency, a world not of truth but of fiction, a world not of finding but of making.

Afterword

Samuel Beckett is the master in our time of the protracted ending, of inconclusive conclusions and interminable terminations. As he hunches over his copybook, clutching the stub of a Venus pencil between thumb and forefinger, the writing flows incessantly, obsessively. Every point of destination becomes a point of departure. Every epilogue becomes a prologue. Speaking at the beginning of *Endgame*, Clov assures us that the end is already in sight: "Finished, it's finished, nearly finished, it must be nearly finished." And yet the consummation that Clov promises seems to recede with each new assertion, to grow less confident and more qualified precisely to the extent that it is affirmed. The play "ends" approximately an hour later with a gesture that answers its "beginning": Hamm places over his face the handkerchief he had removed at the outset. As the curtain has risen, so it now falls. His final words, "You . . . remain," suggest persistence rather than completion, a going on rather than a breaking off. We do not doubt that these two characters will be back tomorrow night. We do not doubt that they will defer their finale once more.

The end of modernity is similarly equivocal. Because the postmodern seeks to free itself from categorical and teleological thinking, to overcome the logic of "overcoming," it has turned to Heideggerian *Verwindung* and Derridean *différance*. As we have seen, this means practicing a "new writing" that brings together the "two motifs of deconstruction," at once undermining the Western tradition from "within" and attacking it from "without." Beckett gave some indication of what this new writing would look like when he remarked, in a 1945 review, "There is at least this to be said for mind, that it can dispel mind."[1] The pentalogy represents, as I have attempted to show, an extended application of precisely this idea, one that "weaves and interlaces" a deconstruction of the Cartesian paradigm with an exploration of its Nietzschean alternatives. At the same time, Beckett's anti-Cartesianism also involves an anti-Balzacianism, and his work therefore mounts an elaborate assault on the realist tradition, including its great modernist practitioners, Proust and Joyce.

In the process of pursuing these philosophical and novelistic ends, the pentalogy develops what we might think of as an anatomy of postmodern themes and devices. Standing behind these themes and devices is Beckett's deconstructive sensibility, his interest in seeing how mind might be used to dispel mind, whether that involves moving beyond the cogito and the metaphysics of presence, or moving toward supplementarity and doubling, the end of the book and the beginning of writing, *différance* and unnamability. Beckett has, as a result, emerged as a de facto theoretician of the postmodern, one who sets forth in his writing a set of ideas and procedures that have figured prominently in French poststructuralism. Indeed, there is a case to be made for the proposition that Beckett has decisively influenced the work of poststructuralism's two leading practitioners, Foucault and Derrida. In separate interviews, both philosophers have acknowledged the importance of Beckett to their own development. Foucault has stressed the extent to which Beckett represented in the 1950s a point of radical departure, a break with all the accepted schools of thought in postwar France:

> I belong to that generation who as students had before their eyes, and were limited by, a horizon consisting of Marxism, phenomenology, and existentialism. Interesting and stimulating as these might be, naturally they produced in the students completely immersed in them a feeling of being stifled, and the urge to look elsewhere. I was like all other students of philosophy at that time, and for me the break was first Beckett's *Waiting for Godot*.[2]

For his part, Derrida has indicated his sense of literary kinship with Beckett, a kinship he describes in terms that, interestingly, evoke both *différance* and unnamability:

> This is an author to whom I feel very close, or to whom I would like to feel myself very close; but also too close. Precisely because of this

proximity, it is too hard for me, too easy and too hard. I have perhaps avoided him a bit because of this identification. Too hard also because he writes—in my language, in a language which is his up to a point, mine up to a point (for both of us it is a "differently" foreign language)—texts which are both too close to me and too distant for me even to be able to "respond" to them.[3]

In this study I have not attempted to argue the case for direct influence, either of the genetic or Bloomian variety. There are two reasons for this. First, such an approach would have involved an entirely different focus, requiring that I devote much more attention to Foucault and Derrida and much less to Beckett. Second, the postmoderns begin by assuming that writers never fully possesses their own voice, that *différance* has always already entered into the economy of origin and copy, and this substantially complicates traditional arguments for influence. I have therefore taken the position that just as Beckett used Proust and Joyce as defining points of reference, so Foucault and Derrida have used Beckett. In other words, the literary negotiations that exist between Beckett and poststructuralism are more a matter of intertextuality than influence, more a matter of allusive engagement than direct imitation.

Where has this intertextuality led, and what has it meant? With *The Unnamable*, Beckett gives us an image of the postmodern itself: out of the two kinds of writing identified with Mahood and Worm, the two motifs of deconstruction, there emerges something that is neither one nor the other, a third term characterized by *différance* and unnamability. This, I have contended, represents the peculiarly self-divided ground that postmodernity has staked out for itself. In taking up these Beckettian pretexts and contexts, in developing them into his own uniquely philosophical and literary idiom, Derrida carries forward the postmodern project that Beckett first articulated at the end of World War II. That project has by now been so fully absorbed by contemporary culture that it has become one of the defining features of our time and place. For better or worse, we are all students of what Beckett has called the "literature of the unword."

Foucault perhaps best conveyed a sense of how pervasive that literature has become when he delivered his inaugural address to the Collège de France. The occasion was Foucault's installation at the college, his country's most august academic body. Among those in attendance on this day of high honor were Georges Dumézil, Claude

Lévi-Strauss, Fernand Braudel, and Gilles Deleuze. Foucault's subject was language and all that it implies, from beginnings and endings to speaking and being spoken:

> I would really like to have slipped imperceptibly into this lecture, as into all the others I shall be delivering, perhaps over the years ahead. I would have preferred to be enveloped in words, borne way beyond all possible beginnings. At the moment of speaking, I would like to have perceived a *nameless voice* [*une voix sans nom*], long preceding me, leaving me merely to enmesh myself in it. . . .
>
> Behind me, I should like to have heard (having been at it long enough already, repeating in advance what I am about to tell you) the voice of Molloy, beginning to speak thus: "I must go on; I can't go on; I must go on; I must say words as long as there are words, I must say them until they find me, until they say me . . . "[4]

More than any other writer of the last half-century, Samuel Beckett has found and said the words that have carried our epoch toward the threshold of its dissolution, the threshold where modernity finally encounters its own equivocal but inevitable end.

Reference Matter

Notes

Introduction

1. In addition to Lyotard, see Habermas, *The Legitimation Crisis*. Please note that the dates given in the text for works by Lyotard, Habermas, and Vattimo are those of the original-language editions. For translations into English, see the Works Cited.

2. Habermas, "Modernity Versus Postmodernity," 12. It should be noted that Habermas hopes to revitalize the modern tradition not by returning to a Cartesian paradigm based on the "philosophy of the subject" but by moving to an intersubjectivity based on "communicative action." For an excellent discussion of the Habermas-Lyotard exchange, see Rorty, "Habermas and Lyotard on Postmodernity," in Bernstein, ed., *Habermas and Modernity*.

3. See "Philosophy as a Kind of Writing: An Essay on Derrida," in Rorty, *Consequences of Pragmatism*.

4. Rorty, *Philosophical Papers*, 2: 1.

5. For social, historical, and political accounts of the postmodern, see Baudrillard, *Simulations*; Huyssen, *After the Great Divide*; Hutcheon, *The Politics of Postmodernism*; and Jameson, *Postmodernism, or, The Cultural Logic of Late Capitalism*. For discussions of related work in the field of science, see Popper, *The Logic of Scientific Discovery*; Kuhn, *The Structure of Scientific Revolutions*, 2d ed.; and Feyerabend, *Against Method*. For theories of postmodern architecture, see Jencks, *The Language of Post-Modern Architecture, Late Modern Architecture, Post-Modern Classicism*, and *Current Architecture*; Venturi, with Brown and Izenour, *Learning from Las Vegas*; and Venturi, *Complexity and Contradiction in Architecture*, 2d ed.

6. See, for example, Newman, *The Post-Modern Aura*; Eagleton, "Capitalism, Modernism and Postmodernism"; and Lethen, "Modernism Cut in Half: The Exclusion of the Avant-garde and the Debate on Postmodernism," in *Approaching Postmodernism*, ed. Fokkema and Bertens. Jameson is also

often read as a critic who regards postmodernism as a form of antimodernism, but in my view his highly complex approach to the subject cannot be reduced to this simple opposition.

7. Derrida, *Writing and Difference*, 292–93.

8. Literary modernism is, of course, a widely varied, often contradictory movement, and there are any number of "modernist" writers who now strike us as "postmodern." One thinks, for example, of parts of Joyce (see Chapter 1), the later Woolf, and a good deal of Stein (whom Beckett cited as an inspiration for his own work: see Beckett, "German Letter," in *Disjecta*, 172).

9. Beckett described what was to become the pentalogy as a "series" in a letter to Thomas McGreevy, dated January 14, 1948; see Bair, *Samuel Beckett: A Biography*, 372.

10. I am quoting Jean Rousset's comments on Proust: see *Forme et signification*, 144.

11. These critical categories are approximate, meant to describe broad trends rather than clearly defined methods. For important examples of the nihilist approach, see Fletcher, *The Novels of Samuel Beckett*; and Federman, *Journey to Chaos*; for important examples of the humanist approach, see Robinson, *The Long Sonata of the Dead*; and Butler, *Samuel Beckett and the Meaning of Being*. Valuable studies that move between the nihilist and humanist approaches are Coe, *Samuel Beckett*; Hesla, *The Shape of Chaos*; and Webb, *Samuel Beckett*.

12. See Kenner, *Samuel Beckett: A Critical Study* (1961); and Cohn, *Samuel Beckett: The Comic Gamut* (1962). See also subsequent work by both authors: Kenner, *A Reader's Guide to Samuel Beckett*; and Cohn, *Back to Beckett*.

13. See Albright, *Representation and the Imagination*; Dearlove, *Accommodating the Chaos*; Rabinovitz, *The Development of Samuel Beckett's Fiction*, and *Innovation in Samuel Beckett's Fiction*; Abbott, *The Fiction of Samuel Beckett*, "Narratricide: Samuel Beckett as Autographer," and "The Writer's Laboratory: Samuel Beckett and the Death of the Book" in his *Diary Fiction*; and Moorjani, *Abysmal Games in the Novels of Samuel Beckett*.

Studies that do not deal directly with Beckett's novels but that I have found especially illuminating are Brater, *Beyond Minimalism*, and *The Drama in the Text*; Brienza, *Samuel Beckett's New Worlds*; Gontarski, *The Intent of Undoing in Samuel Beckett's Dramatic Texts*; and Locatelli, *Unwording the World*.

Because they have exerted little influence, I have omitted from my account of Beckett criticism the Marxist discussions of his work. Georg Lukács has condemned Beckett in particular—and "bourgeois modernism" in general—

as a symptom of the late capitalism that modernism has failed to understand critically: see *The Meaning of Contemporary Realism*. Theodor Adorno has responded to Lukács in several places, arguing that Beckett's radically subjective and negative treatment of reality is the only authentic response to late capitalism: see "Trying to Understand *Endgame*," and *Aesthetic Theory*.

14. See Connor, *Samuel Beckett: Repetition, Theory and Text* (1988); Hill, *Beckett's Fiction: In Different Words* (1990); Trezise, *Into the Breach: Samuel Beckett and the Ends of Literature* (1990). There are also post-structuralist elements in Henning's study, *Beckett's Critical Complicity*; and in Moorjani's *Abysmal Games*.

15. See Culler, *On Deconstruction*; Gasché, *The Tain of the Mirror*; Norris, *Deconstruction*, *Derrida*, and *What's Wrong with Postmodernism*.

16. Rorty, *Contingency, Irony, and Solidarity*, 8.

17. Trezise writes: "The tardy awakening of consciousness to its own illusory priority describes its pre-originary involvement in an economy of signification that both invests or produces and escapes or exceeds consciousness itself" (*Into the Breach*, 31–32). He also quotes Joseph Libertson to the effect that "the *cogito*, in its entirety, is an 'illusion'" (23). Connor comments that "as the consciousness of language as a distorting or constricting force tightens its hold on Beckett, so repetition seems to become more and more necessary in his work" (*Samuel Beckett*, 15), going on to argue that Beckett wants "to have done with language because it is inherently falsifying" (17). Hill makes relatively few theoretical assertions, but when he does write in this vein he sounds like Connor and Trezise: "Foisted on me by others, the [proper] name is an imposition and a falsehood" (*Beckett's Fiction*, 111).

18. The quotation comes from Nietzsche's "On Truth and Lies in the Nonmoral Sense" in Nietzsche, *Philosophy and Truth*, 90.

19. Connor writes: "If being is impure, if there are irresolvable contradictions in human experience, then this, for Beckett, is not to be explained as a fall from grace, a disturbance or complication of original simplicity or unity" (*Samuel Beckett*, 44). Trezise acknowledges that Beckett makes use of the myth of the fall but is quick to distance himself from its Romantic application: "In other words, even though, especially in *Molloy*, Beckett resorts to the metaphor of the Fall, the postlapsarian mood of the trilogy is not be imputed to a fall *from* . . . since, as Moran's experience demonstrates, most incontrovertibly, the paradisiacal repose of the subject is a belated illusion grounded in the oblivion of its intersubjective non-self-coincidence" (*Into the Breach*, 147). Leslie Hill does not address the problem of the fall in Beckett.

20. Trezise, who cites Joseph Libertson to the effect that the "*cogito*, in

its entirety, is an 'illusion'" (*Into the Breach*, 23), does not discuss the autobiographical elements in Beckett. Both Connor and Hill use repetition and indifference as ways of arguing against any conception of the self. Connor does not raise the issue of autobiography, and while Hill mentions it briefly in discussing *Watt*, remarking that "it is difficult not to read" the confrontation between Watt and Sam "as a mode of cryptic autobiography" (*Beckett's Fiction*, 31), he does not pursue the matter.

21. Again, the logic of each of these three studies tends to preclude any analysis that would find evolution or development in the pentalogy. Approaches that focus on "repetition" (Connor) and "indifference" (Hill) predictably discover patterns of recurrence, while the deconstruction of time, space, and subjectivity (Trezise) has the effect of freezing Beckett's work in a perpetual stasis. Thus, Hill proposes that we imagine the novels of the trilogy "to be simultaneous, not sequential" (*Beckett's Fiction*, 58), and Trezise suggests that "this 'future' is already past, just as the 'past' is yet to come; and what is here called the narrator's 'present situation' is no more than the moment at which this past and this future communicate, at which the 'already' returns as the 'not yet'" (*Into the Breach*, 42).

Chapter One

1. Derrida, *Of Grammatology*, 6.

2. Ibid.

3. Some influential studies, which include discussions of themes, techniques, and devices in literary postmodernism, are McHale, *Postmodernist Fiction*; Fokkema and Bertens, eds., *Approaching Postmodernism*; Hassan, *The Postmodern Turn*; and Hutcheon, *A Poetics of Postmodernism*.

4. Abrams's *The Mirror and the Lamp* remains the classic study of imitative and expressive theories of art.

5. Histories of Enlightenment philosophy sometimes contrast Descartes's rationalism with Locke's empiricism. While there are obviously important differences between these two traditions, I use the term *empirical* broadly to refer to the "philosophy of the subject," which has its intellectual roots in Descartes's *Discourse on Method* and *Meditations on First Philosophy*. For a brief discussion of the Cartesian origins of the philosophy of sensory perception, see Straus, *The Primary World of the Senses*, 3–25; for a fuller and more idiosyncratic treatment of this subject, see Husserl, *Cartesian Meditations*. Bernard Williams provides a good general account of Descartes in *Descartes: The Project of Pure Enquiry*.

6. See Abrams, "The Deconstructive Angel."

7. Rorty, *Contingency, Irony, and Solidarity*, 4–5.

8. Foucault, *The Order of Things*, xx.

9. While the emergence of Nietzsche's postmodernity is certainly not an all-or-nothing phenomenon, I locate its beginnings with "On Truth and Lies in a Nonmoral Sense" (1873). Gianni Vattimo concedes that there are postmodern tendencies present in "On the Uses and Disadvantages of History for Life" (1874), but he argues that the real "birth of post-modernity in philosophy" did not occur until the publication *Human, All Too Human* (1878). See *The End of Modernity*, 167.

10. Nietzsche, "On Truth and Lies in a Nonmoral Sense," in *Philosophy and Truth*, 81. Subsequent page references appear in the text.

11. Heidegger saw Nietzsche as the "last metaphysician," much as Derrida has seen Heidegger as the last metaphysician. For Heidegger on Nietzsche, see "The Word of Nietzsche: 'God Is Dead'" in Heidegger, *The Question Concerning Technology and Other Essays*, as well as his four-volume study, *Nietzsche*; for Derrida on Heidegger, see "*Ousia and Gramme*: Note on a Note in *Being and Time*" in Derrida, *Margins of Philosophy*, and *Of Spirit: Heidegger and the Question*.

12. Although Heidegger discusses truth or *alētheia* throughout his work, "On the Essence of Truth," in his *Basic Writings*, serves as a useful introduction.

13. Heidegger, *The Question Concerning Technology*, p. 128. Subsequent page references appear in the text.

14. It is of special importance to Heidegger's larger conception that *Gestell* opens up its own deconstruction and therefore helps bring about the "end of metaphysics." See *The Question Concerning Technology*, 28–32; and Vattimo's discussion of *Ge-stell* in *The End of Modernity*, 171–72.

15. Luc Ferry and Alain Renaut argue this position from a critical perspective in *French Philosophy of the Sixties*.

16. See "Différance," in Derrida, *Margins of Philosophy*.

17. *Discipline and Punish* presents the most fully developed statement of this position in Foucault's works; see also "Truth and Power," in *The Foucault Reader*, 51–75.

18. Derrida, *Writing and Difference*, 292. Subsequent page references appear in the text.

19. I am here drawing on Richard Rorty's use of these terms in *Philosophy and the Mirror of Nature*, 315–56.

20. These oppositions are found in Lyotard's *The Postmodern Condition*; Rorty's *Contingency, Irony, and Solidarity*, especially 3–22; and McHale's *Postmodernist Fiction*, especially 3–40. This is *not* to say, however, that Lyotard, Rorty, and McHale take reductively categorical or teleological approaches to the postmodern. Lyotard has himself argued that the "post" in "postmodern" should not be read as a simple supersession or overcoming: see "Note on the Meaning of 'Post-'," in *The Postmodern Ex-*

plained, 75–80. Rorty has made it clear that one cannot make strong truth claims for the postmodern any more than one could do so for the modern: "To say that we should drop the idea of truth as out there waiting to be discovered is not to say that we have discovered that, out there, there is no truth" (*Contingency, Irony, and Solidarity*, 8). And McHale has insisted, in his most recent book (*Constructing Postmodernism*), that the "categories" of the modern and the postmodern should be treated not as immanent but as pragmatically "constructed." I mention these oppositions because there has been a tendency among critics to treat the postmodern as a simple term of antithesis or negation to the modern; Linda Hutcheon has both remarked on and criticized this tendency: "So much that has been written on this subject has physically taken the form of opposing columns, usually labelled modernist versus postmodernist" (*A Poetics of Postmodernism*, 20).

21. Derrida, "The Ends of Man," in *Margins of Philosophy*, 121. Subsequent page references appear in the text.

22. Vattimo, *The End of Modernity*, 2–3. Subsequent page references appear in the text.

23. Although she evokes neither *différance* nor *Verwindung*, Linda Hutcheon is one of the few literary critics to treat the postmodern as a fundamentally "contradictory phenomenon" (*A Poetics of Postmodernism*, 3). As she puts it, "Postmodern culture, then, has a contradictory relationship to what we usually label our dominant, liberal humanist culture. It does not deny it. . . . Instead, it contests it from within its own assumptions" (ibid., 6).

24. Hassan, *The Postmodern Turn*, 174. Subsequent page references appear in the text.

25. Murphy's "third zone" is described as a "Matrix of surds"; *Murphy*, 112. Hassan, who has written a book on Beckett, is intimately acquainted with the latter's work; Hassan, *The Literature of Silence*.

26. Lyotard, *The Postmodern Condition*, xxiv.

27. Ibid., 81–82.

28. Lyotard, *Heidegger et "les juifs,"* 16; my translation.

29. Kristeva, "Postmodernism?" 141.

30. Derrida, *Margins of Philosophy*, 3.

31. Ibid., 26.

32. Samuel Beckett, quoted in Hobsen, "Samuel Beckett: Dramatist of the Year," 153.

33. Watt, *The Rise of the Novel*, 12.

34. See, for instance, Davis, *Factual Fictions*; and McKeon, *The Origins of the English Novel, 1600–1740*.

35. Descartes writes: "My present aim, then, is not to teach the method which everyone must follow in order to direct his reason correctly, but only

to reveal how I have tried to direct my own. . . . I am presenting this work only as a history [*histoire*] or, if your prefer, a fable [*fable*]." See Descartes, *Discourse on Method*, in *The Philosophical Writings of Descartes*, 1: 112. Subsequent page references appear in the text.

36. Descartes draws a contrast between scientific and poetic knowledge: "Above all I delighted in mathematics, because of the certainty and self-evidence of its reasonings. But I did not yet notice its real use; and since I thought it was of service only in the mechanical arts, I was surprised that nothing more exalted had been built upon such firm and solid foundations. On the other hand, I compared the moral writings of the ancient pagans to the very proud and magnificent palaces built only on sand and mud" (*Discourse on Method*, 1: 114).

37. Descartes's discussion of *histoire* and *fable* appears to be contradictory; indeed, the term *histoire*—which can mean either "history" or "story"—is itself ambiguous. There is, however, a fairly straightforward explanation for what Descartes has written here. When the Catholic Church condemned Galileo's *Dialogue Concerning the Two Chief World Systems* in 1633, Descartes was so alarmed that he voluntarily suppressed his own treatise, *Le Monde*: see Vrooman, *René Descartes: A Biography*, 83–87. No doubt he continued to be concerned three years later, when he was preparing to publish the *Discourse on Method*. By referring to his "scientific discovery" as a "story," Descartes was able to insulate himself from any criticism, should the *Discourse* prove offensive to the Church.

38. It is easy to forget—given our position at the end of the twentieth century—how serious that challenge continued to be in the 1920s and 1930s. An essay like Sartre's "François Mauriac and Freedom" makes it clear that realism was still very much alive during this period. See Sartre, *Literary Essays*, 7–23.

39. Balzac, *La Comédie humaine*, 1: 4; my translation.

40. "De la description," in Zola, *Le Roman expérimental*, 231–32, my translation. For a fuller treatment of these issues in Zola, see his essay "Le Roman expérimental" in the same volume.

41. Balzac, *Le Père Goriot*, 30; my translation.

42. This is especially true of Beckett's fellow "midnight novelists," Nathalie Sarraute and Alain Robbe-Grillet. Although of an earlier generation, Jean-Paul Sartre was also highly critical of Balzac. Here is Roquentin's reaction when he comes on a copy of *Eugénie Grandet*: "I pick it up, mechanically, and begin to read page 27, then page 28: I haven't the courage to begin with the beginning" (Sartre, *Nausea*, 29). Michel Butor, himself a *nouveau romancier*, has provided a useful corrective to the twentieth century's reaction to Balzac: "He is generally used as a sort of bogey to intimidate any attempt at innovation, at invention in the contemporary novel. In

simplistic fashion we contrast the so-called 'Balzacian' novel with the modern novel, that is to say, with all the important works of the twentieth century; yet it is child's play to show that this 'Balzacian' novel is in fact derived from only a tiny part of Balzac's work, and that the only true heirs of this great man during the past fifty years are Proust, Faulkner, etc." See "Balzac and Reality," in Butor, *Inventory*, 100.

43. Modernism's preoccupation with subjectivity and all that it implies (the conscious, preconscious, and unconscious; self, identity, and myth) has been the focus of numerous studies. Ellmann and Feidelson adopt such an approach in their "backgrounds" text, *The Modern Tradition*, one of the standard reference books in the field. Other studies that have taken the problem of subjectivity as their point of departure—whether to elaborate upon this view, qualify it, or argue with it—are Langbaum, *The Modern Spirit*, and *The Mysteries of Identity*; Levenson, *A Genealogy of Modernism* and *Modernism and the Fate of Individuality*; Armstrong, *The Challenge of Bewilderment*; Brown, *The Modernist Self in Twentieth-Century English Literature*; and Pecora, *Self and Form in Modern Narrative*.

44. Pater, *The Renaissance: Studies in Art and Poetry*, 187, 188. We might select any number of figures to represent the modern turn toward the subjective, but Pater—with his famous remark on the "narrow chamber of the individual mind"—seems especially appropriate within a British context: "And if we continue to dwell in thought on this world, not of objects in the solidity with which language invests them, but of impressions, unstable, flickering, inconsistent, which burn and are extinguished with our consciousness of them, it contracts still further: the whole scope of observation is dwarfed into the narrow chamber of the individual mind" (187).

45. "French Society was to be the historian, I had only to be the secretary": Balzac, *La Comédie humaine*, 1: 7; my translation. Please note that the views of Proust and Joyce that I develop in what follows are not my own but Beckett's.

46. Both Barbara Gluck and Nicholas Zurbrugg have written important studies of Beckett's relation to Joyce and Proust. See Gluck, *Beckett and Joyce*; and Zurbrugg, *Beckett and Proust*. For an excellent collection of essays on Joyce and Beckett, see Carey and Jewinski, *Re: Joyce'n Beckett*.

47. See Bair, *Samuel Beckett: A Biography*, 75–77.

48. Beckett, *Disjecta*, 21. Subsequent page references appear in the text.

49. Gluck draws a sharp contrast between Joyce and Beckett on the subject of history. For Joyce history is a "single unified scheme or order" and the "separation of the mental from the physical as anything but a temporary state [is] abhorrent"; whereas for Beckett, history is fundamentally a matter of error and contingency, and the effort to resolve the conflicts that define subject/object relations is a futile exercise (*Beckett and Joyce*, 77).

50. Gluck writes: "Beckett's attitude toward words is vastly different from Joyce's. . . . Where Beckett maligned speech . . . Joyce worshiped the word. A lapsed Catholic, Joyce nevertheless still believed that 'in the beginning was the Word,' and, with Vico, that all language originated from man's effort to arrive at the meaning of the divine thunderclap" (*Beckett and Joyce*, 97).

51. Beckett, *Proust*, 63. Subsequent page references appear in the text.

52. Nicholas Zurbrugg contrasts Proustian and Beckettian conceptions of character. While the former is "immersive," the latter "aspire[s] not so much to this ideal, deep, spiritual reality, as to the neutral, vacuous, absence of reality that Belacqua defines as being neither 'centrifigual' or 'centripetal,' but 'not'" (*Beckett and Proust*, 138).

53. Nathalie Sarraute writes archly of the reverence bestowed upon Balzacian character: "Since the happy days of *Eugénie Grandet* when, at the height of his power, the character occupied the place of honor between reader and novelist, the object of their common devotion, like the Saints between the donors in primitive paintings, he has continued to lose, one after the other, his attributes and prerogatives" (*The Age of Suspicion*, 55). Alain Robbe-Grillet extends this critique of Balzac to ideological as well as aesthetic grounds: "To have a name was doubtless very important in the days of Balzac's bourgeoisie. A character was important—all the more important for being the weapon in a hand-to-hand struggle, the hope of a success, the exercise of a domination. . . . Our world, today, is less sure of itself, more modest perhaps, since it has renounced the omnipotence of the person, but more ambitious too, since it looks beyond. The exclusive cult of the 'human' has given way to a larger consciousness, one that is less anthropocentric" (*For a New Novel*, 29).

54. Beckett, *Dream of Fair to Middling Women*, 119–20. Shortly before his death, Beckett gave permission for the posthumous publication of *Dream*, an edition of which recently appeared (see the Works Cited). For an excellent discussion of Balzac's role in *Dream*, see Rabinovitz, *The Development of Samuel Beckett's Fiction*, 20–35.

55. Beckett, *Dream of Fair to Middling Women*, 12–13. Hippolyte Taine famously argued that character is determined by "la race, le milieu et le moment": see *Histoire de la littérature anglaise*, xxiii.

56. Rabinovitz, *The Development of Samuel Beckett's Fiction*, p. 20.

57. The idea that Proust and Joyce are modern, whereas Beckett is postmodern, is implicit in Gluck and explicit in Zurbrugg. Beckett has been particularly insistent on the subject of his differences with Joyce. Thus, in an interview with Israel Shenker, Beckett remarked, "The more Joyce knew the more he could. He's tending toward omniscience and omnipotence. I'm working with impotence, ignorance." See Shenker, "Beckett: Moody Man of Letters." Some nineteen years earlier, Beckett made a related point in a

letter to Axel Kaun, where he argued for a "literature of the unword," in which language would be "most efficiently used where it is being misused" (*Disjecta*, 171–72). This negative aesthetic was, in Beckett's view, completely at odds with Joyce's own positive aesthetic: "With such a program, in my opinion, the latest work of Joyce has nothing whatever to do. There it seems rather to be a matter of an apotheosis of the word" (*Disjecta*, 172).

58. See Gray, *Postmodern Proust*.

59. Brian McHale offers a subtle and incisive discussion of the modern/postmodern tendencies in *Ulysses*: see *Constructing Postmodernism*, 42–58. For various postmodern approaches to Joyce, see Attridge and Ferrer, eds. *Post-structuralist Joyce*. Phillip Herring's idea of an "uncertainty principle" in Joyce offers a good example of how one can locate both modern and postmodern elements in the same text: see Herring, *Joyce's Uncertainty Principle*.

60. *Disjecta*, 95; the review originally appeared in the *Irish Times*.

Chapter Two

1. As Ferry and Renaut put it, "Foucault opposed the preclassical image of the ship of fools to later representations of confinement: Instead of being locked away, during the Renaissance the 'circulation' of the mad was guaranteed through representations of the madman as the symbol of the human condition, a 'passenger,' passing through: 'The head that will become a skull is already empty. Madness is the *déjà-là* of death.'" See Ferry and Renaut, *French Philosophy of the Sixties*, 73.

2. "Joining vision and blindness, image and judgment, hallucination and language, sleep and waking, day and night, madness is ultimately nothing, for it unites in them all that is negative. . . . There is only one word which summarizes this experience, *Unreason* . . . [which is] all that is constantly in retreat from reason, in the inaccessible domain of nothingness." See Foucault, *Madness and Civilization*, 107.

3. Foucault, *Histoire de la folie à l'âge classique*, 72. I am quoting from a section of *Histoire de la folie* that was not included in the heavily abridged English version, *Madness and Civilization*; the translations are my own.

4. Ibid., 57.

5. Ibid., 58. The "unthinkable" (*l'impensable*) and the "unthought" (*l'impensé*), which play a significant role in the work of both Foucault and Derrida, are related to Beckett's own "unnamable." I discuss both the "unthinkable" and the "unthought" in Chapter 6.

6. Derrida, *Writing and Difference*, 55.

7. Ibid., 56.

8. Ferry and Renaut feel that Derrida wins the interpretive debate with

Foucault: "With respect to the relations between *cogito* and madness in the economy of Descartes's text, Derrida's restatement can hardly be disputed and cuts short the effort to turn the *First Meditation* into the expression or reflection of the great confinement" (*French Philosophy of the Sixties*, 87). Foucault carried forward the debate with Derrida in a response to "Cogito and the History of Madness": see "My Body, This Paper, This Fire." Roy Boyne has written a book-length study on the debate, entitled *Foucault and Derrida: The Other Side of Reason*.

9. Descartes' considerable influence on Beckett has been well documented. While there is no doubt that Beckett greatly admired Descartes and regarded him as one of the defining figures in the development of Western philosophy, I take the position that Beckett was largely critical of Cartesianism. For readings that treat *Murphy* as a Cartesian novel, see Mintz, "Beckett's *Murphy*: A 'Cartesian' Novel"; Kennedy, *Murphy's Bed*; and Morot-Sir, "Samuel Beckett and Cartesian Emblems," in *Samuel Beckett*, ed. Morot-Sir, Harper, and McMillan. Hugh Kenner generally reads Beckett as offering an uncritical endorsement of Descartes's ideas: see *Samuel Beckett: A Critical Study*. More recently, there has been a greater willingness to see Beckett as offering a satirical portrait of Cartesianism in *Murphy*. For a good example of this approach, see Moorjani, *Abysmal Games*, 73, 81.

10. According to Geulincx, the "intercourse" that the mind has with the body occurs through the mediation of God; Coe points out the ironic effect Beckett achieves by dropping God from the Geulincxian formula: see *Samuel Beckett*, 28–30. For the two best general discussions of Geulincx's influence on Beckett, see Hugh Kenner, *Samuel Beckett: A Critical Study*, 83–91; and Ruby Cohn, "Philosophical Fragments in the Works of Samuel Beckett," in *Samuel Beckett*, ed. Esslin. Useful information on the subject will also be found in Federman, *Journey to Chaos*, 77–81; Robinson, *The Long Sonata of the Dead*, 88–91; Hesla, *The Shape of Chaos*, 36–41; and Pilling, *Samuel Beckett*, 114–16.

11. According to Baillet, Descartes sequestered himself in the heated closet on November 10, 1619; that night he had three dreams so "extraordinary" in character that he assumed they were divinely inspired (*Vie de Monsieur Descartes*, 38.) It may be that Murphy's three zones are intended as a reference to Descartes's three dreams.

12. One finds an interesting parallel to what Beckett is describing in certain aspects of the French New Novel. Consider, for instance, Nathalie Sarraute's recommendation, in *The Age of Suspicion*, for a new kind of character, one "devoid of outline, indefinable, intangible and invisible" (56).

13. Again, there is an intriguing connection between Beckett and the French New Novelists. Thus, Sarraute also warns against conventions that make characters stiff, wooden, doll-like: "[The reader has become] wary of

plot, which winds itself around the character like wrappings, giving it, along with an appearance of cohesiveness and life, mummy-like stiffness" (*Age of Suspicion*, 61). In a similar vein, Robbe-Grillet complains in "On Several Obsolete Notions" that "the creators of characters, in the traditional sense, no longer manage to offer us anything more than puppets in which they themselves have ceased to believe" (*For a New Novel*, 28).

14. Quoted in Cohn, "Philosophical Fragments in the Works of Samuel Beckett," 171–72.

15. Beckett also alludes to Geulincx's boat metaphor in *The Unnamable*: "I. Who might that be? The galley-man, bound for the Pillars of Hercules, who drops his sweep under cover of night and crawls between the thwarts, towards the rising sun, unseen by the guard, praying for storm. Except that I've stopped praying for anything. No, no, I'm still a suppliant. I'll get over it, between now and the last voyage, on this leaden sea" (68).

16. A number of critics have remarked on this derivation. See, for instance, Cohn, *Samuel Beckett: The Comic Gamut*, 55.

17. Endon as bird-man parodies the epiphanic moment at the end of part 4 in *Portrait of the Artist as a Young Man* when Stephen beholds the bird-girl.

18. Beckett had already shown his fondness for 1 Corinthians 13.12 in his short story, "A Wet Night": "He set off unsteadily by the Dental Hospital. As a child he had dreaded its façade, its sheets of blood-red glass. Now they were black, which was worse again, he having put aside a childish thing or two" (*More Pricks than Kicks*, 70). For other "face-to-face" encounters, see *Mercier and Camier*, 9; *Molloy*, 10; *The Unnamable*, 37.

19. Cohn also takes notice of the allusion to Descartes: see *Samuel Beckett: The Comic Gamut*, 50.

20. A number of critics have pointed out the ways in which *Murphy* parodies realist fiction. See Kenner, *Samuel Beckett: A Critical Study*, 75; Cohn, *Samuel Beckett: The Comic Gamut*, 46; and Fletcher, *The Novels of Samuel Beckett*, 41.

21. For a calendar that details the chronology of events in *Murphy*, see Kennedy, *Murphy's Bed*, 117–21.

22. See Dearlove's discussion of how Beckett undermines novelistic realism; *Accommodating the Chaos*, 29–37.

23. Kenner, *A Reader's Guide to Samuel Beckett*, 58.

24. Derrida, *Of Grammatology*, 158.

25. Balzac's formulation appears in the "Avant-propos": "La Société française allait être historien, je ne devais être que sécretaire" (*La Comédie humaine*, 1: 7); Stendhal's appears in *Le Rouge et le noir*: "Eh, Monsieur, un roman est un miroir qui se promène sur une grande route" (361).

Chapter Three

1. Derrida, *Speech and Phenomena*, 43. Derrida is here paraphrasing Husserl's position.

2. Derrida, *Of Grammatology*, 12.

3. Rousseau has traditionally been read as a hero of self-consciousness, the man who affirms in the *Confessions* that his purpose "is to display to my kind a portrait in every way true to nature, and the man I shall portray will be myself" (17). Recent criticism has, however, cast doubt on this view of Rousseau. In addition to de Man and Derrida, two studies by Jean Starobinski are especially important: *L'oeil vivant*, and *Jean-Jacques Rousseau: transparence et l'obstacle*.

4. De Man, *Allegories of Reading*, 165. Subsequent page references appear in the text. Please note that, for the purposes of my presentation, I have chosen to treat de Man's work first and Derrida's second, although *Allegories of Reading* was published twelve years after *De la grammatologie*.

5. Of *Narcisse*, de Man writes, "the 'self' to which it ["the disruptive portrait"] claims to point is in fact itself an infinitely deferred condition of indeterminacy between self and other, between identity and difference. . . . The transitive displacement of selfhood upon the other contaminates the other's referential identity and opens up the possibility, that she (or he) too is a 'nothing'" (*Allegories of Reading*, 170). Of *Pygmalion*: "The work no longer originates in the particular will that shaped it, but it is the work that causes the self to exist as its own source and *telos*. . . . When the totalizing identification is about to occur, the exchange between self and other that was to abolish all polarities does not take place or, perhaps more accurately, leaves a surplus (or a deficiency) that prevents the narration from closing" (184).

6. Derrida, *De la grammatologie*, 221; my translation. In the original French the first passage is especially allusive: "En s'affectant soi-même d'une autre présence, on *s'altère* soi-même." *S'affectant* suggests not only being affected oneself by another but also feeling affection (*l'affection*) for oneself with or through another; in addition, there is a punning glance at being infected (*s'infectant*) by another. The primary meaning of *s'altérer* is to change or alter for the worse—to spoil, debase, adulterate, corrupt. Without the pronominal, *altérer* can also mean to "thirst after," which suggests that the onanistic desire of the self for the self (*s'affectant* as feeling affection for) leaves one feeling unsatisfied or "thirsty" (*altéré*).

7. Derrida, *Of Grammatology*, 157.

8. De Man, *Allegories of Reading*, 160.

9. Derrida, *Of Grammatology*, 158. Derrida develops his critique of the metaphysics of presence most fully in *Speech and Phenomena*, where he

shows how the self is both temporally and linguistically displaced. For instances of the former, see especially 60–69; for the latter, see 48–59, where we find passages such as the following: "Husserl thus seems here to apply the fundamental distinction between reality and representation to language. Between effective communication (indication) and 'represented' communication there would be a difference in essence, a simple exteriority. . . . But there is every reason to believe that representation and reality are not merely added together here and there in language, for the simple reason that it is impossible in principle to rigorously distinguish them" (49).

10. For articles that treat *Watt* as a case study in nihilism, see Warhaft, "Threne and Theme in *Watt*"; Senneff, "Song and Music in Samuel Beckett's *Watt*"; Trivisonno, "Meaning and Function of the Quest in Beckett's *Watt*"; and Nielsen, "Beckett's Theory of Knowledge or 'Nihil est in intellectu'". For books, see Fletcher, *The Novels of Samuel Beckett*; Federman, *Journey to Chaos*; Robinson, *The Long Sonata of the Dead*; Harvey, *Samuel Beckett: Poet and Critic*; and Hesla, *The Shape of Chaos*.

Other critics have read *Watt* as a novel that humorously inspects and dissects Watt's analytical character, treating him as a parody of Enlightenment rationalism or logical positivism. For articles that have taken this view, see Hoefer, "*Watt*," in *Samuel Beckett*, ed. Esslin; and Solomon, "A Ladder Image in *Watt*"; for books, see Cohn, *Samuel Beckett: The Comic Gamut*; and Kenner, *Flaubert, Joyce, Beckett*. My own approach to *Watt* shares many of the perspectives set forth in Angela Moorjani's excellent article, "Narrative Game Strategies in Beckett's *Watt*."

11. In "Narratricide: Samuel Beckett as Autographer," Abbott anatomizes the differences between "autography" and "autobiography." The former gives the illusion of a voice speaking in the present, is disjunctive and open-ended in its presentation, and is characterized by a preponderance of nonnarrative discourse; the latter offers a history of events in the past, is chronological and teleological in its presentation, and is characterized by a preponderance of narrative discourse. One of the essay's larger claims is that Beckett "works to disassemble *autobiography*" while carrying forward "the *autographical* project" (36, my emphasis). I am in complete agreement with Abbott's assertion that Beckett is engaged in a form of self-writing but that he, at the same time, "repeatedly sabotages" (40) conventional autobiography. I also find his categorical distinction between "autobiography" and "autography" enormously useful, both for analyzing Beckett and for understanding self-writing in general. For related material, see also Abbott, *Diary Fiction*, especially 183–206 (where he discusses *Malone Dies* as an example of "diary fiction"), and "Autobiography, Autography, Fiction."

12. For a more complete account of the Romantic rewriting of the myth

of the fall, see Frye, *A Study of English Romanticism*; Abrams, *Natural Supernaturalism*; and Cantor, *Creature and Creator*.

13. The allusion is to *Inferno*, canto 1, ll. 113–23: "I shall be thy guide and lead thee hence through an eternal place. . . . Then shalt thou see those who are contented in the fire because they hope to come, whensoever it may be, to the tribes of the blest, to whom if thou wouldst then ascend there shall be a spirit fitter for that than I; with her I shall leave thee at my parting." See *The Divine Comedy*, trans. Sinclair, 1: 19. The well-known passage from *Everyman* reads: "Everyman, I will go with thee and be thy guide, / In thy most need to go by thy side" (ll. 522–23).

14. The image of the winding stair recalls *Purgatorio*, canto 26, ll. 145–46: "Now I beg you, by that goodness which guides you to the summit of the stairway, to take thought in due time for my pain" (*The Divine Comedy*, trans. Sinclair, 2: 343).

15. Samuel Beckett, personal correspondence with the author, April 10, 1986. According to Jacqueline Hoefer, "Do not come down the ladder, Ifor, I haf taken it away" represents Beckett's transcription of a German accent and refers to metaphysical statements that, once mastered, should be abandoned by logical positivists like Watt. See Hoefer, "*Watt*," 74–75. John Fletcher was the first critic to take issue with Hoefer's reading of this passage: "[Hoefer's] interpretation is quite erroneous. Mr. Beckett told me in 1961 that the 'ladder' is a reference to a 'Welsh joke' (an *Itma* classic, I'm informed), making the pronunciation not German but Welsh, and that he had read the works of Wittgenstein only 'within the last two years.'" See Fletcher, *The Novels of Samuel Beckett*, 87–88.

16. James Acheson has collected several versions of the joke. In some cases, obtuseness answers obtuseness: "The joke consists of two lines, a warning and a reply: 'Do not come down the ladder, Ifor, I haf taken it away.' Reply: 'It's too late, man, I'm already half way down.'" See Acheson, "A Note on the Ladder Joke in *Watt*."

17. Beckett, *Proust*, 55.

18. See ibid., 3–7.

19. In my discussion of *Murphy*, I argued that the "dark glass" motif expressed the epistemological process of self-reflection insofar as it involved a mirroring. Of course, here the glass is not a mirror—"not a looking-glass, a plain glass, an eastern window at morning, a western window at evening" (147). Since Beckett consistently equates Knott with the sun, he makes the glass a window through which Watt sees light in the morning and evening. Because the window would be backlit at these times, he would be able to see his own reflection in the pane against the glare beyond; this, I suspect, is the image Beckett wishes to convey. On the equation of Knott with the sun, see Fletcher, *The Novels of Samuel Beckett*, 86.

20. See Morrissette, *The Novels of Robbe-Grillet*, 113–14.

21. See Samuel Beckett's dramatic piece, *Not I*, collected in *Ends and Odds*.

22. Although I do not pursue this line of thought here, the discussion of mirroring, doubling, and the "fall into language" that follows might be developed in terms of a Lacanian analysis. See especially "The Mirror Stage as Formative of the Function of the I," in Lacan, *Ecrits*.

23. There has been some disagreement over whether or not part 3 is set in an asylum or at the Knott establishment, although the evidence overwhelmingly supports the former view. Thus, the rooms where Watt and Sam reside ("in our windowlessness, in our bloodheat," 152) recall the padded cells at the Magdalen Mental Mercyseat and, indeed, are referred to as "mansions," the term used in *Murphy* to describe the padded cells ("There were no open wards in the ordinary sense, but single rooms, or as some would say, cells, or as Boswell said, mansions," *Murphy*, 167). The residents at the present establishment wear uniforms ("Through this hole I passed, without hurt, or damage to my pretty uniform," 160) and appear to be inmates in an institutional setting ("No truck with the other scum, cluttering up the passageways, the hallways, grossly loud, blatantly morose, and playing ball, always playing ball, but stiffly, delicately, out from our mansions, and through this jocose, this sniggering muck, to the kind of weather we liked, and back as we went," 153).

24. Gottfried Büttner reads the gardens as an image of Watt's and Sam's "two spheres of consciousness": see *Samuel Beckett's Novel 'Watt,'* 93.

25. Moorjani, *Abysmal Games*, 31.

26. Büttner claims that this "passage refers to Sam and Watt, who are marching 'side by side' through Mr. Knott's property in a close embrace, the one moving forward, the other backward. I asked Beckett about this passage because it is also possible that it refers to Watt and Mr. Knott; he confirmed that in fact it deals with Watt and Sam" (*Samuel Beckett's Novel 'Watt,'* 98–99). Büttner's reading is, however, at odds with the passage, which explicitly speaks of the two men who are side by side as Knott and Watt ("Knott look at Watt? No. Watt look at Knott? No."). Moreover, the two men are side by side "all day, part of the night," yet Sam and Watt are together only during exercise hours, which do not extend into the night. In the letter to which Büttner refers (and which he has kindly made available to me), it seems that Beckett did not look up the passage but was relying on what proved, in this case, to be a lapse of memory.

27. Moorjani has also observed the connection between Hackett's deformity and "existence off the ladder": see *Abysmal Games*, 85.

28. See Robbe-Grillet's parody of the realist character: "A character—everyone knows what the word means. It is not a banal *he*, anonymous and transparent, the simple subject of the action expressed by the verb. A char-

acter must have a proper name, two if possible: a surname and a given name. He must have parents, a heredity. He must have a profession. If he has possessions as well, so much the better. Finally, he must possess a 'character,' a face which reflects it, a past which has molded that face and that character" (*For A New Novel*, 27).

29. Büttner has also remarked on the birth imagery in this section: see *Samuel Beckett's Novel 'Watt,'* 125.

30. "The Expelled," written approximately a year after *Watt*, begins with an equation between birth and the fall. See Beckett, *Stories and Texts for Nothing*.

31. Raymond Federman has also pointed out the connection between Sam Hackett and Sam Beckett: see *Journey to Chaos*, 110.

32. Balzac, *La Comédie humaine*, 1: 7; my translation.

33. Heath, *The Nouveau Roman*, 15.

34. Ibid., 16, 17.

35. "By that [molestation] I mean that no novelist has ever been unaware that his authority, regardless of how complete, or the authority of a narrator, is a sham. Molestation, then, is a consciousness of one's duplicity, one's confinement to a fictive, scriptive realm, whether one is a character or a novelist." See Said, *Beginnings: Intention and Method*, 84.

36. Quoted in Bair, *Samuel Beckett: A Biography*, 327.

37. Ibid.

38. *On* is the present participle of *einai* (to be). Beckett's Greek was good enough that Joyce often enlisted his help in philological work.

39. Proust, *Le Temps retrouvé*, 14.

40. "The entire history of Rousseau's work, the passage from 'theory' to 'literature,' is the transference of the need to name the world to the prior need of naming oneself"; however, "le sujet est l'innommable." See Grosrichard, "Gravité de Rousseau," quoted in de Man, *Allegories of Reading*, 146–47.

Chapter Four

1. Part 1 of Rorty's *Philosophy and the Mirror of Nature* is entitled "Our Glassy Essence." For works that deal with mirroring and representation, see, in addition to Rorty, Abrams, *The Mirror and the Lamp*; Dällenbach, *The Mirror in the Text*; Gasché, *The Tain of the Mirror*; and Lyons and Nichols, ed., *Mimesis*.

2. Quoted in Kenner, *A Reader's Guide to Samuel Beckett*, 94.

3. On supplementarity, see *Of Grammatology*, 141–64; on *différance*, see Derrida's essay of that title in *Margins of Philosophy*, 3–27. Leslie Hill argues that in the trilogy we encounter "not cumulative totality" but "limping supplementarity"; what is "crucial" to the novel "are the gaps and ex-

cesses, the shortfalls and overspills of narrative organisation which make of each additional narration both a necessary supplement and an inevitable overstatement" (*Beckett's Fiction*, 57).

4. Derrida, *Of Grammatology*, 144, 145.

5. For more extensive treatments of "hyperrealism," see Baudrillard, *Simulations*; and Eco, *Travels in Hyperreality*.

6. "Thus one could reconsider all the pairs of opposites on which philosophy is constructed and on which our discourse lives, not in order to see opposition erase itself but to see what indicates that each of the terms must appear as the *différance* of the other, as the other different and deferred in the economy of the same (the intelligible as differing-deferring the sensible, as the sensible different and deferred; the concept as different and deferred, differing-deferring intuition; culture as nature different and deferred, differing-deferring; all the others of *physis—tekhnē, nomos, thesis,* society, freedom, history, mind, etc.—as *physis* different and deferred, or as *physis* differing and deferring." See Derrida, *Margins of Philosophy*, 17.

7. Ibid.

8. In *Positions*, Derrida argues that *différance* is "*the* economical concept, and since there is no economy without *différance*, it is the most general structure of economy, given that one understands by economy something other than the classical economy of metaphysics, or the classical metaphysics of economy" (8–9).

9. *Différance* moves along two essentially opposed trajectories of meaning. On the one hand, Derrida explains, it gestures toward presence or self-identity: "In the element of the same, [it] always aims at coming back to the pleasure or the presence that [has] been deferred"; on the other hand, it gestures toward absence or difference: "As expenditure without reserve, as the irreparable loss of presence . . . [it] interrupts every economy" (*Margins of Philosophy*, 19). Derrida says of this double movement: "Here we are touching upon the point of greatest obscurity, on the very enigma of *différance*, on precisely that which divides its very concept by means of a strange cleavage" (19).

10. Critics have observed points of identity and difference between the Molloy-Moran narratives. They have not, however, treated these characters and their stories as "identified contraries" or viewed them as examples of *différance*. For other discussions of the connections between the two narratives, see Janvier, "Molloy," in *Twentieth-Century Interpretations*, ed. O'Hara; and Edith Kern's "Moran-Molloy: The Hero as Author."

11. Angela Moorjani also argues that Moran and Molloy "face each other as inverted spectral doubles" (*Abysmal Games*, 108). She develops this idea through an oedipal reading of the novel, which is at once original and persuasive: see *Abysmal Games*, 96–120.

12. The novel contains numerous references to Molloy's mother. For ex-

ample: "Yes, so far as I was capable of being bent on anything all of a lifetime long, and what a lifetime, I had been bent on settling this matter between my mother and me" (87); "And my mother, to settle with her, and if I would not do better, at least just as well, to hang myself from a bough" (106); "So I knew my imperatives well, and yet I submitted to them. It had become a habit. It is true they nearly all bore on the same question, that of my relations with my mother, and on the importance of bringing as soon as possible some light to bear on these" (117); "I was on my way to mother. And from time to time I said, Mother, to encourage me I suppose" (122). Angela Moorjani offers a powerful mythic reading of the figure of the mother in *Molloy*. See "The Magna Mater Myth in Beckett's Fiction," in *Women in Beckett*, ed. Ben-Zvi.

13. According to Deirdre Bair, *Molloy* was composed between September 1947 and January 1948 (*Samuel Beckett: A Biography*, 368). "Le Monde et le pantalon" dates from the end of World War II; "Peintures de l'empêchement" was published in June 1948 (Beckett, *Disjecta*, 176–77).

14. Vivian Mercier offers a good overview of these essays in chapter 5 of *Beckett/Beckett*. The translations from both "Le Monde et le pantalon" and "Peintre de l'empêchement" are my own.

15. See "Recent Irish Poetry," where Beckett writes, "The breakdown of the object . . . the breakdown of the subject. It comes to the same thing— rupture of the lines of communication" (*Disjecta*, 70).

16. For Hugh Kenner, "A Molloy is simply what a Moran turns into when he goes looking for a Molloy" (*Samuel Beckett: A Critical Study*, 65); for John Fletcher, "Moran only finds Molloy in the sense that and in so far as he becomes Molloy" (*The Novels of Samuel Beckett*, 149); and for Edith Kern, Molloy's journey is "a continuation of the trek begun by Moran" ("Moran-Molloy," 188).

17. Connor, *Samuel Beckett*, p. 56. On Moran as the originary term, see ibid., 56–60; and Trezise, *Into the Breach*, 57–60.

18. Connor, Hill, and Trezise have all taken up this point, and Connor and Trezise in particular have shown how *différance* enters into the novel's temporal organization, reversing chronological coordinates such as "before" and "after." My own analysis focuses on the way *différance* affects a number of the novel's spatial metaphors (reversing "inside" and "outside," "figure" and "ground," "reflection" and "reality"), which it then relates to Beckett's treatment of Moran-Molloy as an identified contrary.

19. In one of the "mirror communications," Watt describes Knott as "krad klub" (i.e., "dark bulk"): *Watt*, 165.

20. Like Larry Nixon, A and C have often been ignored by critics, and there has consequently been little interest in drawing a connection between them and supplementarity.

21. In the original French, A and C are "A" and "B." We can only spec-

ulate on why Beckett decided to change the designations for these two characters when he and Patrick Bowles translated the novel into English. One explanation, however, is that Beckett has deliberately dropped out "B" (for "Beckett") to remind us that the author is the ultimate "missing person" in the novel's literary manhunt.

22. The French original likewise insists on a stream: *ruisseau* (*Molloy*, 225).

23. Beckett is here satirizing a literary tradition that associates an elevated prospect with narrative point of view. Perhaps the most memorable use of this device is to be found in Thomas Hardy's novels, but there are many instances of it in poetry as well, from Denham's "Cooper's Hill" to Wordsworth's "Tintern Abbey."

24. Even though Molloy retreats from his assertion ("oh not quite as much, but much younger," 112), there is nothing surprising in this; the game throughout has involved a play of identity *and* difference.

Chapter Five

1. "The Death of the Author," in Barthes, *Image, Music, Text*, 159, 160.

2. Ibid., 142.

3. The quotation, which comes from Beckett's *Textes pour rien*, reads as follows in French: "Qu'importe qui parle, quelqu'un a dit qu'importe qui parle" (*Nouvelles et textes pour rien*, 129). In quoting Beckett, Foucault adds a comma, which does not appear in the original: "Qu'importe qui parle, quelqu'un a dit, qu'importe qui parle" ("Qu'est-ce qu'un auteur?" 77). The added comma has the effect of bracketing the phrase "quelqu'un a dit," thereby individualizing the "author" of "qu'importe qui parle" more fully than Beckett does himself. In quoting the text in English, I have departed from the Josué Harari translation in "What Is an Author," preferring Beckett's own more vernacular rendering of the French: see *Stories and Texts for Nothing*, 85.

4. In the last chapter of *Diary Fiction* ("The Writer's Laboratory: Samuel Beckett and the Death of the Book"), H. Porter Abbott searchingly explores how *Malone Dies* breaks down the conventions of diary writing in a way that brings "into focus not just a type of writing but writing itself," while at the same time having the effect of "undoing the book" (185). Although Abbott does not read Beckett as a traditional metaphysician, he argues against viewing him as either an heir to Nietzsche or an avatar of poststructuralism: "The spirit in which [Beckett] writes is, therefore, at an opposite remove from most current versions of *fröliche Wissenschaft*—as, for example, the Barthesian spirit that rejoices in 'the infinite deferral of the signified'" (*Diary Fiction*, 204).

5. Derrida also discusses the speech/writing dichotomy in *Speech and Phenomena*, and in "Plato's Pharmacy," in Derrida, *Dissemination*.

6. Derrida, *Of Grammatology*, 18.

7. Derrida, *Positions*, 3–4.

8. See "From Work to Text," in Barthes, *Image, Music, Text*.

9. Derrida, *Of Grammatology*, 18.

10. "The Death of the Author," in Barthes, *Image, Music, Text*, 142.

11. Ibid.

12. Ibid., 146.

13. Foucault, "What Is an Author?" in *The Foucault Reader*, 102.

14. As Derrida puts it in *Of Grammatology*: "The secondarity that it seemed possible to ascribe to writing alone affects all signifieds in general, affects them always already, the moment they *enter the game*. There is not a single signified that escapes, even if recaptured, the play of signifying references that constitute language. The advent of writing is the advent of this play" (7). See also "Structure, Sign, and Play," in *Writing and Difference*.

15. Foucault, "What Is an Author?" in *The Foucault Reader*, 102. For a discussion of Foucault's fascination with writing and death, see Miller, *The Passion of Michel Foucault*, especially chapter 1, "The Death of the Author."

16. Foucault, "What Is an Author?" in *The Foucault Reader*, 102–3. Eric Rothstein has pointed out to me Foucault's pun on *le mort* as a "dummy" in the "game" (*jeu*) of Bridge.

17. Angela Moorjani offers a fascinating analysis of *Malone Dies* as a "metanarrative game" on the analogy of Freud's famous *fort/da* game: see *Abysmal Games*, 51–53.

18. See the discussion of Mr. Hackett in Chapter 4.

19. This sense is conveyed even more emphatically in the French: "Je me demande si ce n'est pas de moi qu'il s'agit, malgré mes précautions" (*Malone meurt*, 23).

20. In the French, "cause to live" is "faire vivre" (*Malone meurt*, 34)—an expression that is often used to describe the way novelists "bring their characters to life."

21. I take this expression from Roger Shattuck's book, although I use it, with an emphasis slightly different from Shattuck's, to mean an unmediated vision, one that is not constrained by a situating frame of reference. See Shattuck, *The Innocent Eye*, 413–24.

22. Macmann's greatcoat and hat are mentioned at 53–54 and 55; his boots at 54.

23. In *Proust*, Beckett describes the "essence of ourselves, the best of our many selves and their concretions that simplists call the world" as (citing Proust) that "gouffre interdit à nos sondes" (18–19). Actually this fragment

comes from Baudelaire's poem, "Le Balcon" and is quoted by Saint-Loup in the last volume of the *Recherche*. See Proust, *Le Temps retrouvé*, 91.

24. A number of critics have described *Molloy* as a quest romance and/or spiritual journey. See Janvier, "Molloy," and Kern, "Moran-Molloy," both in *Twentieth Century Interpretations*, ed. O'Hara.

25. Like the earthly paradise of *Purgatorio* (canto 28, ll. 16–27), the park is traversed by a river and filled with birdsong (108).

26. *Askesis* is one of Harold Bloom's revisionary ratios: see *The Anxiety of Influence*.

27. However multiple, successive, and temporal Proust's conception of the self, it is a mistake to identify his work with the character of indeterminacy. Indeed, Proust does on occasion, especially in *Le Temps retrouvé*, speak of a "deep" self, which he discusses in terms that are unapologetically essentialist. As I pointed out earlier, Proust draws a distinction between "notre moi permanent" and "nos moi successifs" (14), between "notre moi véritable et l'autre" (*le moi social*) (367).

28. John Fletcher offers a more complete catalogue of these autobiographical details but then remarks—incorrectly in my view—that "the strands of autobiography in this novel are not of great importance" (*The Novels of Samuel Beckett*, 175–76).

29. "Beckett has admitted that Sapo, with his 'gull's eyes,' bears an uncanny resemblance to himself": see Bair, *Samuel Beckett: A Biography*, 376.

30. See ibid.

31. The letter is quoted in ibid., 328.

32. As Bair points out, Beckett "insists that he was born on Good Friday, April 13, 1906, a date to which he has not discouraged scholars of his writings from attaching undue importance, but his birth certificate gives the date May 13, 1906" (ibid., 3).

33. H. Porter Abbott observes that "*Malone Dies* depicts the impossibility of escaping one's self" (*The Fiction of Samuel Beckett*, 114–15).

34. Derrida, *Positions*, 3.

35. This particular formulation echoes Murphy's own failure to know Endon when they were separated by the "merest hand's-breadth": see *Murphy*, 248.

36. In *Mercier and Camier* (110) Watt is described as a "figure of towering stature."

37. David Hesla makes the same identifications in *The Shape of Chaos*, 110.

38. Leslie Hill shrewdly observes that Lemuel's "hatchet" puns on the French publishing firm "Hachette" (*Beckett's Fiction*, 108).

Chapter Six

1. Foucault, *The Order of Things*, 387.
2. Nietzsche, "On Truth and Lies in a Nonmoral Sense," in *Philosophy and Truth*, 84–86. Heidegger expresses much the same idea in *The Question Concerning Technology*: "However, when man becomes the primary and only real *subiectum*, that means: Man becomes that being upon which all that is, is grounded as regards the manner of its Being and its truth. Man becomes the relational center of that which is as such. But this is possible only when the comprehension of what is as a whole changes" (128).
3. Foucault, *The Order of Things*, 342.
4. A passage like the following is representative: "This means that, unlike the human sciences, which, even while turning back towards the unconscious, always remain within the space of the representable, psychoanalysis advances and leaps over representation, overflows it on the side of finitude" (*The Order of Things*, 374). For Foucault's apotheosis of psychoanalysis, ethnography, and linguistics, see the fifth section of his concluding chapter in *The Order of Things* (373–86). In his later work, Foucault makes no claims for a master discourse and therefore escapes the charge that he is simply replacing an old metaphysics with a new metaphysics. See, for example, the introduction to *The Use of Pleasure*: "But, then, what is philosophy today—philosophical activity, I mean—if it is not the critical work that thought brings to bear on itself? In what does it consist, if not in the endeavor to know how and to what extent it might be possible to think differently, instead of legitimating what is already known? There is always something ludicrous in philosophical discourse when it tries, from the outside, to dictate to others, to tell them where their truth is and how to find it, or when it works up a case against them in the language of naive positivity" (*The Use of Pleasure*, 8–9). Eric Rothstein offers a valuable account of differing attitudes towards truth in early-to-middle Foucault versus late Foucault in "Foucault, Discursive History, and the Auto-Affection of God."
5. Derrida, *Margins of Philosophy*, 121.
6. Ibid., 135.
7. Ibid.
8. I am grateful to Eric Rothstein for having pointed out Beckett's pun on in-homme-able.
9. Samuel Beckett, *Disjecta*, 171–72.
10. Foucault, *The Order of Things*, 323. "Unthought" is "l'impensé" in the original: see Foucault, *Les Mots et les choses*, 333. Several passages from *The Order of Things* have an especially Beckettian resonance. In "Man and His Doubles," for example, we read: "The whole of modern thought is imbued with the necessity of thinking the *unthought*—of reflecting the con-

tents of the *In-itself* in the form of the *For-itself*, of ending man's alienation by reconciling him with his own essence, of making explicit the horizon that provides experience with its background of immediate and disarmed proof, of lifting the veil of the Unconscious, of becoming absorbed in its *silence*, or of straining to catch its *endless murmur*" (327; my emphasis). Likewise: "To all those who still wish to talk about man, about his reign or his liberation, to all those who still ask themselves questions about what is in his essence, to all those who wish to take him as their starting-point in their attempts to reach the truth . . . to all these warped and twisted forms of reflection we can answer only with a philosophical laugh—which means, to a certain extent, a *silent* one" (342–43; my emphasis).

11. Derrida, *Writing and Difference*, 278–79, my emphasis. The French reads "l'impensable lui-même" (*L'Ecriture et la différence*, 409).

12. See, for example, Derrida's recent interview with Derek Attridge, in Derrida, *Acts of Literature*, 90.

13. Derrida, *Writing and Difference*, 293. Derrida is here wandering not only into Beckett's margins but into Nietzsche's as well. See the conclusion to *The Gay Science*, which also evokes an unnamable birth: "Being new, nameless [*Namenlosen*] hard to understand, we premature births [*Frühgeburten*] of an as yet unproven future need for a new goal also a new means" (346; see also *Die fröhliche Wissenschaft*, in *Werke in zwei Bänden*, 1: 532).

14. See *Speech and Phenomena*, 77; "White Mythology," in *Margins of Philosophy*, 270; "Plato's Pharmacy," in *Dissemination*, 168; "La Parole soufflée," in *Writing and Difference*, 185; and *Of Grammatology*, 14. In all cases, the French gives "innommable" for "unnamable" (see *La Voix et le phénomène*, 86; *Marges de la philosophie*, 323; *Dissemination*, 194; *L'Ecriture*, 276; *De la grammatologie*, 25). For the passage cited above from "La structure, le signe et le jeu," see *L'Ecriture*, 428.

15. Derrida, *Positions*, 6; again, the French is "innommable" (*Positions*, 15).

16. Derrida further emphasizes the grammatical mobility of the "unnamable," its vacillation between and across categories, not only by employing the word as both a noun and an adjective, but also by collapsing these two functions into each other; see, for example, "devant l'encore innommable qui s'annonce" (*L'Ecriture*, 428), where *l'innommable* syntactically functions as a noun, but where its more common adjectival usage is suggested by the adverbial modifier (*encore*). For other passages where Derrida uses "innommable" as a noun, see *La Voix et le phénomène*, 86; and *Marges de la philosophie*, 28; for passages where he uses it as an adjective, see *Marges de la philosophie*, 323; *Dissemination*, 194; *L'Ecriture*, 276; *De la grammatologie*, 25; and *Positions*, 15.

17. In some cases the connection Derrida draws between *différance* and

the "unnamable" is implicit, but in others it is quite explicit. In "Structure, Sign, and Play," he relates the appearance of the "unnamable" to the "*différance*" that at once separates and joins the Rousseauian and Nietzschean traditions (*Writing and Difference*, 292–93); in *Speech and Phenomena*, he associates the deconstruction of voice as presence with both the "unnamable" (77) and "the movement of *différance*" (82); and in "Plato's Pharmacy," he identifies the deconstruction of truth as presence with, again, the "unnamable" and "*différance*" (*Dissemination*, 168).

18. Derrida, *Margins of Philosophy*, 3, 26.

19. Ibid., 26–27.

20. Critics have written about Beckett and *différance* (see, for example, Connor's *Samuel Beckett*, Henning's *Beckett's Critical Complicity*, Hill's *Beckett's Fiction*, and Trezise's *Into the Breach*), but they have not identified Derrida's use of the "unnamable" as a specific figure or drawn the intertextual connections between *différance* and the "unnamable" that I develop here. Leslie Hill, whose book deals with issue of Beckett's "indifference," goes the farthest in seeing a relation between "unnamability" and *différance*: "The crux of Beckett's writing [is what] . . . cannot be named. . . . The something I want to name in Beckett's writing may be located more effectively in what could be called the figure of indifference or, to borrow a word from the essays of Blanchot, the neuter. Indifference, the neuter, is that which is in-between positions of meaning, neither positive nor negative, constantly shifting and irreducible to either object or subject" (*Beckett's Fiction*, 8–9).

21. See, for example: "All these Murphys, Molloys and Malones do not fool me. They have made me waste my time, suffer for nothing, speak of them when, in order to stop speaking, I should have spoken of me and of *me alone*" (21, my emphasis); "Basil and his gang? Inexistent, invented to explain I forget what . . . all invented, basely, by *me alone* . . . to put off the hour when I must speak of me" (22, my emphasis).

22. See Kenner, *A Reader's Guide to Samuel Beckett*, 94.

23. Beckett's French version of "I, say I" reads "Dire je" (*L'Innommable*, 7). While the disruptive play that I identify in the English is lost in the French, the latter exploits another kind of *différance* in the word "dire," which can function as either an infinitive or an imperative—as either the formulation of a problem (to say I) or an exhortation to speech (say I).

24. Fritz Senn uses "dislocution" as a catchall term to describe "all manner of metamorphoses, switches, transfers, displacements" (202) in Joyce's work: see *Joyce's Dislocutions*, 199–212. My own use of the term is meant to have a narrower focus, one that relates the operations of *différance* to narrative.

25. A number of critics have noted that "mahood" puns on "manhood."

26. For another example of how Worm might degenerate into a character of determinacy, see 125–26: "But my dear man, come, be reasonable, look, this is you, look at this photograph, and here's your file, no convictions, I assure you, come now, make an effort, at your age, to have no identity, it's a scandal, I assure you, look at this photograph, what, you see nothing, true for you, no matter, here, look at this death's-head, you'll see, you'll be all right, it won't last long, here, look, here's the record, insults to policemen, indecent exposure, sins against holy ghost, contempt of court, impertinence to superiors, impudence to inferiors, deviation from reason."

27. Compare this with the passage in *Discourse on Method* where Descartes derives the whole universe from a few "first causes": "I derived these principles only from certain seeds of truth which are naturally in our souls. Next I examined the first and most ordinary effects deducible from these causes. In this way, it seems to me, I discovered the heavens, the stars, and an earth; on the earth, water, air, fire, minerals, and other such things which, being the most common of all and the simplest, are consequently the easiest to know" (144).

28. Mahood is "speechless" (*The Unnamable*, 55).

29. For Derrida's discussion of the "gap" that defines the difference between "speech" as presence and "writing" as absence, see "Signs and the Blink of an Eye," in *Speech and Phenomena*.

30. Steven Connor is one of the few critics to have noticed the circle imagery in *The Unnamable*, but his approach to this material—concerned with "ontological supremacy and subordination" (79)—is different from my own: see *Samuel Beckett*, 78–87.

31. See sections 33b–34b of the *Timaeus*.

32. Derrida, *Writing and Difference*, 279.

33. Ibid., 279–80.

34. See "Peintres de l'empêchement," in *Disjecta*, 137.

35. Although critics have discussed binary structures in Beckett (see, for example, Abbott, *The Fiction of Samuel Beckett*, 100–101), they have largely ignored the interplay in *The Unnamable* between binary and ternary structures.

36. It will be remembered that Geulincx, Beckett's favorite reviser of Descartes, posited a complete sundering of body and soul, while evoking God as the mediating term that enables them to function in concert.

37. Derrida's translator, Alan Bass, retains the original French title, "Tympan," which of course means "tympanum." In the French version of *The Unnamable*, "tympan" is the word Beckett uses (*L'Innommable*, 160).

38. "In the familiarity of the languages called (instituted as) natural by philosophy, the languages elementary to it, this discourse has always insisted upon assuring itself mastery over the limit (*peras, limes, Grenze*). It has rec-

ognized, conceived, posited, declined the limit according to all possible modes; and therefore by the same token, in order better to dispose of the limit, has transgressed it. *Its own limit* had not to remain foreign to it. Therefore it has appropriated the concept for itself; it has believed that it controls the margin of its volume and that it thinks its other." See Derrida, *Margins of Philosophy*, x.

39. Ibid., xxiv.

40. Ibid., xxiii.

41. In the French, "weave of differences" is "tissu de différences" and "weave and interlace" is "tisser et entrelacer." See Derrida, *Marges de la philosophie*, xix, 163.

42. *L'innommable* has the sense not merely of something unnamable but also of something unmentionable or unspeakable; it is often applied as an adjective to describe garbage: *les ordures innommables*.

43. What I have called "contingent ramification" has become one of the favorite plot devices of the New Novel. Robbe-Grillet specifically pays tribute to Beckett's use of this technique in his opening to *In the Labyrinth*, which echoes the contradictory weather reports in *Molloy* (see *In the Labyrinth*, 29). In "On Several Obsolete Notions," Robbe-Grillet discusses Beckett's use of contingent ramification: "Even in Beckett, there is no lack of events, but these are constantly in the process of contesting themselves, jeopardizing themselves, destroying themselves, so that the same sentence may contain an observation and its immediate negation" (*For a New Novel*, 33).

44. Rousset, *Forme et signification*, 144, quoted in Derrida, *Writing and Difference*, 22.

Afterword

1. *Disjecta*, 95; the review originally appeared in the *Irish Times*.

2. "Postscript: An Interview with Michel Foucault" in Foucault, *Death and the Labyrinth*, 174.

3. Derrida, *Acts of Literature*, 60.

4. Foucault, *The Archaeology of Knowledge*, 215; my emphasis.

Works Cited

Abbott, H. Porter. "Autobiography, Autography, Fiction: Groundwork for a Taxonomy of Textual Categories." *New Literary History* 19 (1988): 597–615.

———. *Diary Fiction: Writing as Action*. Ithaca: Cornell University Press, 1984.

———. *The Fiction of Samuel Beckett: Form and Effect*. Berkeley: University of California Press, 1973.

———. "Narratricide: Samuel Beckett as Autographer." *Romance Studies* 11 (1987): 35–46.

Abrams, M. H. "The Deconstructive Angel." *Critical Inquiry* 3 (1977): 425–38.

———. *The Mirror and the Lamp: Romantic Theory and the Critical Tradition*. New York: Oxford University Press, 1953.

———. *Natural Supernaturalism*. New York: W. W. Norton, 1973.

Acheson, James. "A Note on the Ladder Joke in *Watt*." *Journal of Beckett Studies* 2 (1992): 115–16.

Adorno, Theodor. *Aesthetic Theory*. Ed. Gretel Adorno and Rolf Teidemann. Trans. C. Lenhardt. London: Routledge and Kegan Paul, 1986.

———. "Trying to Understand *Endgame*." *New German Critique* 26 (1982): 119–50.

Albright, Daniel. *Representation and the Imagination: Beckett, Kafka, Nabokov, and Schoenberg*. Chicago: University of Chicago Press, 1981.

Armstrong, Paul B. *The Challenge of Bewilderment: Understanding and Representation in James, Conrad, and Ford*. Ithaca: Cornell University Press, 1987.

Attridge, Derek, and Daniel Ferrer, eds. *Post-structuralist Joyce: Essays from the French*. Cambridge: Cambridge University Press, 1984.

Baillet, Adrien. *Vie de Monsieur Descartes*. Paris: La Table Ronde, 1946.

Bair, Deirdre. *Samuel Beckett: A Biography*. New York: Harcourt, Brace, Jovanovich, 1978.

Balzac, Honoré de. *La Comédie humaine*. Vol. 1. Ed. Marcel Bouteron. Paris: Bibliothèque de la Pléiade, 1966.

———. *Le Père Goriot*. Paris: Garnier Flammarion, 1966.

Barthes, Roland. *Image, Music, Text*. Trans. Stephen Heath. New York: Hill and Wang, 1977.

Baudrillard, Jean. *Simulations*. Trans. Paul Foss, Paul Patton, and Philip Beitchman. New York: Semiotext(e), 1983.

Beckett, Samuel. *Disjecta: Miscellaneous Writings and a Dramatic Fragment*. Ed. Ruby Cohn. New York: Grove Press, 1984.

———. *Dream of Fair to Middling Women*. Ed. Eoin O'Brien and Edith Fournier. New York: Arcade Publishing, 1993.

———. *Ends and Odds*. New York: Grove Press, 1976.

———. *L'Innommable*. Paris: Editions de Minuit, 1953.

———. *Malone Dies*. New York: Grove Press, 1956.

———. *Malone meurt*. Paris: Editions de Minuit, 1951.

———. *Mercier and Camier*. New York: Grove Press, 1974.

———. *Molloy*. Paris: Editions de Minuit, 1951.

———. *Molloy*. New York: Grove Press, 1955.

———. *More Pricks than Kicks*. New York: Grove Press, 1972.

———. *Murphy*. New York: Grove Press, 1957.

———. *Nouvelles et textes pour rien*. Paris: Editions de Minuit, 1958.

———. *Proust*. New York: Grove Press, 1957.

———. *Stories and Texts for Nothing*. New York: Grove Press, 1967.

———. *The Unnamable*. New York: Grove Press, 1958.

———. *Watt*. New York: Grove Press, 1959.

Ben-Zvi, Linda, ed. *Women in Beckett: Performance and Critical Perspectives*. Urbana: University of Illinois Press, 1992.

Bernstein, Richard J., ed. *Habermas and Modernity*. Cambridge, Mass.: MIT Press, 1985.

Bloom, Harold. *The Anxiety of Influence*. New York: Oxford University Press, 1979.

Boyne, Roy. *Foucault and Derrida: The Other Side of Reason*. London: Unwin Hyman, 1990.

Brater, Enoch. *Beyond Minimalism: Beckett's Late Style in the Theater*. New York: Oxford University Press, 1987.

———. *The Drama in the Text*. New York: Oxford University Press, 1994.

Brienza, Susan D. *Samuel Beckett's New Worlds: Style in Metafiction*. Norman: University of Oklahoma Press, 1987.

Brown, Dennis. *The Modernist Self in Twentieth-Century English Literature: A Study in Self-Fragmentation*. New York: St. Martin's Press, 1989.

Butler, Lance St. John. *Samuel Beckett and the Meaning of Being: A Study in Ontological Parable*. London: Macmillan, 1984.

Butor, Michel. *Inventory*. Ed. Richard Howard. New York: Simon and Schuster, 1968.

Büttner, Gottfried. *Samuel Beckett's Novel 'Watt.'* Trans. Joseph Dolan. Philadelphia: University of Pennsylvania Press, 1984.

Cantor, Paul A. *Creature and Creator: Myth-making and English Romanticism*. Cambridge: Cambridge University Press, 1984.

Carey, Phyllis, and Ed Jewinski. *Re: Joyce'n Beckett*. New York: Fordham University Press, 1992.

Coe, Richard. *Samuel Beckett*. New York: Grove Press, 1970.

Cohn, Ruby. *Back to Beckett*. Princeton: Princeton University Press, 1973.

———. *Samuel Beckett: The Comic Gamut*. New Brunswick, N.J.: Rutgers University Press, 1962.

Connor, Steven. *Samuel Beckett: Repetition, Theory and Text*. Oxford: Basil Blackwell, 1988.

Culler, Jonathan. *On Deconstruction: Theory and Criticism After Structuralism*. Ithaca: Cornell University Press, 1982.

Dällenbach, Lucien. *The Mirror in the Text*. Trans. Jeremy Whiteley, with Emma Hughes. Chicago: University of Chicago Press, 1989.

Dante Alighieri. *The Divine Comedy*. 3 vols. Trans. John D. Sinclair. New York: Oxford University Press, 1979 [1939].

Davis, Lennard J. *Factual Fictions: The Origins of the English Novel*. New York: Columbia University Press, 1983.

Dearlove, J. E. *Accommodating the Chaos: Samuel Beckett's Nonrelational Art*. Durham, N.C.: Duke University Press, 1982.

De Man, Paul. *Allegories of Reading: Figural Language in Rousseau, Nietzsche, Rilke, and Proust*. New Haven: Yale University Press, 1979.

Derrida, Jacques. *Acts of Literature*. Ed. Derek Attridge. New York: Routledge, 1992.

———. *De la grammatologie*. Paris: Editions de Minuit, 1967.

———. *La Dissémination*. Paris: Editions du Seuil, 1972.

———. *Dissemination*. Trans. Barbara Johnson. Chicago: University of Chicago Press, 1981.

———. *L'Ecriture et la différence*. Paris: Editions du Seuil, 1967.

———. *Marges de la philosophie*. Paris: Editions de Minuit, 1972.

———. *Margins of Philosophy*. Trans. Alan Bass. Chicago: University of Chicago Press, 1982.

———. *Of Grammatology*. Trans. Gayatri Chakravorty Spivak. Baltimore: Johns Hopkins University Press, 1974.

———. *Of Spirit: Heidegger and the Question*. Trans. Geoffrey Bennington and Rachel Bowlby. Chicago: University of Chicago Press, 1989.

———. *Positions.* Paris: Editions de Minuit, 1972.

———. *Positions.* Trans. Alan Bass. Chicago: University of Chicago Press, 1981.

———. *Speech and Phenomena.* Trans. David B. Allison. Evanston, Ill.: Northwestern University Press, 1973.

———. *La Voix et le phénomène.* Paris: Presses Universitaires de France, 1967.

———. *Writing and Difference.* Trans. Alan Bass. Chicago: University of Chicago Press, 1978.

Descartes, René. *The Philosphical Writings of Descartes.* 2 vols. Ed. and trans. John Cottingham, Robert Stoothoff, and Dugald Murdoch. Cambridge: Cambridge University Press, 1984–85.

Eagleton, Terry. "Capitalism, Modernism and Postmodernism." *New Left Review* 152 (1985): 60–73.

Eco, Umberto. *Travels in Hyperreality.* Trans. William Weaver. New York: Harcourt Brace, 1986.

Ellmann, Richard, and Charles Feidelson, Jr. *The Modern Tradition: Backgrounds of Modern Literature.* New York: Oxford University Press, 1965.

Esslin, Martin, ed. *Samuel Beckett: A Collection of Essays.* Englewood Cliffs, N.J.: Prentice-Hall, 1965.

Federman, Raymond. *Journey to Chaos: Samuel Beckett's Early Fiction.* Berkeley: University of California Press, 1965.

Ferry, Luc, and Alain Renaut. *French Philosophy of the Sixties: An Essay on Antihumanism.* Trans. Mary H. S. Cattani. Amherst: University of Massachusetts Press, 1990.

Feyerabend, Paul. *Against Method.* London: Verso, 1978.

Fletcher, John. *The Novels of Samuel Beckett.* London: Chatto and Windus, 1964.

Fokkema, Douwe, and Hans Bertens, eds. *Approaching Postmodernism.* Amsterdam: John Benjamins, 1986.

Foucault, Michel. *The Archaeology of Knowledge.* Trans. A. M. Sheridan Smith. New York: Pantheon, 1972.

———. *Death and the Labyrinth: The World of Raymond Roussel.* Trans. Charles Ruas. Berkeley: University of California Press, 1987.

———. *Discipline and Punish: The Birth of the Prison.* Trans. Alan Sheridan. New York: Vintage Books, 1979.

———. *The Foucault Reader.* Ed. Paul Rabinow. New York: Pantheon Books, 1984.

———. *Histoire de la folie à l'âge classique.* Paris: Editions Gallimard, 1972.

———. *Madness and Civilization.* Trans. Richard Howard. New York Vintage Books, 1988.

———. *Les Mots et les choses.* Paris: Editions Gallimard, 1966.

————. "My Body, This Paper, This Fire." *Oxford Literary Review* 4 (1979): 9–28.

————. *The Order of Things: An Archaeology of the Human Sciences.* Trans. Alan Sheridan. New York: Vintage Books, 1973.

————. "Qu'est-ce qu'un auteur?" *Bulletin de la société française de philosophie* 63 (1969): 73–103.

————. *The Use of Pleasure.* Trans. Robert Hurley. New York: Vintage Books, 1986.

Frye, Northrop. *A Study of English Romanticism.* New York: Random House, 1968.

Gasché, Rodolphe. *The Tain of the Mirror: Derrida and the Philosophy of Reflection.* Cambridge, Mass.: Harvard University Press, 1986.

Gluck, Barbara Reich. *Beckett and Joyce: Friendship and Fiction.* Lewisburg, Pa.: Bucknell University Press, 1979.

Gontarski, S. E. *The Intent of Undoing in Samuel Beckett's Dramatic Texts.* Bloomington: Indiana University Press, 1985.

Gray, Margaret. *Postmodern Proust.* Philadelphia: University of Pennsylvania Press, 1992.

Grosrichard, Alain. "Gravité de Rousseau." *Cahiers pour l'analyse* 8 (1972): 43–64.

Habermas, Jürgen. *The Legitimation Crisis.* Trans. Thomas McCarthy. Boston: Beacon Press, 1975.

————. "Modernity Versus Postmodernity." *New German Critique* 22 (1981): 3–14.

————. *The Philosophical Discourse of Modernity: Twelve Lectures.* Trans. Frederick Lawrence. Cambridge, Mass.: MIT Press, 1987.

Harvey, Lawrence E. *Samuel Beckett: Poet and Critic.* Princeton: Princeton University Press, 1970.

Hassan, Ihab. *The Literature of Silence: Henry Miller and Samuel Beckett.* New York: Alfred A. Knopf, 1967.

————. *The Postmodern Turn: Essays in Postmodern Theory and Culture.* Columbus: Ohio State University Press, 1987.

Heath, Stephen. *The Nouveau Roman: A Study in the Practice of Writing.* London: Elek, 1972.

Heidegger, Martin. *Basic Writings.* Ed. David Farrell Krell. New York: Harper and Row, 1977.

————. *Nietzsche.* 4 vols. Trans. David Farrell Krell. New York: Harper and Row, 1979–87.

————. *The Question Concerning Technology and Other Essays.* Trans. William Lovitt. New York: Harper and Row, 1977.

Henning, Sylvie Debevec. *Beckett's Critical Complicity: Carnival, Contestation, and Tradition.* Lexington: University Press of Kentucky, 1988.

Herring, Phillip. *Joyce's Uncertainty Principle*. Princeton: Princeton University Press, 1987.

Hesla, David. *The Shape of Chaos: An Interpretation of the Art of Samuel Beckett*. Minneapolis: University of Minnesota Press, 1971.

Hill, Leslie. *Beckett's Fiction: In Different Words*. Cambridge: Cambridge University Press, 1990.

Hobsen, Harold. "Samuel Beckett: Dramatist of the Year." *International Theatre Annual* 1 (1956): 153–55.

Husserl, Edmund. *Cartesian Meditations: An Introduction to Phenomenology*. Trans. Dorion Cairns. The Hague: Martinus Nijhoff, 1977.

Hutcheon, Linda. *A Poetics of Postmodernism: History, Theory, Fiction*. London: Routledge, 1988.

———. *The Politics of Postmodernism*. London: Routledge, 1989.

Huyssen, Andreas. *After the Great Divide: Modernism, Mass Culture, Postmodernism*. Bloomington: Indiana University Press, 1986.

Jameson, Fredric. *Postmodernism, or, the Cultural Logic of Late Capitalism*. Durham, N.C.: Duke University Press, 1991.

Jencks, Charles. *Current Architecture*. London: Academy Editions, 1982.

———. *The Language of Post-Modern Architecture*. New York: Rizzoli, 1977.

———. *Late Modern Architecture*. New York: Rizzoli, 1980.

———. *Post-Modern Classicism: The New Synthesis*. London: Academy Editions, 1980.

Kennedy, Sighle. *Murphy's Bed: A Study of Real Sources and Sur-real Associations in Samuel Beckett's First Novel*. Lewisburg, Pa.: Bucknell University Press, 1971.

Kenner, Hugh. *Flaubert, Joyce, Beckett: The Stoic Comedians*. Boston: Beacon Press, 1962.

———. *A Reader's Guide to Samuel Beckett*. New York: Farrar, Straus and Giroux, 1973.

———. *Samuel Beckett: A Critical Study*. Berkeley: University of California Press, 1961.

Kern, Edith. "Moran-Molloy: The Hero as Author." *Perspective* 11 (1959): 183–93.

Kristeva, Julia. "Postmodernism?" *Bucknell Review* 25 (1980): 136–41.

Kuhn, Thomas. *The Structure of Scientific Revolutions*. 2d ed. Chicago: University of Chicago Press, 1970.

Lacan, Jacques. *Ecrits: A Selection*. Trans. Alan Sheridan. New York: W. W. Norton, 1977.

Langbaum, Robert. *The Modern Spirit: Essays on the Continuity of Nineteenth- and Twentieth-Century Literature*. New York: Oxford University Press, 1970.

———. *The Mysteries of Identity: A Theme in Modern Literature.* New York: Oxford University Press, 1977.

Levenson, Michael. *A Genealogy of Modernism: A Study of English Literary Doctrine, 1908–1922.* Cambridge: Cambridge University Press, 1984.

———. *Modernism and the Fate of Individuality.* Cambridge: Cambridge University Press, 1991.

Locatelli, Carla. *Unwording the World: Samuel Beckett's Prose After the Nobel Prize.* Philadelphia: University of Pennsylvania Press, 1990.

Lukács, Georg. *The Meaning of Contemporary Realism.* Trans. John Mander and Necke Mander. London: Merlin Press, 1972.

Lyons, John D., and Stephen G. Nichols, ed. *Mimesis: From Mirror to Method, Augustine to Descartes.* Hanover, N.H.: University Press of New England, 1982.

Lyotard, Jean François. *Heidegger et "les juifs."* Paris: Editions Galilée, 1988.

———. *The Postmodern Condition: A Report on Knowledge.* Trans. Geoff Bennington and Brian Massumi. Minneapolis: University of Minnesota Press, 1984.

———. *The Postmodern Explained: Correspondence, 1982–1985.* Ed. and trans. Julian Pefanis and Morgan Thomas. Minneapolis: University of Minnesota Press, 1992.

McHale, Brian. *Constructing Postmodernism:* London: Routledge, 1992.

———. *Postmodernist Fiction.* London: Methuen, 1987.

McKeon, Michael. *The Origins of the English Novel, 1660–1740.* Baltimore: Johns Hopkins University Press, 1987.

Mercier, Vivian. *Beckett/Beckett.* New York: Oxford University Press, 1977.

Miller, James. *The Passion of Michel Foucault.* New York: Simon and Schuster, 1993.

Mintz, Samuel. "Beckett's *Murphy*: A 'Cartesian' Novel." *Perspective* 11 (1959): 156–65.

Moorjani, Angela B. *Abysmal Games in the Novels of Samuel Beckett.* Chapel Hill: North Carolina Studies in the Romance Languages and Literatures, University of North Carolina, 1982.

———. "The Magna Mater Myth in Beckett's Fiction: Subtext and Subversion." In *Women in Beckett: Performance and Critical Perspectives.* Ed. Linda Ben-Zvi. Urbana: University of Illinois Press, 1992.

———. "Narrative Game Strategies in Beckett's *Watt*." *L'Esprit créatur* 17 (1977): 235–44.

Morot-Sir, Edouard, Howard Harper, and Dougald McMillan III, ed. *Samuel Beckett: The Art of Rhetoric.* Chapel Hill: North Carolina Studies in the Romance Languages and Literatures, University of North Carolina, 1976.

Morrissette, Bruce. *The Novels of Robbe-Grillet*. Ithaca: Cornell University Press, 1971.

Newman, Charles. *The Post-Modern Aura: The Act of Fiction in an Age of Inflation*. Evanston, Ill.: Northwestern University Press, 1985.

Nielsen, Erland. "Beckett's Theory of Knowledge or 'Nihil est in intellectu.'" *Language and Literature* 1 (1973): 57–82.

Nietzsche, Friedrich. *The Gay Science*. Trans. Walter Kaufmann. New York: Vintage Books, 1974.

———. *Human, All Too Human*. Trans. R. J. Hollingdale. Cambridge: Cambridge University Press, 1986.

———. *Philosophy and Truth: Selections from Nietzsche's Notebooks of the Early 1870's*. Ed. and trans. Daniel Breazeale. Atlantic Highlands, N. J.: Humanities Press International, 1979.

———. *Werke in zwei Bänden*. 2 vols. Ed. Ivo Frenzel. Munich: Carl Hanser, 1973.

Norris, Christopher. *Deconstruction: Theory and Practice*. London: Methuen, 1982.

———. *Derrida*. Cambridge, Mass.: Harvard University Press, 1987.

———. *What's Wrong with Postmodernism: Critical Theory and the Ends of Philosophy*. Baltimore: Johns Hopkins University Press, 1990.

O'Hara, J. D., ed. *Twentieth-Century Interpretations of 'Molloy,' 'Malone Dies,' and 'The Unnamable.'* Englewood Cliffs, N.J.: Prentice-Hall, 1970.

Pater, Walter. *The Renaissance: Studies in Art and Poetry*. Ed. Donald L. Hill. Berkeley: University of California Press, 1980.

Pecora, Vincent. *Self and Form in Modern Narrative*. Baltimore: Johns Hopkins University Press, 1989.

Pilling, John. *Samuel Beckett*. London: Routledge and Kegan Paul, 1976.

Popper, Karl. *The Logic of Scientific Discovery*. New York: Basic Books, 1961.

Proust, Marcel. *Le Temps retrouvé*. Paris: Editions Gallimard, 1954.

Rabinovitz, Rubin. *The Development of Samuel Beckett's Fiction*. Urbana: University of Illinois Press, 1984.

———. *Innovation in Samuel Beckett's Fiction*. Urbana: University of Illinois Press, 1992.

Robbe-Grillet, Alain. *For a New Novel: Essays on Fiction*. Trans. Richard Howard. New York: Grove Press, 1965.

———. *In the Labyrinth*. Trans. Richard Howard. New York: Grove Press, 1960.

Robinson, Michael. *The Long Sonata of the Dead: A Study of Samuel Beckett*. London: Rupert Hart-Davis, 1969.

Rorty, Richard. *Consequences of Pragmatism*. Minneapolis: University of Minnesota Press, 1982.

———. *Contingency, Irony, and Solidarity.* Cambridge: Cambridge University Press, 1989.

———. *Philosophical Papers.* Vol. 1: *Objectivity, Relativism and Truth.* Vol. 2: *Essays on Heidegger and Others.* Cambridge: Cambridge University Press, 1991.

———. *Philosophy and the Mirror of Nature.* Princeton: Princeton University Press, 1979.

Rothstein, Eric. "Foucault, Discursive History, and the Auto-Affection of God." *Modern Language Quarterly* 55 (1994): 383–414.

Rousseau, Jean-Jacques. *The Confessions.* Trans. J. M. Cohen. Harmondsworth, Eng.: Penguin Books, 1987.

Rousset, Jean. *Forme et signification: Essais sur les structures littéraires de Corneille à Claudel.* Paris: José Corti, 1962.

Said, Edward. *Beginnings: Intention and Method.* Baltimore: Johns Hopkins University Press, 1975.

Sarraute, Nathalie. *The Age of Suspicion.* Trans. Maria Jolas. New York: George Braziller, 1958.

Sartre, Jean-Paul. *Literary Essays.* Trans. Anette Michelson. New York: Citadel, 1955.

———. *Nausea.* Trans. Lloyd Alexander. New York: New Directions, 1964.

Senn, Fritz. *Joyce's Dislocutions: Essays on Reading as Translation.* Ed. John Paul Riquelme. Baltimore: Johns Hopkins University Press, 1984.

Senneff, Susan. "Song and Music in Samuel Beckett's *Watt.*" *Modern Fiction Studies* 11 (1964): 137–49.

Shattuck, Roger. *The Innocent Eye.* New York: Washington Square Press, 1986.

Shenker, Israel. "Beckett: Moody Man of Letters." *New York Times,* May 6, 1956, sec. 2.

Solomon, Philip. "A Ladder Image in *Watt*: Samuel Beckett and Fritz Mauthner." *Papers on Language and Literature* 7 (1971): 422–27.

Starobinski, Jean. *Jean-Jacques Rousseau: transparence et l'obstacle. Suivi de sept essais sur Rousseau.* Paris: Editions Gallimard, 1971.

———. *L'oeil vivant.* Paris: Editions Gallimard, 1961.

Stendhal. *Le Rouge et le noir.* Paris: Garnier Flammarion, 1964.

Straus, Erwin S. *The Primary World of the Senses.* Trans. Jacob Needleman. New York: Free Press, 1963.

Taine, Hippolyte. *Histoire de la littérature anglaise.* Paris: Hachette, 1891.

Trezise, Thomas. *Into the Breach: Samuel Beckett and the Ends of Literature.* Princeton: Princeton University Press, 1990.

Trivisonno, Ann. "Meaning and Function of the Quest in Beckett's *Watt.*" *Critique: Studies in Modern Fiction* 12 (1970): 28–38.

Vattimo, Gianni. *The End of Modernity: Nihilism and Hermeneutics in*

Postmodern Culture. Trans. Jon R. Snyder. Baltimore: Johns Hopkins University Press, 1991.

Venturi, Robert. *Complexity and Contradiction in Architecture.* 2d ed. New York: Museum of Modern Art, 1977.

———, with Denise Scott Brown and Steven Izenour. *Learning from Las Vegas.* Cambridge, Mass.: MIT Press, 1981.

Vrooman, Jack Rochford. *René Descartes: A Biography.* New York: Putnam, 1970.

Warhaft, Sidney. "Threne and Theme in *Watt.*" *Wisconsin Studies in Contemporary Literature* 4 (1963): 261–78.

Watt, Ian. *The Rise of the Novel.* Berkeley: University of California Press, 1957.

Webb, Eugene. *Samuel Beckett: A Study of His Novels.* Seattle: University of Washington Press, [1970].

Williams, Bernard. *Descartes: The Project of Pure Enquiry.* Harmondsworth, Eng.: Penguin Books, 1978.

Zola, Emile. *Le Roman experimental.* Paris: Garnier Flammarion, 1971.

Zurbrugg, Nicholas. *Beckett and Proust.* Gerrards Cross, Eng.: Colin Smythe, 1988.

Index

In this index "f" after a number indicates a separate reference on the next page, and "ff" indicates separate references on the next two pages. A continuous discussion over two or more pages is indicated by a span of page numbers.

Index

Begam, Richard
Samuel Beckett and the end of modernity / Richard Begam.
        p.   cm.
Includes bibliographical references and index.
ISBN 0-8047-2731-7 (cloth : alk. paper)
1. Beckett, Samuel, 1906– —Criticism and interpretation.
2. Postmodernism (Literature)—Ireland. 3. Postmodernism
(Literature)—France. 4. Modernism (Literature)—Ireland.
5. Modernism (Literature)—France.   I. Title.
PR6003.E282Z5728   1996
848'.91409—dc20   96-27406
                                                            CIP

∞ This book is printed on acid-free, recycled paper.

Original printing 1996

Last figure below indicates year of this printing:

05   04   03   02   01   00   99   98   97   96